Qigong Journey

Nine-Five Maintenance of Qi

Protect Your Life
with
Nine Palaces Daoist Qigong

by

Dr. Baolin Wu

Jessica Eckstein & Di Wu

With Original Artworks
by
Oliver Benson

Three Pines Press
St Petersburg, FL
www.threepinespress.com

9 8 7 6 5 4 3 2 1

Printed in the United States of America
This edition is printed on acid-free paper that meets
the American National Standard Institute Z39. 48 Standard.
Distributed in the United States by Three Pines Press.

Cover Design: Brent Cochran

Illustrations: Oliver Benson

Library of Congress Cataloging-in-Publication Data

Names: Wu, Baolin, 1954- author. | Eckstein, Jessica, author. | Wu, Di,
    1983- author.
Title: Qigong journey: nine-five maintenance of Qi : protect your life with
    nine palaces Daoist qigong / by Dr. Baolin Wu, Jessica Eckstein & Di Wu
    ; with original artworks by Oliver Benson.
Description: St Petersburg, FL : Three Pines Press, [2021]
Identifiers: LCCN 2021000420 | ISBN 9781931483476 (paperback)
Subjects: LCSH: Qi gong. | Physical fitness.
Classification: LCC RA781.8 .W72 2021 | DDC 613.7/1489--dc23
LC record available at https://lccn.loc.gov/2021000420a

Contents

Dedicated

to

Dr. Uddhava Om.

As he learned and taught in turn,

with joy and kindness,

so shall he continue his journey,

for eternity in the Dao.

Preface

I am in the unusual position to be the student, tasked to write, of a master, tasked to teach.

The contents of this book are taken from many hours of classes taught in Mandarin by Dr. Baolin Wu and translated on the spot by his son Eric Wu. I transcribed the transcripts word for word and then cross-referenced the wealth of material into a form that closely follows the experience of taking a class in person. Dr. Wu always begins with extensive discussion on the philosophical underpinnings of the practice, but eventually the qigong form itself is presented silently, shown, not discussed. Questions from the class are taken and then discoursed upon at length, sometimes in relation to what we have already learned and sometimes as a complete digression, which still maintains pertinence to the study at hand.

Ultimately, to learn qigong means to watch the master demonstrate, stand up and repeat on your own. It is a physical lesson, despite the concepts and explanations presented along with it. Even as the words in this book are the words of the master; that I was asked to set them down inevitably causes my words, the words of the student to come through, intercepting the teachings, which at their core are non-verbal. After many years of reflecting upon the implications of this conundrum, the resolution of the problem is actually simple, just as is everything of the Dao.

That these words are the words of the master and the student combined is a gift to you, the reader. You are not just another student at the feet of a teacher. Rather, these words will spark something within you and you shall be your own teacher, as well as your own student, eager to reveal knowledge and to learn. The ultimate message is that the voice of the teacher and the mind of the student are both a part of you. These lessons are the lessons you find from within your heart. My personal mission in accepting the challenge of writing this book is to convey this message and my deepest wish is for you to find this message to be true.

— Jessica Eckstein, Los Angeles, California. Year of the Rat, 2020

Qiu Chuji
Master of the Eternal Spring

Dr. Baolin Wu
Daoist Master and Physician

Chapter One

A Journey

Setting Out

An early morning in winter in the White Cloud Monastery, the sun has been up for less than an hour and mist still hangs in the silence. All the monks have convened in the main courtyard to say farewell to their brother, who is leaving that day, sent on a mission of great importance to another monastery on the other side of the country. Ranged by rank before their masters, all rise and solemnly perform a parting ritual, a ceremony of protection to grant their fellow initiate safety and strength along his journey. At the end, he hands his teacher a small plant he had been tending. This would be his token of honor he would leave behind in his place. As he sets out beyond the solid walls that surrounded his only home, his master will continue to care for this plant and through it, view his pupils varying fortunes as it withers or blooms.

    This book is dedicated to the teaching of this ritual practice of Daoist internal alchemy. It is presented here the way it has been taught within the Complete Reality school (Quanzhen pai) of Daoism since the days of Qiu Chuji (1148-1227), the great mystic who traveled far and wide, met with favor as an advisor in the court of Genghis Kahn, and returned to Beijing in honor, to found the White Cloud Monastery (Baiyun guan) and remain there until his death. He developed this practice for his own safety during his many years of wandering and it has been held closely in great esteem by the monks of the White Cloud Monastery for over eight hundred years. It has been performed for the safety and defense of all those who were tasked to leave on difficult journeys, and those

who stayed behind studied its effects and kept the record of its use for generations. It is with great honor presented to you now, not only to continue its heritage, but to offer you a powerful tool for your own personal growth and protection.

In *Qigong for Total Wellness* (St. Martin's Press, 2006), we presented a Daoist
qigong form, involving the cultivation of yang energy from the sun, known as
Nine Palaces Facing Heaven Qigong. The form in this book is another version
of Nine Palaces Qigong, known as Nine-Five Maintenance of Qi Practice (*jiuwu
yangqi fa*). It is considered an "amulet" or talismanic style of qigong that forms
part of the nine palaces category of qigong practice. It is a special appeal to the
heavens to give the practitioner a charm or ward, to prevent sickness or misfortune while traveling. Right now, there is much sickness and upheaval in the world,
in an ecological sense, as well as in the man-made structures of society. This is
the reason for introducing this practice publically. It is meaningful to learn this
form right now, because times are difficult for all of us and for the world we live
in.

Origins of the Form

Nine Palaces Qigong originated in the White Cloud Monastery, one of the oldest
and most prominent Daoist institutions in China. It can loosely be described as
the Vatican of Daoism, in that many different schools and sects where represented within its halls, and a formal study of Daoist doctrine and practice was
carried out, in the style of a university. Today, worldwide there are probably
thousands of forms of qigong, but the main origin of all the modern forms of
qigong comes from Daoism, branching out over many hundreds of years from
the original Daoist teachings. Laozi (6th - 4th c.), Confucius (aka Kongzi, 551-479
BCE), and Sunzi (aka Sun Wuzi, 544-496 BCE) are the three great philosophers
who are worshiped by Daoists as three essential gods and venerated in temples
across China.

You could say that the tenets of Daoism are a part of Chinese thought as a
whole and at the same time, the important elements of Chinese thought are direct
products of Daoism. In China today, *The Book of Dao and Its Virtue* (*Daode jing*),
one of the great works of Laozi, is again taught, along with *The Art of War* (*Sunzi
bingfa*), the great work of Sunzi, as well as the *Analects* (*Lunyu*) of Confucius. Even
though Confucius and Laozi coexisted in the same generation, technically speaking, Confucius is the student of Laozi. Sunzi is the student of Confucius, and all
three share a student and mentor relationship between them. It is quite remark-
able that China's three greatest philosophers lived within one generation of each
other.

Confucius studied, or "asked Dao," with Laozi, posing the question "What
is Dao." He sought knowledge and teachings from Laozi. And Sunzi in the same
respect sought knowledge and teachings from both Confucius and Laozi. So with
that relationship some people could say that Sunzi in a way is a student of Laozi

as well. In traditional historical lore, Confucius would bring Sunzi with him when he would go to visit Laozi and both sought knowledge and teachings from the great master. Of course, there is little hard evidence to back up this legend, but the few reliable historical records from the time indicate this as a reasonable possibility.

The Nine Palaces is a qigong form originally created by Laozi. In his writings, he discusses the nine palaces and the eight trigrams, although only touching on the five elements theory in passing. The historical evidence of this is recorded in the texts of Wenzi, however the nine palaces was not publicly taught until Wang Chongyang (1113-1170), the master of Qiu Chuji and founder of the White Cloud Monastery, nearly 1500 years after the days of Laozi. Only then was Nine Palaces Qigong spoken of and taught in an organized manner. Laozi's contributions to this form were recorded, the details of how to practice, the benefits of the practice, in the tablets of Wenzi. However it was Wang Chongyang, the later master, who actually practiced it as an art form and showed others. Nine Palaces Qigong was enriched by his further explanations of each movement and recorded into the doctrines of Complete Reality Daoism. The school flourished within the White Cloud Monastery when they preserved the art and discipline of Nine Palaces Qigong, for seventeen generations, all the way up to today. Dr. Wu, 17th generation lineage holder, has been tasked to teach its details through these books so that they may continue on as the world changes around us.

While Laozi's teachings focused on the nine palaces and the eight trigrams, five elements philosophy only became strongly developed from Confucius' works. Confucius had studied the *Book of Changes* (*Yijing*) and poured through the pages of his copy so diligently, so many times that it's said he "tore through its cow tendon bindings three times." Laozi instructed him to study the *Book of Changes*, so he studied so hard he wore out the bindings. This is the classical idiom that is used and it's very apt, as Confucius' theories are pervaded with the wisdom of the *Book of Changes*. He is known as an innovator of Laozi's philosophies, building upon them. Laozi had taught "as big as no boundaries, as small as a speck" and "everything goes with the flow of nature." Through observation and the studies of Laozi's theories, Confucius found that everything has a pattern. As we try to go with the flow of existence, the flow has a pattern of its own flowing through it. This pattern is bound by the five elements.

Laozi did not speak of the restrictions, parameters or refining of these patterns, as for him, there are no boundaries or limits to be made. We say the rat is afraid of the cat, and then the cat is afraid of the dog. Elephants aren't afraid of tigers or lions because they are so mighty, but they are afraid of rats. Confucius sees the world in terms of cycles such as this. In the midst of the cycle, there is also the human capacity to make adjustments within the natural order of things. Cats are afraid of dogs and as humans, we can train dogs to take advantage of this natural advantage if we so choose. Thus, Confucius's teachings contrast with Laozi's. Not everything goes with nature its flow. There are networks of constraints as well as affinities between all building blocks of existence, embodied by the five elements. Confucius advanced the thought that everything has a central focal point, like a fruit has a pit in its center. No matter how big a family is, there is always a head of the household. No matter how big the flock of birds, there's always a navigator in the flock during migration. There's always a leader or driving force.

Confucius believes in the supremacy of nature and the five elements as the basis of it patterns and cycles, then matches these theories to Nine Palaces Qigong practice. Yin-yang is the center of the entire flow of nature, or the pit of the fruit, the flesh and skin surrounding the pit are the five elements and the eight trigrams and the nine palaces are the shell surrounding the pit. You can't just let kids run around wild. You have to teach them. This is Confucius's thought. Laozi may disagree and advice letting them be free to grow up as they will. This is what is best for nature, but for a helpless infant, it's certainly not the most beneficial method. You have to show children limits and boundaries, so they can be safe to grow. Even a tree still has to be trimmed, if you want the fruit harvest for the next year to be plentiful. This is why Confucius is considered the first teacher of Chinese history, for his emphasis that children should be taught and go to school.

Dr. Wu feels that China has truly moved on from pure Communism, since the government is promoting Confucius again as the teacher and originator of social science, due to his theories of higher education. Now we understand the connection between the five elements and Nine Palaces and its development from the relationship between Laozi and Confucius. From their teachings, Sunzi derived and taught the understanding of the environment and using strategic positioning for a particular purpose, on which the Nine-Five Maintenance of Qi practice is particularly focused. As one travels outside the monastery, one is also traveling through the ups and downs of life. We use all the theories wrapped up in Daoist qigong to aid us on our way.

Cosmic Numbers and the Body

Working with qi means harmonizing Heaven, Human and Earth. There is no way to separate qigong practice from this. Theoretically speaking, when we say nine palaces, we mean the nine stars in the celestial heaven. In ancient times, the mathematics and astronomy of China was very advanced. This science was in service of astrology and divination, comparable to civilizations such as the Mayans. The Chinese methodology for calculating the alignments between stars and predicting the future, and its pervasive influence on the culture is quite comparable, especially in terms of astronomy.

In this ancient cosmology, the earth is placed in the center and around earth, the nine stars revolve. And what is this earth? Essentially, it is us. Every single one of us represents his or her own little earth. You are earth, and your eyes might be the moon or the sun rotating around you. And your meridians, collaterals and the blood in your veins represent the rivers and the oceans that flow upon the earth. Your skeleton and bones represent the mountains that support the earth and your muscles and muscular system represent the earth's crust. That's how the ancient Daoists make connect the earth to each individual human being. Embodying the earth is the primal perspective that governs the principles of Nine Palaces Qigong. The body is the earth.

To continue the analogy, the nine orifices of the body, the eyes, ears, nose, mouth, urethra and anus, represent the nine palaces and in that respect, each of the organs within your body have a special relationship with the nine different stars in the skies. Even today, we still have an awareness of this correspondence, saying "men are from Mars and women from Venus." Whenever one of your organs is unwell or whenever you want to maintain or tonify that organ, you can accomplish it by enhancing that particular organ's relationship with each of these stars, all nine or just its particular companion star. The body is communicating with the universe, just like the plant that was tended by the monks as a stand-in for their brother while he was away on his mission.

The Chinese expression, "impulse and response of heaven and humanity" (*tianren ganying*) means or heaven and human corresponding to each other. *Ying* means response, so you can consider an organ in your body that is weak is still connected to its star and can gain renewed energy from the star's response to its weakness. There is a chart of nine characters that symbolize the nine treasures of the universe. In heaven, there are three treasures. They are the sun, moon, and the star. On earth there are three treasures as well, water, fire and wind. And as humans, we also have three treasures, our essence (*jing*), our breath (*qi*), and our spirit (*shen*), which is the soul.

Based on this magic square chart, we can assign different numbers, one through nine. We can replace, or fill in numbers horizontally, or vertically or diagonally and whatever way you add them up, it will always total fifteen. Fifteen, according to the *Book of Changes*, can be broken down to the numbers one and five. $1 + 5 = 6$. So therefore the number six is representative of peace and tranquility and smoothness, as in the way our fingers fit together perfectly and comfortably when we interlace them. You can make a symbol using the four directions, east, west, north and south. Draw a square with four points in the corners. East is in the upper left, west is the upper right, north is in the lower right and south is in the lower left, drawn in that order. Now add heaven and earth by drawing two diagonal lines from the corners, bisecting in the middle of the square. These are the six elements, whose harmonization of these we stress here as an integral concept in the Nine-Five Maintenance of Qi.

Yin and Yang

What is born within heaven and earth and the four directions, harmonized together? Humanity. The *Book of Changes* concept is "Within the six harmonization, is "Humankind." Explored further, this concept embodies the relationship between yin and yang. Observe the image of the Taiji symbol, the circle bisected with a curving line to form the white and the black segments, each with their opposing energy lying within as a circular seed.

Yin and yang are in constant correspondence with each other. They are dependent on each other. They are both continuously present, constantly modulating their relative percentages. Place your left hand palm up, for yang, and your right hand palm down, for yin, and move them in a slight weighing motion, weighing the balance of qi, to feel the physical sensation of this concept. You will feel the two different qualities of their pull.

There is a movement we can make to experience every category of yin or yang energy. For example, day is considered yang and night as yin. Stand and move your left palm going up, its open palm facing your chest with the elbow bent vertically, while the right palm is held with the elbow bent horizontally forming loose fist facing in to chest. Experience the different sensations. We categorize males as yang and females as yin. Reach out as if grasping with the respective hands, forming strong fists as you grasp and feel the distinctions. That which rises is yang; both hands rising up, palms up. That which falls is yin; palms turning over at brow level to face downwards, slightly cupped, passing down to the chest level. Movement is yang, stagnation is yin; open each palm up and thrust slightly outwards. Yet there is no absolute yin or yang, no concept to point to or sensation to feel. They always coexist, in one proportion or another to each other, always oscillating respective to each other. They move in accordance to each other.

To illustrate this key point, as we said before, males are yang. However, even though males are categorized as yang, we have to appreciate that only seventy percent of their structure is yang and thirty percent is yin. The same applies to women. We have already established that females are yin, but they are not absolutely all yin. Two thirds of their existence is yin and one third is yang. This is how yin and yang change in accordance with each other.

The key to this theory of constant change is that within every yang there is yin and within every yin there's yang. There is always a spark of one being born from the other. For instance in the Taiji symbol, the white half pointing up represents yang, and the black half pointing down is yin. In the White Cloud Monastery, the circles that are contained in both hemispheres are usually drawn rather large. They portray the "yang within the yin," on the black half and the "yin within the yang" on the white half. To even further denote that for every yang there's yin, usually the drawing will also contain some dark shading on the lower curve of the yang portion) to signify that yin shadows yang from the outside. On the yin side, you will see a bit of white highlight around the fullest part of its upper outer curve. This is done on purpose to further denote the fact that yang highlights yin from above. So there is always the opposite force growing from within, as well as radiating towards the other from outside.

From here we may ask, what is sinuous line that partitions the two halves of the circle? This line is a representation of the twenty-four seasonal changes of qi within the year. Rather than just having four seasons or twelve months, in the

Chinese system, for every month, there are two individual seasonal periods, each with their own unique climate and balance of yin and yang. From the upper tip of where the curve begins at the outer upper edge we begin in spring, and tracing down to the lower ending point at the lower outer edge on the bottom right of the circle, we finish with winter. This is the peak of yang, at the fullest point of the white curve's "head" where yin's "tail" is at its thinnest. It represents the height of summer. The opposite peak of yin, represent the coldest days of winter. Tracing along this line separating yin and yang, we can see the shape of the time-line of the twenty-four seasonal changes within a year. Yin and yang are reflected by the twenty-four seasonal changes and adjust throughout every period in a particular combination.

This is a unique way of explaining yin and yang developed by the Daoist scholars over millennia. No other culture has delineated the substance of these two energies and their interplay with nature's seasons in this way. There are many layers of meaning to this symbolism. Spring's emphasis is on "rising," when everything comes to life. For summer, the emphasis is growth. Summer is divided into two main seasons, summer, which is growth, and "long summer" or Indian summer, which symbolizes changes, and the inevitability of change. Autumn means the day of fruition, where you harvest the fruits of your labor, and winter is hibernation, as in the hibernation of silkworms in their chrysalis. You can symbolize each of the twenty-four seasonal changes with different kinds of trees and other seasonal plants, such as grain crops. .

Every seed that is planted will eventually sprout with life. Even though you might accidentally plant the seed facing down, when it sprouts, it will sprout upwards. This is the inevitable cycle of life. The ten heavenly stems and twelve earthly branches combine to denote the changes will occur within every sixty-year cycle. If you trace along the outer edge of the Taiji symbol's circle, starting with the exact point at the top where the tip of yang meets the thinnest tail of yin, once around the edge represents the changes of the sixty-year cycle.

If you travel this way along the internal curve separating yin and yang that represents the changes within one year, as we have said. These two timelines form the original meaning of what is yin and what is yang. The most important knowledge to take away is that yin and yang cannot be separated from the seasonal changes. Making the choices in your life based on these seasons is "The harmonization of heaven and human," in its fullest sense. Knowledge of the seasonal changes shows us the ebb and flow of yin and yang. We know when to plant the crops and also when to raise new opportunities for ourselves. To work with qigong, especially the Nine-Five Maintenance of Qi form presented here, means working with the twenty-four seasonal changes and the fluctuations of yin and yang within nature.

Heaven, Humanity, and Earth

When we discussed the proportions of yin and yang within men and women, it should be clear that we were not simply referring to a body mass to water ratio. The seventy percent yang and thirty percent yin ratio for men might appear connected to this idea, but then how would you explain the reversed ratios for women? Yin and yang fluctuate and adapt to each other. This is a factor that goes beyond the physical makeup of the body. Take the earth as an example. Land covers about one third and water covers roughly two thirds of the total surface area of the planet. Even though Nine Palaces Qigong practice emphasizes training yang energy, "yang originates from yin." It is critical to understand this. For instance, snap open a lighter. A flame sparks on. The flame is yang, but where does the flame come from? The source of the flame is the liquid inside. The lighter fluid is yin. It doesn't matter if you're male or female. We all came from our mother, who is yin. Even though we're striving to cultivate yang, ultimately in the very end you will become yin in the cycle of life and death.

Our practice is inseparably linked with the five thousand year old heritage of Chinese thought. It is a worldview that never ceases to find parallels between our individual lives and the cycles of nature. For example, females go through a menstrual cycle of twenty eight days on average. There are three or four days where the egg starts to move, as menses occurs. Chinese medicine directly correlates the phases of the menstrual cycle to the moon's phases and position in the sky. Treatment is applied based on the moon cycle for regulating menstrual cycle imbalances. This is a perfect example of Chinese culture and Chinese medical culture as well. Traditional Chinese Medicine (TCM) is deeply ingrained in traditional Chinese culture, which is based on adjusting to the seasonal weather patterns of the earth, as well as the universe. This is the main reason why TCM treatments are holistic and the focus is treating the patient as a whole rather than treating individual symptoms or parts of the body. It's a different way of looking at things. Again it goes back to the Taiji symbol as the root guideline for enhancing our life. The Taiji symbol is the source of inspiration for our practice.

In this world, we are surrounded by yin and therefore we endeavor to develop the yang to balance the yin out. Nine Palaces Qigong is a yang practice, most often focusing on the yang-based systems in the body, primarily the nervous system. Five Centers Facing Heaven is the sister practice to the nine palaces and usually done at night with the moon. It focuses on enhancing the yin body systems, particularly the endocrine system and hormonal balance.

Nine Palaces is the number nine, and Five Centers is five. Putting the characters for the number 9 and the number 5 together is a classic Chinese figure of speech, praising something as the pinnacle, the top or the peak. It means the ultimate. The Nine-Five Maintenance of Qi practice is indeed a very high level of qigong, heavily involved with the cycle of yin and yang, life and death, all in service of building new energy and opportunities. The interplay of yin and yang within the seasons of the year and the cycle of birth, death and rebirth permeates this practice in every movement and breath taken. It is the guiding principle behind the way it trains the body physically, harmonizes the heart and mind psychologically, and influences our safety and opportunities on a mystical level.

For Nine Palaces Qigong we present in this book, about two thirds of the form is involved with yang energy and yin comprises the other third. As we talked about earlier, the nine stars are categorized as yang and the earth itself is categorized as yin. Following from this, if we compare earth to a human being, then earth would be yang and we would be yin. So too, when looking at our opportunities and general fortune in life, seventy percent is heaven's will and thirty percent are factors we can influence or change.

To return to the Mayan astronomers and astrologers, as we know, the Mayans have made major contributions to the history of forecasting and astrological prediction. Their mathematical system uses a base of twenty. Computers use a binary system of using two integers, 0 and 1. So do the *Book of Changes*'s calculations. The Mayan system uses base 20, with twenty integers, from 0 to 19. To count a number above twenty, you would have to use a much more complex calculation to express it, especially compared to the binary system of the computer or the *Book of Changes*. Mayan calculations sacrifice the streamlined efficiency of the binary system in favor of complexity and discrete detail. In this respect the Mayan culture is a very profound culture with very finely developed astronomical and astrological calculations. The detailed numeric system allows for extensive mathematical models that they used to predict events far into the future.

According to the Mayan calculations, they projected that the year 2012 would be a year of extreme catastrophes and crises, due to a rare conjunction of the sun to the center of the Milky Way galaxy. Modern scientific methodology verified this alignment would indeed take place and it created a certain amount of anxiety across the world, wondering what would actually come to pass.

In 2009, Dr. Wu decided to run *Book of Changes* calculations for the year as well, out of his respect for the Mayan calendar's accuracy. The *Book of Changes*, being a binary system, relies upon its agility to make up for the lack of mathematical density of the Mayan system. After he completed the calculations, it confirmed the Mayan belief that 2012 would bring a sea change in the health of the planet. Based on the *Book of Changes* calculations, there was no prediction of massive loss of life. However, the losses would be significant and on a global scale. There was one significant detail. It would not be a sudden crisis, but an increase in hazardous conditions, not just for humans, but for the entire animal kingdom, we included. It was these calculations that decided Dr. Wu to teach the Nine-Five Maintenance of Qi publically.

It is very interesting to look back on the notes of our discussions on this topic from 2009, as they appear to be more accurate now in 2020 than they seemed even in 2009, 2012, or 2016. Dr. Wu's feeling was the crisis indicated by the *Book of Changes* was related to the rise of new viral strains, particularly ones that would be passed from animal species to humans at an unusual rate of potency and transmission. In 2009, we were dealing with a looming H1N1 epidemic, that the World Health Organization had assigned a level six severity. Level six severity indicates a pandemic, where a virus spreads globally.

At the time, H1N1 was primarily swine influenza, initially originating from pigs, which had then crossed over the capability of infecting humans. Some research at the time even pointed to humans being able to transmit the disease back to pigs as well, a potentially deadly scenario that was previously unheard of. Of course, since then, we have also experienced severe outbreaks of avian flu or SARS, MERS, Ebola, and in 2016, powerful strains of Zika virus and Chikungunya. As of this writing, in 2020, we struggle in the throes of the COVID-19 Novel Coronavirus outbreak, a global pandemic that is unprecedented in its severity and reach, striking all continents and all socioeconomic levels, violently destabilizing the foundations of world financial and political structures, with millions of infected and tens of thousands of deaths. We have passed the threshold where human/animal viral transmission has become an established phenomenon on a planetary scale.

Daoist theory posits that there is more to brace for. It's a trickledown theory, in that major catastrophes such as a nationwide or global epidemic, will be followed by smaller disasters afterwards. For instance, after a major earthquake or flood, the devastation results in conditions ripe for breeding disease or hazards, which in turn cause further damage. This belief is the source of the Chinese saying "Heavenly disasters and human disasters are together in the same place" (*tianzai heren huo tamen yiqi*). Human suffering follows from heavenly disasters. What Westerners would call natural disasters, in the Daoist worldview are often considered acts of heaven. Heaven's decree can be invoked by imbalances in the natural order caused by the actions of mankind. Or they simply occur due to the inevitable events that compose the cycles of the universe that take place within the patterns formed along the pathways of the *Book of Changes*.

We are here today to learn the art of Nine-Five Maintenance of Qi. Practicing it will boost our mental and physical immunity, so that we are more resistant to the natural disasters that surround us. Beyond that, it will also increase our positive opportunities as well. In the face of danger, it will bring the kind of fortune that allows us to escape or lessen impending harm. Many people have stories of missing a plane that then crashes, or less dramatically, just missing being hit by a falling tree branch or toppling bookshelf. What do we call the phenomenon that draws us away from brink of catastrophe? Is it luck, reflex, intuition, heavenly blessing? Call it what you will, these moments of being snatched away from harm are beyond what we can comprehend scientifically.

According to Daoist worldview, the course of a person's life as dictated by numbers from birth to death. The family you were born into, your gender, and your base lifespan potential are all in the numbers, outside of your direct control. However, according to the *Book of Changes* interpretation of this string of numbers, about one third of the calculations are under your influence. You control this third of your fate. You can manipulate the numbers about a third of the time. Marriage, career, if and when you have children, are all factors you have power over and are able to change. Some of this is obvious. For instance, if you don't have a happy marriage, then you can get a divorce. If you're not happy with a career or job, you can always find another one. However, practicing qigong can bring those opportunities into clearer focus and give you the clarity to follow through on them. The Nine-Five Maintenance of Qi takes this to an ultimate degree by generating the power to bypassing harm, or even fate itself. What you put into your practice is what you will get from it, each person to his or her own needs.

Accepting and Adapting to Nature

This brings up an important question that new students of qigong often ask, especially if they have a background in other spiritual, religious or esoteric traditions. When we practice Nine-Five Maintenance of Qi, are we manipulating the forces of the earth for our own ends? Are we taking earth energy and putting it into our bodies for personal gain?

There are many examples of bringing in the living energy of animals or plants to adjust our fortunes in Daoist tradition. For instance if you're sick and a male, there are forms of qigong that you practice in front of flowers because flowers belong to the category of yin and men belong to the category of yang. Conversely if you were a female in the same situation, you would want to practice with trees instead, for their yang properties. The practice involves sensitizing your hands with a combination of qigong exercises and external training using bowls of raw rice filled with water. You then approach the tree or flowering plant, perform sigils with hand gestures and breathing to initiate communication and if a connection is made, breathe together with the plant to absorb their healing qi.

There are other Nine Palaces Qigong practices with trees that are not specifically for improving your health, but for growing various special relationships with them. What method you pick depends on your situation or what you want to achieve. For example, Dr. Wu spent a number of years teaching varying stages of a Nine Palaces practice that you had to practice with a tree, standing facing it or with your back to it, sometimes right next to it and sometimes further away but still within range. Initially when you began the practice, you needed to select the tree knowing its age and usual life span, the reason being that this tree was going to become a partner in your life. Ideally, you would pick a young tree or a tree with a remaining lifespan proportionate to your age and you would practice and grow old together. For instance, you are seventy years old and you have found a large pine tree that really appeals to you. You search for information about the tree and find that it was planted two or three years ago and its species' natural lifespan is two hundred years. This would be a good match. So as the tree is growing, you are growing. You are mutually growing together. So that's scenario number one.

Another option for a slightly different effect might be that you have found a tree that is already two hundred years old, but you feel like this tree is projecting to you that it has good qi. You see it's blooming and flourishing, not withering or dying. It feels lively when you stand near it and its qi is very animated. For this circumstance, if you choose to practice with that tree, it would also be good. As long as its qi is able to carry you with it as the two of you continue to practice, you have found a good partner. The scenario that we don't want and would hope to avoid is as you are practicing with this tree, it unexpectedly sickens to the point of death, struck by lightning or an aggressive wasting away. You don't want that kind of tree. You would have to be concerned that this negativity will be applied to you as well, because you've been practicing with that tree. But on the other hand, there still is some good to be gained in the sense that this tree took a hit for you. Its death has foreshadowed your own bad luck, misfortune and mishaps. You can use it as a warning to take preventative measures in your day to day life, shoring up against danger. There are things that can't be explained with science.

There are bonds that are so strong, the one can absorb the misfortunes of the other. For instance, the Daoists have studied the scenario where a person with cancer has a dog as a pet. Later on, the dog also gets cancer and dies as a result. A Daoist doctor would tell the person he now might have a better chance of being cured of his own cancer. It's because the dog took that cancer on itself and in a way cured its master. For pets, only dogs have this special ability. No other pet has it.

Science cannot explain this phenomenon. Even the data accumulated by the Daoists is not definitive. Not all dogs capable of taking the sickness for their masters. You can't just buy a dog and start taking care of it once you've been diagnosed with cancer. It has to be a dog you were with long before you became ill. In a sense, the dog had to be fated from birth to be with that master and save him. This degree of loyalty and bonding is an innate ability of dogs, but there also has to be an aspect of destiny and special connection. In general, though, dogs are the number one animal with this ability. Horses are also sometimes able to do this. Other animals such as cats are not as certainly capable and others, such as fish or birds, do not have this capacity. These are natural conditions, the natural order of things. Some animals, like snakes and pythons, might not be appropriate pets at all. Those animals are not for everybody. As pets, it's based on where you live and your own zodiac animal whether they will be beneficial for you.

The main goal is to accept and adapt to nature. Just as the trees and animals are enlisted to help us, we must respect the laws of nature to properly integrate them into our lives. Whether we are making adjustments using fengshui and *Book of Changes* principles or practicing qigong in search of better energy and opportunities, we only receive a benefit if we recognize nature's laws as our guide.

A student asked Dr. Wu what seemed like a simple question. If your animal sign is the Dog, can you have a dog as a pet? The answer is intricate. There are unexpected variables involved. In Chinese characters, if you take the character for "dog" and double it, those two characters together form the character for "crying" or "sadness." Because of this, it is considered an inauspicious sign to own two dogs at the same time. One dog, three dogs or four dogs are fortunate, but not two. To follow from this, it is recommended that if you are born in the Year of the Dog, never keep only one dog. You are a dog and one more dog makes two, the sign of crying. If your sign is the Dog, you can raise a pair of dogs so you all add up together as three dogs. If you're not a Dog, one dog is acceptable, or have three or four if you like. It's very important to take note of this.

If you're of a certain animal sign, whether or not you can raise that same animal or how many you can raise, are issues you have to be careful about. The same thing goes with fish, how many fish should your raise in a tank, and even their color varies depending on the person and the situation and getting every detail right is very important. All these calculations are derived from the *Book of Changes*. It's a matter of numbers. Besides numeric calculations, the doctrine of "same qi" (*tongqi*) is a factor. If you are the sign of the Monkey, it's helpful if you are able to raise a monkey, especially during hard times. This means you have the same spirit and the same qi, and you can mutually help each other. Of course, caring for a live monkey is not always possible, but you can raise an animal that's similar in spirit or behavior to one. For instance, you can keep a bird. Birds can crawl and climb well like monkeys and have similar impish and intelligent personalities.

A lot of people are not aware this principle is fundamental to Daoist shamanic belief. In the West, we could term this sympathetic magic and there is certainly a tradition of its practice in Western culture going back millennia. In Chinese culture, its principles run very deep and have been inexorably intertwined with the impulse to harmonize with nature. Daoist scholarship has spent thousands of years studying its effects without suffering the persecution that cut down its pagan practitioners in the West. It's more than just putting like with like. Instead, it is a means to completely align yourself with nature's guidelines. It can be a powerful tool and is put to great use in the Nine-Five Maintenance of Qi.

Please do not underestimate all the assistance that nature has to offer you for help and guidance. When you're walking down the middle of a dusty road on a hot, summer day and the leaves of a tree shade you as you pass by, that's what nature has to offer you. It is offering you a great comfort. A moment of shade can seem very small and inconsequential, but that is just one moment. Multiply that by every tree that releases oxygen into the atmosphere and every moment you take a breath of that air. The sense of scale suddenly becomes immense. Stop for a moment to contemplate its vastness and we start to see what nature really has to offer. If there's one thing to understand, just know that in our lifetime, everybody needs help.

The Nine-Five Maintenance of Qi practice teaches us how to dissolve into nature. Every object and every endeavor has its own qi. There are the five elements of wood, fire, earth, metal and water, each with its own balance of yin and yang and its own underpinnings of *Book of Changes* calculation. Everything can be categorized by the five elements. If you can break a plan for your future down to the element that represent it, you now have an archetype or basic image you can use to conceptualize its qi. Along with the same qi, you have the two cycles of the five elements, generating (which can also be called nourishing) and controlling, to work with in order to enhance your plans and prevent them from problems. This is fundamental Daoist fengshui. If you're in the field of construction or architecture, you are part of earth. You are categorized as the element of earth. If you're in the business of restaurants, then you are part of fire, categorized as the element of fire. If you are involved with banking, it is related to metal and also to water, as metal nourishes water in the generative cycle.

Now, let's say that there's a two story building. Downstairs is a restaurant and upstairs is an acupuncture clinic. Acupuncture also belongs to the element of fire, so as fire/fire, they do not conflict. If instead of acupuncture, you have a bank upstairs from the restaurant, there is going to be a problem. Banking belongs to water and metal. The fire of the restaurant will melt the metal of the bank, which is bad for the bank's business. Even worse, because the bank is positioned on the top floor, its water will run down onto the fire of the restaurant, which is bad for the restaurant's business and also bad for the bank.

Water will not coexist with fire. In the mundane world when they meet, at best you will get some steam as the water extinguishes the fire or the fire evaporates the water. However, Daoist internal alchemy takes another direction. Even though water and fire are in direct conflict with each other, if they eventually do merge, much energy is generated and out of this fusion, creates something new. That new substance will be the best. It's this ideal substance that we seek, that everyone who practices qigong should be in pursuit of. This ideal can be seen as a distillation of contrasting forces. The original energies dissolve and a refined, ultimate essence is left. If we recall that "Nine-Five" is an idiom for "ultimate," we can see another layer of purpose within the Nine-Five Maintenance of Qi. In point of fact, creating this new qi is the purpose of all Daoist qigong.

How do we dissolve? The details of the physical training will be discussed in the course of this book. This qigong form is designed to soften your body. You will practice to the point where you are an infant, newborn, very soft, completely malleable. Only then will you be able to adjust your opportunities and adjust yourself. You will have the fluidity to finally pull away from all the factors that have tightened you into misalignment. All the forces of nature will come to help you reach this state, because alignment means aligning with nature. Dissolving into nature occurs first and foremost in one's consciousness and perception of self. You are changing your perception of the universe from within your physical body and emotional state.

It's true that we use intention and will to go through a series of exercises. It's easy to feel you are at the center of your practice and you stand in that center as its guiding force. In reality, it's not about "You." You're not practicing with the earth. The earth is practicing with you. Why is this? As much as self-determination is a guiding principle in *The Book of Dao and Its Virtue*, Laozi's emphasis is that we have to adapt to nature in order to achieve it. Even though as humans we have the capacity to change nature and alter certain portions of it, the truth is that even with all our efforts, these changes are very minimal and should be recognized as such. Our main goal should be to accept and adapt to nature. When we ignore this and impact the environment without care, geological catastrophes will follow, earthquakes, floods and droughts. If we disturb the natural order of life, we are presented with new diseases and imbalances in the ecosystem, as we are already experiencing. Whatever consequences we are suffering today, we brought upon ourselves, by elevating human agency above its place in nature's design.

The main take away from these lessons is that we are here to adapt to nature. We accept nature on its terms. We are a part of its whole. This is our true relationship with nature. It is also the source of our true sense of self. Even though we do change our natural environment a bit just by our presence on the planet, our impact will be kept to a minimum. In turn, we will share in wisdom of nature's rhythms. This is the theory and philosophy of Laozi.

Daoism emphasizes being one with nature, going with the flow of nature. In this spirit, the Nine-Five Maintenance of Qi is an attunement with nature. As we practice, we harmonize ourselves with heaven and earth, yin and yang, life and death. Everything that doesn't matter dissolves away and what is left is a will that finds its motivation in the cycles of nature. We perceive our humanity anew in the awareness that at once, we are infinite as the cosmos itself and small and imperceptible as a grain of rice. With this knowledge, we take our rightful place on that sinuous line that curves across the Taiji symbol and forms the timeline of the universe.

Chapter Two

Beginning to Practice

The Form's Structure

Qigong forms practiced in the White Cloud Monastery are always structured as a deepening sequence of operations, usually starting with warming up the joints, moving on to unlock channels of communication between the internal organs and the external environment, and then finally bringing the practitioner to a fully opened state where the actual form is enacted as an alchemical ritual, in profound meditation. The Nine Palaces Qigong form outlined in *Qigong for Total Wellness* closely follows this pattern.

In the warm-up stage, basic muscle tension is released and posture is balanced. Breathing and heart rate are regulated. This is simply achieved, with sets of fluid movements designed to bring motion and circulation into the joints. There may also be varying types of self-massage and patterned breathing, so that the body relaxes and readjusts more completely. These basic warm-ups are what the general public most commonly recognizes as qigong, both in China and abroad. They are found in many kinds of qigong and martial arts practice, both of Buddhist and Daoist traditions.

In qigong practiced across the White Cloud Monastery's main schools, after the warm-up stage, your body's basic systems are activated and ready to unfold, expand and flow with the world around it. At this point, practice commonly shifts to more static postures, where it is time to relax deeply and allow oneself to merge with the rhythms of nature inside the body and outside the body. At this level, you are also tuning into rhythms and patterns held within your memories of the past and your emotions of past, present and future, which are all deeply rooted within your physical body, as well as your mind. The ideal goal is to experience your body as a conduit for universal energies passing through it, as is also the case in many other yoga traditions. This phase is also a preliminary step to reaching the perfect physical and mental state for the "main event," which is performing the actual form itself, either the Nine Palaces Solar Qigong or the Five Centers Lunar qigong.

These two root forms of qigong practice are traceable back to the earliest organized forms taught by the White Cloud Monastery's founding masters and even earlier. In the monastery, these forms are considered mystical ceremonies of union with heaven and earth. At their core, they embody pure shamanic transformation and renewal of consciousness. It is impossible to discuss qigong practice without referencing seemingly mystical or philosophical concepts such as harmonizing heaven, humanity, and earth. Again, though, it is very important to reiterate that the source of these esoteric ideas is rooted in physical practice. You are developing your body, mind and consciousness, but starting with your body first and foremost. Then emotions come into play as a result. New types of awareness and spiritual interaction are born from fundamental improvements you are making to your physical, and by extension, mental health.

This brings us back to the purpose of Nine Palaces Qigong this book explores. This form is structured somewhat differently than the standard stages discussed above, with special emphasis placed on bringing qi into the body from the outside. Rather than simply being a conduit for qi flowing through us, in this practice we are coming to the sun as individuals seeking personal communication and aid. Rather than just an empty vessel serving as a channel for the vast, shifting tides of the cosmos, with the Nine-Five Maintenance of Qi practice, we step up and ask for heaven's power to protect us. On a physical and psychological level, we are boosting our health and focusing our sense of self, so that we cannot be harmed. This is, simply put, a practice of self-defense. It is defensive strength training for the body and will.

Right now, more than ever, we must take into consideration all the problematic trends of our planet and their direct impact on our lives. We must take into account the things that are not going well in our environment and the society we have created. We have global health pandemics, viruses like H1N1 transferring to humans for the first time from the animal world, and worse. Our international economy is volatile. The political climate is unstable. We need a self-defense mechanism to help protect us from all these external harms. From the Daoist point of view, these difficult conditions are both of heavenly and human origin, and must be counteracted with heavenly assistance and our own human effort.

The *Book of Changes* calculations that expose these difficulties are deeply entwined with the exercises of the Nine-Five Maintenance of Qi practice. We do the movements with our bodies while the heaven-derived numbers infuse them with deeper meaning and the power to make contact with the forces that can help us. A profound connection is created. A sacred equation develops between us and the forces we are tapping into. While there is no straightforward way to discuss it scientifically, before beginning this practice, the student of Nine Palaces Qigong does well to be aware of how innate this connection is and honor its implications. In this way, we have one of many, many examples of how the simplest actions, even just one breath, weave a tapestry of meaning in the art of qigong.

As an illustration of how numbers become an integral part of the practice, in the Nine-Five Maintenance of Qi practice, we have five stages of bringing qi into the body, developing it and then allowing it to revitalize the nine openings of the body. These are welcome qi, intake qi, adjust qi, tonify qi and utilize qi.

•   We begin with welcoming the qi, to let our presence be known to the sun and the forces of the universe.

•   After greeting and inviting the sun to our practice, we gently intake qi, allowing it to grow up from the earth into the body, which then grows even further out, as far as it can go until finally dissolving back into the earth like water.

•   Once the body has been expanded and dissolved by the flow of qi, the next step is to adjust the qi. This will vigorously remove blocks within the muscular structure of the body, as well as further harmonize with the rotation of the planet.

•   After this grounding phase, it is time to tonify the qi, in a very powerful series of internal isometric exercises.

•   Finally, after this profound clearing and purifying, we are able to go back in and utilize the qi to open the nine palaces, through simple, yet highly effective self-massage.

At this point, we have energized our total body-mind system and can further concentrate the sun's power into healing internal illness and uplifting psychological conditions. These five stages allow us to harvest the boundless power of the sun and put it to use for vitality and vibrant rejuvenation. After reaching this peak state, we then complete the practice with the actual Nine Palaces form, for a total of six stages in all.

As we can see, the cosmic numbers that represent heaven (9), human (1) and the six directions and five elements of earth are all being embodied within the steps of this qigong form. There will be further use of numbers within each stage, in the different numbers of sets and repetitions of the exercises and as mantras to increase the mental intensity of certain other exercises.

Given the differences in the way this form is structured, what do we do with previous Nine Palaces practices, such as the "Healthy and Happy Practice" in *Qigong for Total Wellness*? One thing all my years of study with Dr. Wu has taught me is that it is most important to develop the harmony of your body with heaven and earth and feel the qi of the universe bringing to you the information you need to know from the world around you. This might sound philosophical, but it is very literal. It truly is a physical awareness you develop as your train your body over time.

Even if you already practice a different version of Nine Palaces, it's best to stop and focus on this method for now, to learn it in full. Practicing this form for seven days, one month or three months in a row, without missing a day, results in a deeper understanding. You will certainly contact this special awareness and afterwards, you may find that your questions about qigong and spiritual consciousness will be formed from new insight. The answers and inspirations that will follow will be of a very different order. Even a single week of focused study of this form will bring you great gains, as suited to your own personal needs.

There are nine levels of Nine Palaces Qigong, each with nine sub-levels, and so in theory, there are eighty-one stages. In practice, however, these differences can be very subtle. Again, the goal is to achieve harmony between yourself, the forces of the earth and the wisdom of heaven. For this reason, what we study with Dr. Wu in his classes changes every year. He bases what he will teach on the astrological and *Book of Changes* calculations for the year. This allows us the most progress with our training, because we are practicing in harmony with the general influences for that year. In this sense, we are not going through the levels in numerical order, but in an order that corresponds with nature's order. If you knew it was going to be a rainy year, you would make sure in advance to fix the roof of your house. The same principle applies to how we learn qigong from a traditional teacher like Dr. Wu.

Of course, each facet of Nine Palaces Qigong builds upon the others. They're not in conflict with each other. The Nine-Five Maintenance of Qi presented right now in this book is for special circumstances, in times of hardship, based on today's world conditions. This practice works in tandem with what you have already learned and developed with your previous practice. Just because you go to college doesn't mean you can simply discard everything you learned in high school. It is wrong to think that this is a more advanced form of Nine Palaces. If you train your body one day with swimming and one day with dance, you are training different systems, but it still is your own body and individual effort each time. One discipline does not supplant the other.

The form taught in this book is another facet of the entire scope of what we can learn and accomplish with Nine Palaces Qigong. If you have come to this form first, without previous qigong practice, you are still going to achieve as much as another student who has tried other versions, based on the sincerity and consistency of your efforts. It is the right time and place to learn what is here. For that reason, it is best to concentrate on this form as your single Nine Palaces Qigong practice for the day for at least a week to three months. Afterwards, you will know what will be best for you to continue, whether it is exploring this form further, returning to your previous Nine Palaces Qigong practice or even coming to meet Dr. Wu and studying what the current year or circumstance has to offer.

How to Stand: the Circle, Square and Triangle

Just as numbers are used as triggers within qigong practice on physical, as well as esoteric levels, we also use geometry and basic shapes for not only philosophical symbolism, but also as part of how we exercise our bodies when we practice. The symbolism and the physical sensations of the circle, the square and the triangle go hand in hand as integral parts of the experience. These are not only concepts to be vaguely aware of. Before we start to practice for the day, we must not only clear our minds of all the usual daily thoughts. We must replace them with the knowledge of the circle, the square and the triangle. We must know how to stand.

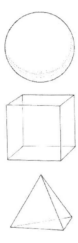

We have already talked at some length about yin and yang energy and how it can be conceptualized as a circle, as in the Taiji symbol and also as a square, as in the six harmonization of heaven, humanity, and earth. There are many different energetic pathways in the body, but the basic shapes of circle, square and also triangle are this qigong form's key means of experiencing our body sensations during practice. We use these shapes to adjust our posture and our perceptions during Nine Palaces Qigong, at one and the same time. Simply put, they are not mental visualizations. They are the postures we fit our body into as we train our muscles, joints and breathing. These shapes show us how to stand and how to move as we practice.

We have explored some of the philosophy behind the symbolism of the circle and the square in the previous chapter, how these shapes are used as metaphors for the fundamental process of harmonizing heaven, humanity, and earth. These simplest, most archetypal shapes illustrate our twin goals of merging with the flow of nature and simultaneously perceiving the universe in its infinitely vast and infinitely minute states. This is more than theoretical. Qigong is a method of physically experiencing these concepts at deeper and deeper levels.

How do we experience the relationship between the square and circle? First off, as you learn the practice, you will see many examples of circular movements. You will be making circular motions with the arms or head or hips, for example, as well as training the ability to expand the torso to fuller, rounder proportions from the inside out, using breathing and stretches. The universe is circular, a circle, the earth is a circle and within humans to a certain extent, much of our existence is circular as well. As the body becomes more rounded, breathing becomes more gently circular and even our awareness is also rounder. Over time, the practice coalesces into a definite sensitivity to a full, rounded field of perception surrounding the body. This is one of the new perceptions that is automatically gained with daily practice, as sure as ones muscles grow stronger when lifting weights.

When we cultivate ourselves with Nine Palaces Qigong, even though there are circular movements and circular sensations, our goal is also to become more solidly square as well. Human consciousness is centered inside the circle of the universe, but sometimes you also have to practice bringing that consciousness into the square of earthly matters. There's a saying in Chinese: "Heaven is a circle and earth is a square" (*tianyuan difang*). Before you practice this Nine Palaces form, be sure you have it in mind that within a circle, there's also a square.

What is this concept and how do we use it in our practice? There's a simple way to view the practical, physical understanding of this goal. Frequently, when we are analyzing the fengshui for people's houses, what we first want to do is to find the center point of that house, by connecting two lines drawn from the four corners of the house. Where the two lines intersect, we find the most important power point in the house. Dr. Wu illustrates this with a diagram of an X inside a square with the center point surrounded by a circle that is somewhat spacious:

In essence, this symbol represents how the center point of your house should be empty. It should not be blocked or filled with furniture or other objects. When adjusting the fengshui in a home, there's a concept called "The five elements inside of the house and the five elements outside of the house." This involves adjusting the balance of all the elements, to improve the qi so that it can flow more freely, bringing more harmony and opportunities, as needed. It's different for different people and circumstances, but in general, for any room, we count from one corner to the opposite corner and repeat for the other two opposing corners and the center point will be right here in the middle. It has to be empty. Furniture or other objects there would hold the qi down. You are trying to make the qi float free, not sink it, so by keeping this space clear from any furniture or obstructions, you are in fact promoting the qi to float. In other words, two lines of opposing force are meeting in the center, so keep that space clear, in order to make a place for new energy to arise.

In some special fengshui circumstances, you may want to place a particular object in this center point, in order to attract a particular qi to the area. This is heavily dependent on the energies of that particular astrological year and how they connect with the astrological makeup of the people living in the house. For example, in the Year of the Horse, specially dried manure collected from white stallions is prepared by the monks and sprinkled on the ground in this center point, in order to invoke the heightened yang energy that is uniquely present in this year. In the year of the Sheep, you would put a small bamboo plant sprinkled with salted water in the same spot, as an offering to the spirit of the Sheep, which loves to eat tender leaves and drink salted water. Generally speaking, though, the primary objective is to keep the area clear, for maximum lightness and flow.

We are using this same principle in qigong cultivation, when we bear in mind that within the overall circular space we create when we practice, there is an inner space that is square; our "house" so to speak. Within this square, we are clearing a special field for our qi to be freed and refined. This isn't just an esoteric concept. We work our way up to some of the most important exercises in the entire form especially to make square movements for generating a sense of solidity around a clear and empty core within the torso, as well as to release old memories, feelings and tensions at a very deeply held level within those core muscles. We use the escalating stages of the form to relax into a comfortable, rounded sensation of ease and then build a strong, inner sheath, formed of four-sided movements.

Regular practice not only develops a uniquely stable physical structure in posture and balance. It can also unleash sensations of enormous power and release, as the newly rebalanced body is re-energized. The final movements of the form train us to harness all that energy and store it back within one's core for even more clarity and stability of body and mind. Heaven is the circle and earth is the square. As soon as you stand up to begin your Nine Palaces practice, remind yourself of this important concept. Take your place knowing that within a circle, there is also a square. This is the first step in aligning yourself with the universe as you cultivate.

Qigong practice takes it as a given that your posture directly affects your state of mind. Furthermore, posture is always influencing your luck and opportunities, both due to how it improves or detracts from your health and also in how other people view and relate to you on a subliminal level because of how you carry yourself. Daoists believe that there are certain basic indicators of good fortune in a person's carriage. For example, a woman who holds herself with her chin held high to the sky will have more opportunities, while a man does best when he keeps his head down, looking at the ground. We could say that on one level this could be because confident women and humble men appear more appealing to others. However, a Daoist would say that they do better because they are each balancing their natural tendencies, women with the yang energy of heaven and men with the yin energy of earth.

This balance point is central to every aspect of Daoist cultivation, as we can see looking further at the proper posture to maintain while practicing Nine Palaces Qigong. If we must begin our practice with the sensation of the square inside the circle, how can we stand with the best posture to feel this enveloping roundness and internal solidity?

First off, the primary posture adjustment that must always be made when beginning to practice is to keep the body curved. This curve is our body's phys-ical manifestation of that sinuous central line divid-ing yin and yang in the Taiji symbol. Just as all the seasons of the year take place along this line, our day-to-day life events are reflected in the natural curvature of the spine. Daily activities cause stress, pressure and over time, misalignment. In the mon-astery, the monks sleep in shallow circular baskets that allow them to not only position their heads facing the best direction for any time of the year, but keep their bodies curled up while they rest. It's very important to sleep gently curled, rather than stretched out stiff and straight, in order to promote spinal health and replenishment while we sleep.

Regular qigong practice gives the body an even greater opportunity to relax and readjust the weight-bearing alignment so crucial to pain-free health and well-being. When practicing, at all times we keep the lower body very stable, with the knees slightly bent and the feet kept shoulder-width apart, toes pointing inwards. In this position, we can sit down into our stance, which is crucial for keeping the torso properly curved during practice. Whether our arms are up or down or mov-ing in any given qigong exercise, this curve is essential.

In the West, we think of good posture as standing up straight, with the neck elongated and the chin held high, with the abdomen sucked in and the shoulders square. During Nine Places practice, we actually must throw out this standard and instead, keep the body soft and curled into an almost opposite posture, in order to put the spine back into a more neutral state. Instead of a straight line or the natural S-curve of the spine, we are forming the head, neck, torso, hips and bottom of the pelvis into more of a "C," with the head slightly down, the chest caved inwards and the back rounded.

Curving the posture from the head down to the hips in this way lets us position the muscles to better take that pressure off the spine. Instead of fighting against stiffness and blockages we have accumulated over the years with standard standing and seated posture, we are bypassing them entirely by using the large muscles of the abdomen and upper back to form the rounded "C" shape. Always keep the lower abdomen very soft, rather than pulled in. Instead, allow the upper chest and sternum sink down in the same way they relax after you let out a big sigh.

At the same time, focus your awareness on rounding and curving the upper back outwards, opposite and proportional to the front of the chest sinking down, in the area between the shoulders and shoulder blades. This will automatically engage the muscles around the diagraph and upper abdomen, from the inside out. The main point is to sink the upper chest and keep the lower abdomen loose. The rest of the muscles in the upper back, as well as around the diaphragm area, will naturally trigger, without having to put much thought or force into the effort. The qigong exercises themselves will help further develop these muscles, so that they will align, build and strengthen from this starting point. The Nine Palaces Qigong form we present in this book is very heavily designed to focus on strengthening this "C" positioning, using breath and internal isometric stretches.

Strengthening the upper back, relaxing upper chest and loosening and articulating the muscles around the diaphragm, puts the spine into a neutral position and allows the organs packed into the chest and abdominal cavities to hang down more freely, also realigning them over time. Importantly, this posture also disengages the shoulders from their constant struggle to keep balanced with the hips and upper chest, by removing them from the posture equation. The shoulders are exercised and then relaxed to keep them sloped downwards as much as possible. Added to the basic C-curve, this lets the shoulder sockets and all the joints down the arms into the tips of the fingers relax, open and generate very soft, delicate movements that can generate a lot of momentum with the least amount of effort or force. When the shoulders are so greatly relaxed, the muscles and tendons along the sides and back of the neck that connect to them are also finally allowed to let go and unwind.

We use this opportunity to better position the head, chin and neck to promote our C-curve, all without tension or fighting against any stiffness and misalignment or breathing blockages that have already built up over the years. With the rest of the body properly aligned, you will only need to make the slightest, easiest movements with the head to completely readjust yourself, breathe more easily and feel many new sensations. We want the chin held pressed lightly into the neck and tipped down, bowing the head down with it ever so slightly.

This serves to further stretch the upper back of the neck where it connects with the skull and all the surrounding muscles. There is no need to position the teeth or tongue in any special way, unless specifically stated, although an advantage of keeping the chin in and down is the relaxation it brings to the mouth and other muscles at the front of the face and head.

This also holds for keeping the eyes open or closed. Unless otherwise mentioned, keep your eyes open, with the eyelids very relaxed, throughout the practice. In general, the eyes are always open during yang practices such as Nine Palaces, plus it promotes more relaxation in the facial muscles overall. While practicing, if you feel you need to close your eyes momentarily to relax, you may, but surprisingly, most people wind up tightening their foreheads and the area around the eyes if they keep them closed for extended periods of time during practice. Closing the eyes impedes the body's ability to keep itself balanced while standing and as a result, many minute muscular adjustments will be automatically made and held in response. Keeping the eyes open but with relaxed, hooded lids removes this subtle stress and by result, helps augment one's total alignment and relaxation.

It's not necessary to keep the chin tucked in with muscular effort. If there were already any stiffness issues or misalignment in the area, tucking the chin would just exacerbate them. Instead, just a general awareness at all times to hold the proper position will over time reposition, strengthen and lengthen the neck, in conjunction with the nine palaces exercises themselves. The key is always to choose ease, relaxation and gentleness over effort and excessive muscular force when practicing qigong. This is true both for breathing and for movement. In keeping with the basic tenets of the Daoist world view, going with the flow aligns us with our body, our breath and the universe around us. Over the twenty-five years of my own qigong practice, I've personally gained over an inch in height, as well as eradicating persistent neck and shoulder stiffness. The particular exercises in this form have accelerated this progress to a great degree.

Of course, it would not be so easy to reap the benefits of standing in a C-curve posture without the help from a supremely stable lower body. Again, the symbolic geometry of the universe finds its mirror in the human body. Besides the roundness of the sphere and the solidity of the cube, we make use of the dual qualities of the triangle at the basis of the way we stand and our entire practice. The pyramid is both immovable and immutable and dynamically bursting with upwards energy. Daoist belief mirrors the more familiar Egyptian esoteric traditions in revering the pyramid as a symbol of vitality and immortality, as well as considering a primary diagram of

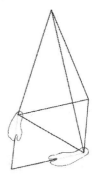

yang energy at its most active. The human body is considered to be made up of many triangles, whether from the shoulders down to the pelvis, or the feet up to the head, to the male or female sexual organs and the planes of the face. We want to utilize the symbolic power of the triangle when practicing Nine Palaces Qigong, as well as imitate its structure to create a solid physical starting point for cultivation.

The very first thing a qigong practitioner does when beginning the form is to put the feet and lower body in the proper stance. This is done before aligning the upper body. Interestingly, one's posture is put in place before what one would think would be the first order of business, clearing one's mind. This is how important a solid stance is considered. You cannot begin to clear your mind of its many thoughts or even regulate your breathing properly before you stand correctly. The triangle is key.

First, you want to stand with your feet shoulder width apart. They can be held slightly wider than shoulder width if comforta-  ble, but they must be well aligned with the shoulders. Double check visually if you have any doubts. You need this width as the first component of a very stable, low exertion stance that will take as much load off the upper body as possible. The goal is to feel as if you are standing not only on two legs, but as if you are a tripod, with its third "leg" growing from the bottom of the tail bone down into the ground. It's very common for people with stiff backs to not position their feet wide enough, so it pays to check how wide you think you are standing before you begin to practice. Use a mirror to get a clear feeling for where your feet, legs, knees and hips are, and where they need to be to be able to sit down well into your "tripod."

Along with the feet being shoulder width apart, the knees must be slightly bent. It will be easier to keep them properly bent when the feet are properly far enough apart. We bend the knees in order to form the third leg of our tripod. Bending the knees allows us to sit down with the hips and pelvis into a very solid stance. It's almost as if you are just about to sit in a chair, with the third leg of your tripod being the seat. This is where we gain a lot of assistance from standing relaxed in a C-curve, as a loose lower abdomen frees the pelvis to relax and easily tuck in and curve forward in that near-seated position, which in turn straightens the coccyx, letting the tripod's third leg grow down into the ground.

Besides bending the knees, it's most important to point the toes inwards as much as possible. This is the crucial, final element that will allow you to maintain this rooted stance comfortably for the duration of your practice. Don't be afraid to exaggerate how much your toes point in. This lets the hips, especially the back of the pelvis, fully open up. Then the hips will be at their maximum load-bearing ability, with the weight of the body most evenly distributed across the pelvis and down the legs. The more you allow the width of your hip bones to support your stance, the more you take pressure off the spine, which will hang freely and very centered. You also take any residual pressure off of the knee and ankle joints, as well as the delicate joints of the feet and toes. Just remember, as your feet point in, your hips will open out, counterbalancing your posture. When your hips open wide across, the center line of your body, including head, neck, spine, will adjust and straighten, and your shoulders and knees and lower abdomen can relax and sink down into the tripod stance sensation.

Keeping the toes pointed inwards is the key adjustment that lets the rest stay comfortably in place. It's the foundation of the entire qigong stance, just like the foundation of a house. If you stood for half an hour with your toes pointed straight ahead or for the same amount of time with toes pointed in, you would have very different physical sensations. Pointing inwards allows the rounded sensation field of the circle to be experienced more fully by the body. It also creates the interior space needed to feel the sensations of the square, solidifying the core of the body. You will feel the strong base and dynamic upward-flowing energy of the triangle. It will also relax and sink down any tension deep into the earth, so that you may completely dissolve away into a brand new realm of sensitivity, perceived across the entire body as you practice and afterwards, for the rest of your day.

The Lower Dantian: A Deeper Understanding

Most people who have some familiarity with qigong will have heard about the three locations of *dan* (elixir): upper, middle, and lower. The upper *dan* is in the center of the head between the two eyebrows. Dr. Wu demonstrates this point by pressing into the spot just up from the center point between them, as if you were touching the top edge of what would be considered dead center. Try pressing into this point yourself with your first or middle finger and observe your sensations.

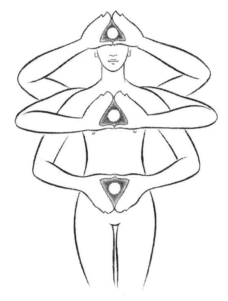

Between the two pectoral muscles, using the nipples as the guideline, the middle *dan* is at the center point. The lower is right below the navel. Find it the way Dr. Wu demonstrates, by pressing into the center of the navel with one hand while pressing at the center top edge of the pubic bone with the other hand. These are actually the perimeter points of the lower, which form a circular area between them.

For every human being, there are these three, but the main one is the lower one. Why do we call it *dantian*, rather than just *dan*, like the other two? *Tian* means a field where one cultivates crops, in particular, a rice field. In women, the childbearing ability is located here, in the ovaries. We can explain many principles following from this. In fact, to explore the ideas that come from within the simple strokes that form the character for *tian*, we can for the first time fully understand the true importance of the lower *dantian* within the body, and its connection to the most profound purpose of the nine palaces Nine-Five Maintenance of Qi form that we present here.

Tian is the Chinese character for rice field. Draw the character for heart below it, like so. According to Chinese culture, we believe the heart does more than just pump blood. Its function has an element of thinking or thought to it as well. From the western medical standpoint, the only organ that processes thought is the brain. According to traditional Chinese medical theory, in addition to thoughts that are created in the brain, we can also think with the heart. This heart thinking accounts for situations commonly heard about, such as people who get overly excited in highly stimulating conditions, like at a major sporting event, and then have a heart attack.

Sometimes this is also the Chinese medical perspective on why people who have a heart condition and get into an angry excited state, from an argument for example, could suddenly trigger a heart attack. Why? Because we believe there is a thought process generated by heart function, not just the brain, and it can affect the whole body as directly as the mind's thoughts, if not even more powerfully. The question becomes: do you want to let the powerful forces of the heart erupt automatically at this or that stimulation, or do you want to learn how to make use of its power and harness it for the greater good of your mental and physical health?

In Chinese culture, words hold a very high degree of importance. Over millennia, the culture has become completely enmeshed with the characters, their pronunciation, and their every stroke when written. Layer after layer of meaning has developed from this intense relationship, so that the language itself is reflective of the most fundamental cultural beliefs. Putting two characters together to form a third is a significant act.

The character for field on top and the character for heart beneath it, combine together to make a third word, *sī*. This is the word for thought, meaning your thoughts, beliefs and intentions. To take this even further, there is another word made of two characters, the character *jīn*, which means "now," that is also drawn on top of *xīn*, the same character for heart. Combined together, these two characters form the word *niàn*, which means a remembrance. When the characters of *sī* and *niàn* are placed together, they form a new word, which means "to think of, to long for, or to miss." In other words, something you have had and fondly remember as your heart's desire, as if it was here with you now.

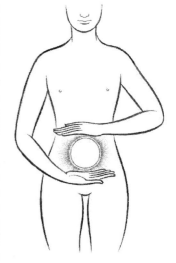

You have a field, where new growth forms, you have your heart, combined together, you have your intention. Placing your intention with the desire of your heart brings you to your most real and innate desire, your True Will. Our lower *dantian* is where we energize the development of new forms of consciousness. It is where we give birth to the power of our true heart and mind. The Nine Palaces Qigong presented in this book focuses specifically on the lower *dantian* in certain special exercises that are unique to this particular form. It will bring you to this new awareness.

Another energetic spot that will come into play in unique ways in this practice is the Baihui acupoint. It is located at the very top of the head. If you draw a line between the two highest points of the ears and another line from the tip of the nose and its corresponding point at back of the head where the skull curves outwards the most, the Baihui acupoint will be right at the center where these two lines intersect. It is often recognized as the topmost spot in the body when cycling the Microcosmic Orbit.

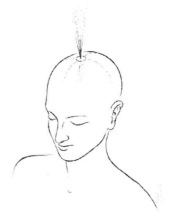

However in this practice, the Baihui is not used as a station point that is part of the Microcosmic Orbit. We are not exercising the Microcosmic Orbit. Instead, this Nine Palaces Qigong focuses on the general structure of the body, taken as a whole, rather than simply circulating energy along a single closed circuit such as the Microcosmic Orbit or particular columns of energy, such as the three vertical columns that were explored in the nine palaces form in *Qigong for Total Wellness*. We are aiming to integrate our entire body into a single unit. We want the body to be a solid, unified whole, above and beyond the energy pathways within it; and then pass that place towards a complete dissolving into the energy of the universe. Specific points, such as the Baihui or the lower *dantian* may come into play, but they do so in order to direct the physical body and mental, emotional and spiritual consciousness into these profound states.

The importance of approaching this practice divorced from preconceptions based on other discussions of qigong or energy pathways in the body cannot be stressed more highly. It's another way of thinking, of using thoughts and emotions to stimulate the body's energetic systems. You could call it a yearning, the way a mother and child would yearn for each other if they were separated, or if your lover was far away on a long trip and you were waiting for him or her to return. This is the kind of thought you must place inside of your body in order to practice Nine Palaces Qigong form presented here. Only when you can put this feeling, which is a physical state as much as it is a mental state, into your lower *dantian*, which is as much influenced by a physical area in the body as it is by the emotional energy put into it, then you are truly practicing this form. You must use this level of emotional identification as the connection to your physical feelings to act as the springboard for your cultivation. The synergy between thought, emotions and physical sensation is the source of the consciousness behind this practice, as well as its motivating force.

As we were saying, Chinese culture and language are inextricably combined, especially when exploring the ancient byways of knowledge in the teachings of Laozi and the practice of qigong. We are talking about exercises and locations in the body, states of mind, and philosophical ideals to aspire to on an esoteric level as well as pragmatically in everyday life. They are all combined together as one, passed down through words and images used as dense symbols with many layers of teachings. To learn qigong is to be struck all at once with knowledge that instructs the body, mind, heart and spirit. A concept can be presented in one word and resonate at any level you wish to approach your practice. It's important to underscore this point, which is so crucial in the understanding of how a teacher teaches qigong and how a student learns from being exposed to the teachings.

For example, there are ten or more established English translations of the *Book of Changes*. A noted professor from a major Ivy League university came to Dr. Wu to talk about the *Book of Changes*, referencing the different translations. Dr. Wu told him bluntly there was really nothing to talk about, because a lot of the translations are not accurate. If he used the English versions as a basis for his study, he had to recognize the degree of inaccuracy in the currently available translations. A lot of the translations neglect accuracy on small things the individual translator didn't judge important. But quite on the contrary, those small details are the essence of the *Book of Changes*.

For instance, in the *Book of Changes* there are two characters, *yue* and *shou*. When translated into English, these two words are commonly given the same translation of "talk" and would be considered synonyms of "talking. However, culturally speaking, a native Chinese speaker with a background steeped in the old texts understands when these characters appear together, it is recited out loud and the pronunciation then is changed to *shu-ey*, which has more subtle meaning than just talk. It means persuasive talk in hopes of influencing the other person. That's what this *shu-ey* means. It's a deeper meaning than just talk. If you used it in a sentence it would mean persuading the person you're talking to, not just talking to them. This is no different than understanding subtle nuances of meaning in English that another culture might not understand. Even contemporary native English speakers need books filled with references and annotations to fully grasp the word play in Shakespearian drama. A translation of the *Book of Changes* would not only need a detailed understanding of modern and archaic Chinese characters, there would also need to be a cultural understanding of classical recitation, which has unique properties compared to spoken language, not to mention the inner teachings of *Book of Changes* divination that are rarely if ever presented in public.

When talking about any Chinese traditional studies, one is automatically talking about old texts where the written and spoken word go together, hand in hand. There is an interaction between classical Chinese writing and recitation that colors and deepens the meaning of every word. In Traditional Chinese Medicine, when the texts discuss diagnosis by taking the pulses on the wrists, the Chinese character recognized as *mai* is often referred to, one of its meanings understood as "meridians." Diagnosis via palpating the pulses on the wrist is called *haomai*; literally "sensing the meridians." Because of this general usage, much study of TCM in the West has conceptualized the meridians as vessels or channels related to or functioning similarly to blood vessels, veins and arteries.

Actually, this is an incorrect understanding of *mai*. Although today the character is pronounced *mai* in the classical Chinese of the era of the early medical texts, it was pronounced as *luo*. When you talk about *mai*, it can be understood as meridians, but when you talk about *luo*, as in the original Chinese texts, there is a subtle element of qi in the definition as well, qi that is not palpable or tangible. It's referring to air and qi's innate ability to move. Cultures all over the world have studied the health and energy flow in the body, but it is the Daoist cultivation of qi and qigong practice that has led Chinese medicine to conceptualize and categorize this flow in its unique and highly detailed way. The practice of qigong led to the realization there is a certain movement of qi that exists within the body and through the Daoists' discovery, they were able to write down and eventually verify and confirm all the collaterals and meridians in the body. Only through cultivation will you be able to increase your understanding and appreciation of the subtlety of qi and collaterals and meridians within the body.

Returning to the character *luo*, it has another meaning where you're actually going to a person and with your finger are palpating or touching the body. Beyond this, there's another meaning where you are not just palpating, but actually intentionally guiding the qi, directing it to where you want it to go. Going back to the original *mai*, we see the superficial meaning is correct, but there are all these other deeper meanings, brought about by the cultural history built up around the shifting and developing usages of an ancient word. The cultural differences between our Western norms and the Chinese traditions are constantly creating gaps when exploring these topics.

As another example, we are used to using the family name second, after the personal name. Meanwhile, the family name always is given first in Chinese. When doing *Book of Changes* calculations, if one must write the personal name first and the family name second, this would be a huge distinction with many ramifications for a Chinese student that could easily be missed by a Western student, without being reminded of the Chinese cultural norms it upends. The understanding of the power and use of a name would be reversed. The cultural perspective so heavily informs the message that it takes extra care and explanation to convey what is so succinctly put forth in a few brushstrokes in Chinese.

In this way, we come all the way back to the lower *dantian* and the words *sī* and *sīniàn*, to see how it encompasses many of Daoism's primary beliefs. You have the field and the heart combining together to form the thoughts. Laozi teaches that in order to achieve something, no matter what it is, it has to be given up first to attain it at last. To have the object of my desire in the end, I have to relinquish my ties to it beforehand. This might be considered a very complicated and circuitous way of striving for the things you want, but from the Daoist perspective, this isn't in order to challenge a person or raise the bar on one's personal expectations or even to find a more superior way of being. It's simply the recognition of the ebb and flow of yin and yang. There are always two ways to look at a situation, yin or yang. If you set your sights on something you really want, it doesn't mean you necessarily will have it and the more hope of having it you have, the more disappointment you will have in the end if you don't get it. It's a disappointment that is a kind of harm to the mind, psychologically speaking. This is the Chinese way of seeing things.

Let's say a boy sees a beautiful girl and ultimately wishes she would fall in love with him. A Chinese mindset would have the boy saying to himself "You're beautiful and I really like you. I want to get to know you but if you don't want to get to know me, that's fine too." Initially, in his heart and mind, he doesn't take her that seriously, with a fatalistic attitude of either it happens or it doesn't. He will reason that since she is so beautiful, she must have many other suitors much more eligible and appealing than he is. Even though he'd appreciate earning her love, he would find it perfectly understandable if it couldn't be attained.

It's a little different in Western society, where we see something and are immediately determined to get it. The launching point on how to approach the matter is a little different, perhaps more extreme. One could say he would give it his all in pursuit of his goal, but if he doesn't get it, the stakes have been set so high from the start, the defeat feels all the more crushing. The Chinese boy has doubts from the first moment the attraction arises and at once also knows it'll be fine if it doesn't work out. The uncertainty instantly creates a nonchalant attitude. Either he'll be with her or not. His thought process already has the awareness of yin and yang well developed within it. He can get her or not and everything will be fine either way. He will still pursue her love, but he won't go to *dan*gerous extremes or subject himself to emotional or physical harm. His motivation's launching point is based on the objective understanding that she will have many others interested in her. He can't react too tragically if it doesn't work out, because of her obvious opportunities.

Just like the reason a cup can hold water is because it starts out empty, he will approach the girl and speak his heart to her. He will tell her that his situation is not the most elevated, he may not be a high level executive, but he has the sincerity of wanting to get to know her. He tells her his circumstances in full truth and honesty. He may not have a big house or a fancy car or a lot of money. He just has a heart that loves her and the will to try his best for their future together. In this way you let everything go, in hopes of attaining it. By telling her the truth and all the unflattering or unattractive facts of his circumstances, he has already let go of his hopes to impress her. People can be more or less superficial, but some women would see the sincerity in what he said and would appreciate it, developing deep feelings towards him in return.

If he had not been sincere in his intentions and put up a false front of success and material wealth in their stead, what would he have achieved by marrying the object of his affections? Eventually, that person would find out the extent of the trickery and lies. How long could the marriage last after this? In a sense, this is a practical example of Laozi's teachings in action. To give up everything first means admitting the truth about yourself and the situation you are in, facing your circumstances with realism and sincerity and understanding that even with your best efforts, if the outcome doesn't go your way, accepting it for what it is, is the only way to continue on. It's about taking one step back to advance a step further. If you understand your life at this level, you begin to see the truth of what is and isn't meant to be. This is Laozi's message for us. Use sincerity in all your dealings, be truthful and the end result will be correct.

To speak of *sīniàn* in concrete terms means to live life from this standpoint. It's not an abstraction. It's the perspective that helps you when you are confronted with problems. It's what gives you the strength of character to take a square look at hardship, without sugar coating or excuses. It's what builds confidence in your integrity so that you can deal with others honestly, respecting their dignity and intelligence. It's about seeing clearly what is real and what is fake, bravely, without fear.

Ultimately, in this Nine Palaces Qigong form, we are courageously allowing our wildest fears and hopes to come up from within, asking the universe for protection and a new strength. What is this protection? It is found dissolving the barriers between the body and the universe in a state of complete physical relaxation. A special resilience is formed. A consciousness of totally open awareness is born from this state. This is the strength that we receive. We have let go everything we normally cling to in this practice of deep release and gain new and more capacity to revitalize and rejuvenate, physically and emotionally. We have let go of what we thought we wanted and have remembered what we really require. The perception of the body is gone and is replaced with flowing energy to be enjoyed, enhanced and redirected in harmony with the whole. This is the true alchemy of the nine palaces.

Chapter Three

Welcoming Qi

The First Phase

Nine-Five Maintenance of Qi qigong consists of five stages of interacting with qi, finished with the sixth stage, which is the core Nine Palaces form itself. To begin, the first phase is "welcoming qi" (*yingqi, yingjieqi*). *Ying* means "to welcome" as used in modern Chinese (*huanying*). It signifies an invitation, an accepting of qi. Qiu Chuji, in his description of this practice, states that welcoming qi is the key to Nine-Five Maintenance of Qi practice. That the originator of these teachings ascribes such importance to this first portion of the form can be explained with an example. As has been said already, traditionally, if the Daoists masters left the monastery on a long journey, to compete in a martial arts tournament or act in other official capacities as a representative of the monastery, they would have to practice this form before they went. It was understood as a ceremonial practice to ask for heaven's power to protect them, as well as to boost themselves physically and mentally so that they were not harmed on their way.

Simply put, this practice is a self-defense method to help us and protect us from all the harms of the external world. In order to begin practice, we must use the analogy of a nation ceremonially raising its flag every morning as a symbol of national identity. This is the welcoming of qi. It is the crucial opening stage of the nine palaces form presented here. Just as a country must raise its flag every morning as a declaration of national sovereignty, this beginning set of movements is like raising your own flag, a salute to yourself. This is welcoming the qi.

37

When to Practice

In *Qigong for Total Wellness*, when practicing Nine Palaces Qigong, you must stand facing the direction corresponding to your birth season. If you are born in spring, face east. Born in summer, you face to the south. Those born in fall face west and winter face north. Facing your birth direction positions you between where you came from and where you will go. If you're born in the summer, you will be leaving this life in the winter. When people pass away and move on, they will usually fit this pattern. We face our birth direction, then, in order to feel that flow; letting it pass through us, from the energy of birth to the stillness of death. In Daoism, there is a great emphasis on this transition and its ties to the seasons of heaven and earth.

Following this same line of thought, there is detailed Daoist study on the best positions for sleep. Normally, the usual healthful position is thought of in relation to the position of the earth's poles, with the head in the north, facing south and the feet, in turn facing north. For a more fine-tuned adjustment, instead of following this general rule, for spring and summer, your face should be facing east as you lay. For fall and winter, the face should be pointing west. This pattern is what you should follow if you want to specifically maintain and tonify your health. Your body should be slightly curved like the central dividing line on the Taiji symbol. This line is a representation of the curves in your body and spine, as well as the transitions of the seasons. Although it is a bit exaggerated, compared to the natural curvature of the spine, it does indicate how you should not keep your body stiff and straight as you sleep, but keep slightly curled up. These are the standard postures for healthful sleep, but it is noted that it is also acceptable to sleep facing your birth direction.

However, welcoming qi is an invitation and a reception of qi from a very specific source and for a very specific purpose. Because of this, it has some notable differences to other qigong practices. It does not rely on the birth month and direction. We are not simply enhancing the way our lives fit in as part of the planet. We are seeking change and an increase in power. Therefore, we always face the sun when practicing this type of Nine Palaces Qigong, instead of our individual direction. The sun gives us the special protection and assistance we are asking in.

Since we are reaching out to the sun, we want the ideal time of the day to open the communication and get the best energy from the sun for our purpose. As a result, when practicing this form, prime emphasis is placed on picking the right time of the day to face the sun. The best time to practice is from seven to nine in the morning. It's the best time to welcome qi. This is when the light from the sun is at its best. During this period, you should be standing facing the sun. It will be the best opportunity in the day to make contact.

In the connection between qigong and the *Book of Changes*, timing is always key. A *Book of Changes* practitioner must carefully select the right time to begin the calculations. It has to be done at a time of day that corresponds to the questions being asked, whether about health, business, family, and so on. Beyond this, it must be a moment where the practitioner is most receptive to the messages of the universe coming in. Finally, at a high level of *Book of Changes* divination, besides these factors, the universe must give the practitioner its cue that now is the right time.

There are signals as diverse as if there are birds in the sky at the precise intended moment and the direction they are flying, or how a leaf drifts to the ground in just the right way. These are a few of many cues that tell the practitioner that the divination results will be accurate, but the first element that must be in place is always the timing. As important as harmonizing with the environment is in general Daoist thought and practice, timing is more important here. Timing is more important than positioning because we are trying to make a change, rather than simply staying on the current course, or unifying with the general external trend. Successfully accomplishing goals is dependent on timing. Just as *Book of Changes* calculations require just the right moment for accuracy, in this qigong form, we are seeking certain results, so when to practice becomes the primary consideration.

Obviously, it isn't only *Book of Changes* calculations that require perfect timing. Timing our actions to adjust to the world around us is a basic fact of survival. Human culture has always grown and developed from timing important events with the seasons. There is a certain time of the year to plant crops and to harvest them. In war, there is a time of the year where conquest is favorable, due to the climate, versus the time of the year where increasing defense moves ahead in importance. We instinctively respond to obvious cues, like dressing warmly in the winter. With extra observation, we can pinpoint the best times of the day to eat, sleep or take care of many other functions, based on the circadian rhythms that govern our bodies.

Daoists have accumulated many centuries of information, by careful study and observation of the environment and the living creatures within it. As the study is refined, more and more seemingly esoteric observations can be made with varying degrees of accuracy, but for the most part, they are based first and foremost on careful observation of the natural world.

Going back to the example we've already used about different positions to sleep in, generally, one should sleep with the head in the north, facing to the south, so that the feet face north in turn. This is to align the body with the earth's magnetic fields, the North and South Poles. It's not common knowledge outside of the monastery, but the Daoist monks sleep on circular beds. The prayer mat that they sit on when cultivating in sitting meditation is also a circle. The students use standard mats, but the high abbots and masters have a circular pad to sleep on embroidered with the Taiji symbol. They will change their sleeping direction and body position throughout the year, in accordance with the circle of Taiji, in order to maintain the insight and ability to carry out their monastic duties.

For everyday benefit, following the general sleeping direction is enough, but it can be fine-tuned to a great degree. In spring and summer, the standard north and south is further adjusted, so that you lie on your side with your head still in the south, but facing east. In winter, lie on your other side, so your head is turned to the west. However, let's say you had an important business opportunity that would require careful negotiations. The night before the meeting, you would want to sleep so that your head in the west, facing east and your feet are in the east, face back to the west. This direction axis symbolizes money and career opportunities, which you want to temporarily maximize for your big day, even though we generally want to sleep in the direction that is best for health maintenance.

This qigong practice begins with yingqi, or welcoming the qi and the nature of the entire form is suffused with the intent of inviting and embracing the sun's energy. From seven to nine am, the light is the best for inviting in the sun and making contact. There are always adjustments that can be made to further augment the results of this cultivation. For example, Dr. Wu told me to practice at either five in the morning or three in the afternoon, in order to best learn the form in order to write about it in this book. These hours are the times of the day when the light is changing, just blossoming into dawn or the last light before dwindling into dusk. These are the best times to practice if you need to make many profound transformations to your life.

Also, I am born in the spring, so my birth direction is east. Since the sun rises in the east, five am was particularly good for me to enhance my practice. From seven to nine am will bring in the best quality of light to maximize the protective power of this form, however. If your birth direction happens to correspond with the direction of the sun at this time, it is optimal for the goal of welcoming the qi. Facing the sun is the most important element, though, and it is most important to face the sun, whatever direction it is in, no matter what time you practice, unlike other forms of Nine Palaces Qigong. Continue facing the sun for the entire form.

Facing the sun sets this form apart from other qigong we have learned. Traditionally, this form was only practiced when someone in the White Cloud Monastery was undergoing difficulties or undertaking a long journey away from the monastery. The practice is mentioned in the monastery's oldest records, naming a master Xue Huji, who was about to set out on a perilous journey to visit another master in the Snow Mountains. Once all his other preparations were made, at the last, he performed this same ritual. The Nine-Five Maintenance of Qi practice is a ceremonial style of qigong that is part of the nine palaces, asking the heavens to grant you a talisman of protection against sickness or hardship during travels and travails. Because we are right now going through a strenuous period of illness and obstacles on a global level, is why this practice is being presented in this book.

Whether practicing at 5 a.m. or later, if there is a particular issue to work on that day, it is best to start your practice immediately when waking up from sleep. First, go to sleep the night before, using the correct posture, whether for health or for finances as we have already discussed. Then as you awaken, rise up into a sitting position slowly. Once you are sitting up in bed, do a little stretch, by stretching up one arm at a time, with the hands in light fists and the elbows bent at a right angle outward at chest level, like a cat. Stretch each arm up and down a times until you have warmed yourself up. It's important to stretch every morning. If you have pets, observe your cats and dogs. The first thing they do when they get up from a nap or deep sleep is stretch. Watch how a cat stretches her front paws forward, using her shoulders, rotating them as she stretches one clawed arm forward then the other, also putting her hips into it, so her whole ribcage gets a workout. Your animals are trying to warm their bodies up and wake up their muscles with stretching.

We are just like them. We should stretch to warm up our muscles. After a small stretch while still in bed, we rise slowly, by sitting on edge of the bed for half a minute before standing up. Put on your clothes or stay in your pajamas if you like, but don't brush your teeth, wash your face, shower or do anything else. Just immediately exit the bedroom, and walk out of your house into your back yard or other quiet outdoor spot, and face in the direction of the sun. Stand with the sun in front of you and relax your soul. Relax your mind, body and spirit. Close your eyes and smile within yourself to relax deeply.

Balancing Body and Breath

Whether you are practicing the moment you get out of bed, to deal with a special challenge for the day, or just practicing between 7 a.m. and 9 a.m., or any other time during the day that is right for you, you will always stand facing the sun. Relax deeply with a clear, empty mind. There is no special prayer or mantra to say. Just breathe naturally and be very calm. This is the state of mind necessary for welcoming the qi.

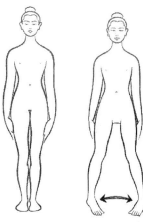

How should you stand? Stand straight but naturally, then step out with some awareness, so that your feet are shoulder width apart, toes pointing in, in that solid tripod position we have discussed in the previous chapter. Opening the feet and legs in this way allows more physical experience of opening your body into the circle with the square inside of it, which is the one thought you should recall before you begin practice. The toes pointing inwards form your foundation, like the foundation of a house. When the toes are facing this way, you are forming a triangle, just as the reproductive organs form the shape of a triangle. You are a pyramid, standing tall. Whatever is inside that pyramid will gain energy, just as the pharaohs in their pyramids did not decay.

When you position your body in the shape of a triangle, the first place that will feel relaxed will be the reproductive organs and anus. You will feel like the third leg is growing out from behind you to form a solid tripod and you will feel good. This relaxed feeling will help you sense the plant that grows within you. Like a young tree needs three poles to support it from the wind, or like the very tall building uses a zigzag triangular framework for structure, this stance will bring you solidity and the means to grow tall.

Daoists say that if an object is not straight, it will naturally become more rounded. As we have discussed, Daoism seeks to explore the numbers and shapes of the universe. The Daoist studies identify one hundred and thirty four shapes. Using shapes to harmonize with the seasons or to increase health is a deep study that has been made over millennia.

In the wintertime, people should focus their eyes and minds on shapes that have angles, to block the perception of cold and the soft, blurry experience of snow, in order to generate heat. In the springtime, focus on triangular shapes, as triangles symbolize growth. In the summer, look at more circular shapes and objects to smooth out the irritation that can result from excess heat. In autumn, rectangular shapes make people feel a sense of accomplishment. Have children look at things with many angles to challenge them.

Daoism is linked with the *Book of Changes*, which is linked with numbers and the geometry of things. When we analyze the Egyptian pyramid, it's enduring energy and everlasting growth is due to the triangle. We see the reproductive systems of male and female as triangular. Also noses are triangular so there is an entire study of analyzing the personality through the shape of the nose. Standing solidly with a sense of your triangular presence is how we begin to open communication with the sun.

Besides posture and a clear mind, you want to give some attention to breathing gently and naturally. Check your pulse at your wrist. Four heartbeats should correspond to one inhale and exhale. The average body breathes about twenty thousand times a day, one thousand, one hundred and forty times per hour. Adjust the speed of your movements based on your breathing. You decide how fast you want to do the practice, as slow or as fast as your body is telling you. Obviously, you may also take your daily situation into account, if you don't have as much time that day to practice. Overall, when you sensitize yourself to the pace of your breathing, you will find that you won't be breathing that slowly, or doing the

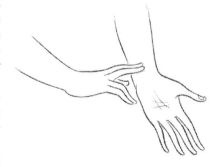

movements of the practice that slowly either. It's based on your body's needs, but this is an energizing practice overall.

The goal is to adjust yourself and your qigong practice to your body's rhythms. A good example is the classic tradition of checking your tongue first thing in the morning after you get out of bed. If your lips are red and your tongue is yellow, it means you're overheated, with too much yang energy. In order to balance yourself, do your practice more slowly that day and avoid eating animal flesh. Fish can produce heat and meat can produce phlegm. However, if your tongue coating is white in the morning, it means the body is more cold than hot, so to balance that, eat hot food through the day, either foods that are hot in temperature or foods that are heating to the body, like fish and turkey.

Daoists emphasize using diet to gain longevity. The belief is that you introduce sickness through your mouth. Whatever you eat is now part of you. You can't take it out again. For every bite you don't eat, you gain one extra day of longevity and for every bite you force yourself to eat, you lose one day of longevity. Monks in the White Cloud Monastery stop eating solid food at noon. At night, no rice or grain products are eaten, even in liquid form. They will only eat soup or fruit juice in the evening, if they are feeling hungry at all. The soup is made of cooked roots some days, or bean soups from different kinds of beans on others, as there is a specific menu for every day, corresponding to the seasons and days of the month.

You can make a similar soup at home with black beans, green mung beans, red adzuki beans, small white beans, and yellow dried soybeans. These are the five beans with the colors of the five elements. Cook them long and slow in water until a rich broth is formed. Strain out the solids and drink the liquid with a sprinkling of sesame seeds on top. It will give you a lot of strength.

Traditional Chinese medical doctors focus on pulse power when forming a diagnosis, but the Daoists determine wellbeing more from the tongue coating. If the right or left side of the tongue has a heavier coating, it means either the liver or the gall bladder is having issues that day. Thickened coating on the tip of tongue indicates the heart, while the back of tongue is the kidney and the center of the tongue is the spleen and stomach. If your tongue is red and you still eat meat, it will make the tongue redder and increase your temper and feelings of stress or agitation. The optimal tongue color is a light, pale natural tongue color. This indicates a slightly more acidic body balance, which is ideal. If the tongue is really red, douse the fire by drinking more water or eating watermelon.

Dr. Wu's teachers would look at his tongue and tell him what to practice for the day, standing posture or tai chi or qigong. The monastery even had two different dining halls and based on their tongue reading for the day, the monks would eat at one or the other. By observing your tongue, you can take many actions for balancing yourself for the day, including how much you should exercise. If you have excess heat, with a yellow colored coating, then move slowly through the day. If the coating is white, move faster to balance your coldness. The monks would look at their tongue coating and even decide how far they would travel for the day. By all means, take this into considering when choosing how fast or slow to practice qigong.

To make a well-considered decision on the speed and intensity of your practice for the day, the same analysis applies for the pulse, as well as the tongue. Analyze your tongue quickly when you wake up, then check your pulse before you begin to practice to determine the speed of your practice. If your pulse is slow, especially so slow, it's out of alignment with the speed of your breathing, you may want to do the practice a little faster. In fact, increase all your general movements for the rest of the day to balance yourself as thoroughly as possible. The Nine-Five Maintenance of Qi practice consists of simple movements, but they can be a real workout even though individual exercises do not require intense exertion. Determining the best pace for yourself will allow you to practice quickly, effectively and without wasteful effort. You will be maximizing your practice to carefully observe your body's cues and respond to them with intention. Harmony begins from within.

Gentleness, Emptiness, Tranquility

This leads to an important general point when practicing this, or any, qigong form. Straining with effort when practicing does not improve the quality or the results of your practice. It is always better to practice gently, with gentle breathing and easy, fluid, effortless muscle movements. If you find yourself holding your breath as your practice, tightening your posture, or tensing your muscles, slow down and do the exercise more gently. It is always better to choose light, easy breathing and movement over physical force. There are physical, mental and philosophical reasons behind this, as is usual in the multilayered nature of qigong.

Laozi teaches us we should not think with our egos, constantly seeing through the filter of "me" and "I." Our sense of self should be dissolved into the flow of the universe. This is the meaning of nothingness or non-existence (*wu*), that which is not there. The cup is hollow so that we can pour water in to drink. This is the metaphor used in Buddhism to illustrate the term "emptiness" (*kong*). Sensuality (*sè*), literally "color," moreover, is a Confucian concept that means the attraction between men and women, the foods we eat, our desire for money. It means the connection to the colorful world, our worldly, material concerns. Non-existence, emptiness, and sensuality, then, are the three core principles of Chinese philosophy.

When Dr. Wu was young, he asked his teacher "What does this nothingness and emptiness mean? What do you mean by sensuality?" Dr. Wu's teacher told him to lie on the bed and then hit him on his bottom with a rattan switch. He told him "This is sensuality. You know it when you feel it on your rear end." Thus, it is easy to explain.

For nothingness and emptiness, he gave him another story. Emperor Tang Taizong (598-649) was very powerful when he was alive. His was a glorious moment in Chinese history, during the Zhenguan era, the great peak of the Tang

Dynasty (618-907). He had limitless power, but governed the nation with fair policies. As a result, during his era, China was prosperous in every imaginable direction, the rule of law, the wealth of the country, great flourishing's of art and philosophy. This emperor made a great contribution to his time and his territory reached far and wide, including Inner and Outer Mongolia and even deep into what is now Russia, the largest sphere of influence of the Tang Dynasty, second only to the conquests Genghis Khan (1162-1227), nearly six hundred years later. The Zhenguan era was China's foremost Golden Age of peace and prosperity.

Emperor Taizong was a devout follower of the Daoist alchemical tradition and established many monasteries in this time, followed by his son, who built even more. Before the emperor died, he commanded his coffin to be constructed with two holes. He was laid in the coffin with his two arms stretched out of the holes. On his right hand, the character for emptiness was inscribed and the left hand, that for nothingness. Not only did he contribute to his kingdom in life, he also used his death to impart his final insight, to be left as an inspiration and warning for posterity. When you are dead this is all you leave in the world, nothingness and emptiness. Not many people can fully grasp the significance of this message.

In this life, the drive for fame blocks our understanding of nothingness and the drive for fortune and wealth blocks our understanding of emptiness. Sensuality is a constant that exists at all times, but becomes a greater and greater challenge as we satisfy our drives for fame and fortune. We spend our whole lives working hard for money to survive but the more we succeed, the more we obtain beyond the subsistence level, the more we are working for fame as much as for money. If you have one, you have the other, or so it seems in our society. Se means the drive for the opposite sex as a symbol of power and success. In modern terms, you could call wanting a trophy wife an example, although history is filled with powerful women who wanted the equivalent.

Wu Zetian (624-705), the wife of Tang Taizong's son and successor, Tang Gaozong (649-683), eventually became China's only independently ruling Empress. In her old age, she surrounded herself with a harem of young men. No matter what your gender is, when you reach a certain level of ambition achieved, sexual conquest is the next motivation. Without money, there is no survival or even existence, but too much money can bring disaster.

We live in a world where it is easy to succumb to the headlong pursuit of fame, wealth and sex. Daoists understood their strong influence and developed theory and method to offset their harmful effects. We are all trying to balance our desires and keep them on the level of what is right, natural and life-giving, rather than be consumed by them. Balancing the endless chasing of fame, fortune and decadence with dissolving into non-existence, becoming an empty vessel and achieving perfect equilibrium of yin and yang within oneself is the subject of profound Daoist alchemical inquiry. The *Yellow Court Classic* (*Huangting jing*) is one of the classic texts that famously explores this balance, but all qigong practice is enriched by its understanding.

It's apparent that psychologically, we use our qigong practice to release our minds from our daily worries and concerns. However, we must always start with releasing the tension physically, from within the body first, where the years of struggle and difficult memories are lodged. This is why we first check our pulse at the wrist and match our breathing to its beat, four beats to one complete inhale and exhale. You can breathe a little faster to match the pulse or slow your breathing down in order to slightly slow your pulse, depending on your previous tongue analysis, when you first awoke. The key is, we are adjusting ourselves to our body's needs, before we have done anything else except stand up. We stand facing the sun and take a step out to the side, so that the feet are shoulder width apart and the toes are pointed in, in the stable, tripod-like posture we have discussed. Now it is time to use the principles of nothingness and emptiness to completely open and relax.

As you stand, breathing naturally in rhythm with your body, you are experiencing nothingness with your gentle, harmonious breathing. This is why gentle motion is such a priority when practicing qigong. Not only is it easier on the body, it helps us to embody the experience of nothingness, or dissolving into non-existence as a part of the universe. This dissolving further frees our minds, along with our bodies, from the chains and strains of our ego drives. As we breathe gently and step out, we now relax the thirteen points, or joints, one by one. Start with the shoulders and let all the tension drop away from them. Then relax the elbows, then the hands, then the hips, knees, and feet. Finally, we relax our head, the thirteenth point. We are facing east to the early morning sun and using our gentle breathing to flow in harmony with its rising energy. This relaxation of the joints and sense of flow is our first step in experiencing emptiness.

Gentle breathing and a sense of dissolving take the body tension out of the equation. You may feel a sore spot or a blockage or tightness when you try to relax, but qigong is not about directly confronting or untying these knots. Over time, the practice will make your muscles and breathing stronger and suppler, more able to release internal tension held in the muscle memory and the mind. However, simply breathing gently and forgetting the little aches and pains is the first step in bypassing the blockages you will eventually release.

You are making yourself empty and receptive to new sensations, not just the same old sore spots and familiar imbalances. Removing tension and effort allows the experience of emptiness. This allows experience of the free flowing of energy passing through you from the sun. Remember, you must have emptiness first to fill yourself with new energy. You will make much more physical progress in the practice of qigong, the more you override the muscles, the pains, the strains and blocks, and will bring the new sensations in quickly. Breathing and posture is all that's needed. Nothingness and emptiness are physical, not visualizations. Together, they assist you in experiencing the circle and the square within, which are the shapes we will be embodying as we practice the Nine-Five Maintenance of Qi.

Of course, we are emptying the mind, but the body is the starting point. Experiencing your body as empty and your breathing as gentle naturally settles the mind. Allow posture and the breath to calm the heart and mind, as you relax the thirteen points. If there are still worries filling your head at this point, make some quick, snap decisions about them for now and then set them aside. You can always go back and change your course of action later, after you have finished your practice. This kind of spontaneous solution brainstorming is a good training for living, just in general. It teaches decisiveness and a sense of will and personal responsibility. It is the last step in fully preparing your body to welcome the qi.

Welcoming Qi

Qigong is an art of personal expression. It is time to begin the practice in earnest. Again, we have adjusted ourselves, stepped out into proper posture and opened the thirteen key joints into a relaxed state. We accept a sense of roundness, with a solid four-sided strength within, supported by the energy and stability of our triangular stance. We are welcoming and embracing the sun as we face its direction. Bring your hands up so that the thumbs touch together on the navel and the rest of the fingers point down and touch to form an open triangle over the lower *dantian*, the lower abdomen over bladder area. This posture allows you to complete your relaxation. As you feel yourself slowly relax to your fullest, open your hands again and drop them to the sides of your body. This is the very first movement we make to welcome the qi.

Let's examine this movement. The very first thing you do is place your hands in this triangular position. The space within the triangle is the exact position, shape and size of your lower *dantian*. Have no doubt about this place and its importance to you energetically. When the tips of the thumbs meet in the navel and the palms rest on the abdomen so that forefingers and middle fingers touch, you are locating the *dantian*, as it is uniquely shaped on your body.

Daoist anatomy dictates that the size of your fist is a reasonable representation of the size of your heart. This may or may not be scientifically accurate down to the millimeter, but the awareness of their similarity is enough for you to have a new way of seeing and a new connection to your internal organ. Where you place your hands in the triangle, it is defining your lower *dantian* in a way you can see and feel. This is why when you flip your triangle hands to point upward and raise them so that the center of the triangle is the center point on your chest between the two nipples, this mirrored triangle outlines the location of your middle *dan*. You don't have to worry if it's a little more this way or that. It's the right spot.

There is also a small triangle between your eyebrows, which is the upper *dan*. Press into the center point between the brows with both forefingers, then trace up and slightly outwards to above the brow with them as if you are touching the sides of an inverted triangle, then back down the center to that first center point, to activate the sensation of the spot. Just remember, the three *dan*, upper, middle and lower *dantian*, are not circular. They are triangular. Just as in billiards, you use a triangular rack to rack up the balls before you begin. The first, or break shot separates the balls all over the table with a great deal of outward momentum, due to this triangular set up. It's the same shape as the pyramids, as we've discussed. Cultivating the *dantian* in its triangular form creates the proper energy and potential force to preserve your body. Nine-Five Maintenance of Qi is an internal practice, and it all begins with the lower *dantian* and the triangle.

San Ban – Three Salutations to the Sun

To welcome qi, we are going to perform a series of three salutations (*sanbān*) to greet the sun, each with its own significance, followed by a final embracement of the sun.

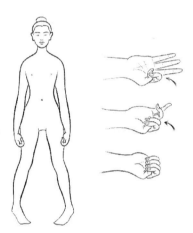

From their position at the lower *dantian*, the hands open up and the arms come to the sides of the body. As you reach this point, bend your thumbs into the center of palms and cover them with the rest of the fingers to form fists.

The thumb is a representation of you, individually. Placing your thumbs in the center of your palms is you placing yourself in the center of your practice. The five fingers are the five elements; earth, which is also the thumb, wood, the forefinger, fire, the middle finger, water, the ring finger, and wind, the pinkie. You need to place yourself in the center and close the rest of your fingers over, so that the four protect you, the one, in the center. One thing to note is that when you cover the thumb, the fingers all close over it in one shot, rapidly and firmly.

The thumb is directly in the center of the palm at the Laogong point, which is related to the heart. It's not so easy to get your thumb flexible enough to do this perfectly, but it is worth it to keep trying and at least be aware of the ideal. An easy way to locate and activate the Laogong point in the palms that Dr. Wu has shown in the past is to press the fingertips together with the tips of the thumbs, with the palms up, to form the peak-shaped mudra known as the Five Finger Mountain. This hand posture allows the palms to cup in just the right way so that they form a hollow activated point at the Laogong. This movement is not a part of what we are learning here, but it is helpful to do on your own, separate from your practice, to get a good sense of the Laogong points in your palms.

Bow your head slightly as you open your hands from the triangle at the lower *dantian* and drop them to the sides, forming the fists, then raise your head again as the hands come up in the first welcoming posture. The arms are going to swing up, with the right hand still in fist with the thumb tucked inside, while the left hand opens up as the arms begin their motion.

The right fist meets with the left palm, which will stay open and flat, with fingers extended. The left wrist is not flexed, so the hand will be at an angle, rather than pointing straight up. The hands are at a level that the fist is slightly in front of and directly below the nose, so that the tip of other hand covering it is higher than the nose. This is the first sign of respect towards the sun. You might remember seeing characters in old martial arts movies using this movement as a sign of fealty, however the difference here is in the martial arts tradition, the fist is formed with the thumb on the outside of the fist. Our emphasis is that the thumb should be within the rest of the fingers and that we are human saluting the sun.

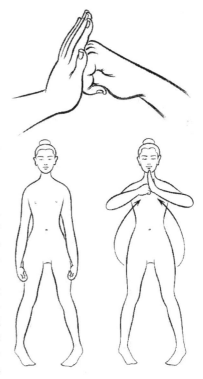

As we've said before, the triangular shape of the pyramid is the key to its enduring energy. The triangle is the symbol of everlasting growth. The reproductive organs of male and female are both triangular. Noses are triangular, too. There is a whole school of personality analysis derived from the nose. Therefore, there is much to be considered when positioning the hands at the proper height and distance to the nose in the three salutations. Bowing the head in tandem with the hand/nose positions accentuates the sensations you will feel while doing this practice.

Slightly bow your head to feel a sense of contact with this first salutation, then straighten your head as you unfold the right fist into a prayer position with both hands palms together. The hands are held together, with the tips of the fingers in line with the bridge of the nose. There is a certain amount of motion in this, so the hands actually rise up a bit once totally unfolded into prayer position, in conjunction with the 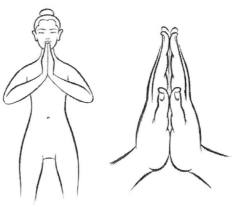 head straightening up, so that the highest finger is at the upper *dan* momentarily. Finalize and feel the movement by pulling the hands down a bit to the nose's bridge, to align with the length of the nose as you very slightly bow your head again in connection. Do not place the hands lower than the tip of the nose. This is the second salutation.

Now, from this position, you will shift into the third salutation. Open up the prayer posture, so that the right hand still stays up in its place, while the left hand starts to slide down the palm, then continues to trace down the length of the forearm, to the elbow. When following along the forearm, the left palm travels along the part of the forearm that is facing outwards from the body.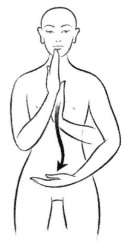

It starts by gently separating from the right hand, caresses its outer edge, as the left wrist turns the moving hand horizontal from vertical. While still lightly touching, the left hand then runs down the forearm to right along the elbow, but not under the elbow. Here, the left wrist turns again so that the moving hand can separate from the right arm and float down palm up, until it reaches a palm up position, very lightly cupped under the center point of the lower *dantian*. The left hand is always touching gently and lightly as it moves down. It doesn't lose contact with the right arm until reaching the end of the elbow. The right single prayer hand is still high at the nose, as the left hand passes down the forearm, but then pull it down slightly with some turgor, or muscular activation, so that the highest finger is just in line with the tip of the nose, as you bow your head slightly to connect with and finalize this third salutation. These are the San Ban, or Three Proclamations, paying respect to the sun.

Both men and women use the same hands for the three salutations. In some cases, men and women might practice certain exercises with the opposite hand or foot. This happens sometimes if there are particular gender adjustments required to properly complete a movement and will be mentioned as such, when necessary. If there is no mention made, women and men practice alike.

Embracing the Sun

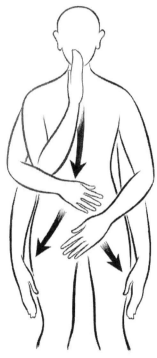

After the third salutation, allow both hands to slowly and gently rotate palms down and float downwards naturally, until they come to the sides. Continuing this smooth movement, allow the wrists to rotate naturally so that the hands again form fists with the thumb placed in the center of the palm with the other fingers covering it. As we have talked about before, for smooth and flowing movements, always allow your limbs to float gently into place, accompanied with gentle and natural breathing. Qi is stored and also dispersed outwards from the joints, so in every motion, use shoulders, elbows and wrists in round, fluid and interconnected motion. Instead of leading your movements with your hands, let your joints rotate first to glide your hands into their special postures with the least amount of effort. Remember this, as it will come up again and again in the Nine-Five Maintenance of Qi practice. It will make many of the exercises much easier to do, and it will also feel wonderful and bring you into a deeper state of qigong awareness.

Using this principle, when your hands float to your sides, continue the motion with a smooth rotation of the wrists to bring your hands into position to easily curl the fingers over the thumbs again into the fists, all in one motion. As you place your thumbs into the center of your fists, remember the Laogong point. You may even very lightly squeeze your palms, as if you were about to do the Five Finger Mountain mudra, but only enough to activate the sensation of the Laogong, rather than bringing the fingertips together. As you sense the point in the palms, place the thumbs there and then cover them with the rest of the fingers.

The fingers each represent one of the five elements, but they also represent our family, friends and ourselves. Covering the thumb with the rest of the fingers in a fist, you are protecting yourself with your mother, father, family and friends. The thumb is you, the first finger is your mother, middle finger is your father, the ring finger represents siblings and children and the pinkie represents our friends.

Daoist *Book of Changes* divination uses this finger theory as part of its calculations, as a means of fine-tuning the interplay of the numbers. The thumb is you, so pay attention to changes in sensation in the thumb. When you wake up, quickly observe how your thumb is feeling. If there is no unusual pain or numbness in the thumb, you will have a good day. These observations are normally quite accurate, unless you already have a serious illness or specific issues with your thumb. Under normal conditions, if you wake up and your thumb feels pretty good, nothing hurts, with no numbness or soreness, then you will have a successful day today. To make personal predictions regarding yourself, look to the subtle cues your body sends you.

Tongue analysis gives you a snapshot of your health. To evaluate your opportunities, evaluate your thumb. For instance, you met someone you like, a boyfriend or girlfriend. How do you know if that person likes you back? Stand away from them, near or far, any distance where you can see each other, then you wave to them, saying hello or goodbye. At that moment you're waving, as long as your thumb has no feelings except for maybe a slight warmth, you know that person likes you. If your finger feels numb or slightly painful, that is a bad indicator for your relationship. We have the faculty to read these messages from the natural order of things, just like other animals that might be more famous for their innate abilities. You can't evaluate this with science or technology. It's just nature.

A bulldog in your back yard will know whenever anyone walks by, but they don't necessarily bark at everybody. If that person is aggressive or malicious, then the dog will act more aggressively than towards a person who is harmless. They have that ability to differentiate, even when they can only hear or smell but not see the passersby. This is part of the natural order. Wild animals don't eat human babies. That's why you hear about feral children, who survive after being abandoned in the wilderness. The wolves or tigers don't necessarily eat those children and sometimes might even care for them instead. They recognize they are babies even though they are a different species. These are instinctual survival mechanisms. We can't fully evaluate this behavior with the science and technology we have today, although we are making some progress studying pheromones and other hormonal and neurological activity. There are still fundamental connections we haven't made yet and might not make. That's just the way things are.

It's the same thing with the sensations in the thumb when waving to someone you like. This is one of our innate abilities, our own little weather forecast. Many people get aches and pains before it's going to rain, which really isn't any different from the animal behavior that can be observed before rain or earthquakes. Watch ants scurry around, dragonflies fly lower, and birds becoming noisy and irritated before a rainstorm. They have this native ability and so do humans, in our own way.

The sensitivity of our fingers is one of our special, natural talents. Feeling in the thumb can convey information about our potential with other people. Sensations in your first finger on a daily basis mean your mother misses you or wants to see you. The same holds true for the other fingers. If you have sensations in your mother, father, family or friends fingers, you will know they are thinking of you or need you. We have full capacity to sense and interpret these cues. Practicing qigong helps develop this awareness, as surely as lifting weights makes your muscles stronger. In turn, when we make a fist with the fingers covering the thumb, we are using the power of this ability to energize ourselves and send out a signal of our humanity to the sun. This is more than a philosophical symbol. We are making full use of the natural aptitudes of the human body. The study, development and preservation of our body's inborn capabilities are the grand achievement of centuries of Daoist scholarship.

To continue the practice, once both hands have curled into fists at the sides, the right arm comes up from the side in an arc, so that the elbow bends at a right angle and the fist is facing palm down, in line with the center-line of the body. Although the fist is not touching the body, feel it align with this center line, at a height that is just slightly below the Tanzhong point, which is the point at the center of the line between the two nipples.

From this position, extend the right fist out from the center, until the arm is fully extended and the knuckles of the fist point forward. Because this extension comes from the center, the arm is not snapping out from the elbow. Rather, the fist is moving and the arm is just

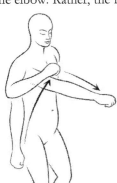

following, staying in close. This keeps the shoulder fully relaxed and the chest slightly sunken in, rather than expanded. It positions the arm so that it is up, parallel to the ground, but not so high that it is creating tension in the shoulders or chest. The aim is to come from the center of the body and move with the fist, to remove as much stress off the shoulder, elbow, wrist and chest. After the arm and fist are extended, repeat in the same way with the left arm, to end with both arms out, knuckles facing forward and the arms held inwards ever so slightly, so that there is no strain on the shoulder joints.

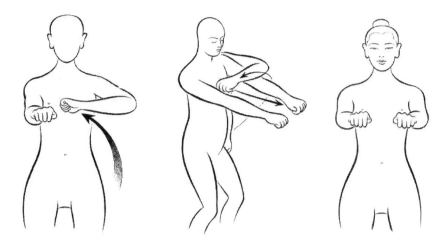

One of the most beneficial aspects of the Nine-Five Maintenance of Qi form is that everything comes from the mid line or center of our body, all the energy coming in and out, as well as the strength and alignment we are building over time with regular practice. This is one the key Daoist philosophies that has gone on to inform all the traditions that have followed in Chinese culture. Confucius uses the term "centered way" (*zhongdao*), meaning everything flows from the center. Confucius's teachings strongly advocate this fundamental dictate, but its origin comes from even more ancient Daoist beliefs.

If you look closely at recordings of Bruce Lee, every motion he makes is perfectly coordinated with the centerline of his body. Every strike and kick is always expressed out from dead center. This is because his master Ye Wen, more famously known as Ip Man, studied in the White Cloud Monastery and only later went out and taught under more public traditions. He taught that every punch you make is always from the middle, always aligned with the central vertical axis of your body. This is why Bruce Lee's most famous blows are not standard punches. They are the notorious one-inch punch, where he aligns his open hand with his center, then closes his fist and then strikes out with very little arm extension but great force.

He uses your own force against you, throwing you off balance, by applying his force in such a pinpointed concentration. The one-inch, or hand punch, is made possible by the extreme centeredness of its power. Because his master Ye Wen was an exceptional martial artist, he was able to meet and study with many of the masters of his era. Although it is little known today, he learned this training from Dr. Wu's own master, studying Daoist internal force with him for almost seven years, after which he incorporated it into his own teaching.

This is the principle of the centered way. Everything comes from the center. With the movement of the fists out from the center of the body, sinking firmly into your solid tripod-like leg and hip stance, with no stress on the shoulders or chest, we embody this paradigm perfectly. It's not just a concept, but a complete physical reorientation of the body's center of gravity. Our movements focus on the midline. The emphasis is from the center out when extending the fists. At this point, we open up our fists, again with the sense of it coming from the center.

When opening them up, the hands open in one decisive motion, so that they are palms down. It's a subtle movement, but the palms are not simply flat with the fingers pointing straight out. More precisely, the fingers and thumbs are pointed down ever so slightly. They might look flat at a casual glance, but they have a hint of a bell shape, just enough to indicate that the centers of the palms are still activated and holding force, rather than just releasing all the momentum of opening out the fists. It is not a slow uncurling, but it is controlled so that you have not let go of the power you are building from your center.

Rather than staying in this posture, this is the beginning of a complete hand movement. Let your wrists continue to roll, allowing your gently bell-shaped palms to turn facing up, along with the forearms, again without losing contact with your center line or placing any effort on the shoulders. Continuing the movement fluidly, the thumbs roll back into the centers of the palms, and each finger folds over them in turn, to reform the fists, facing up this time.

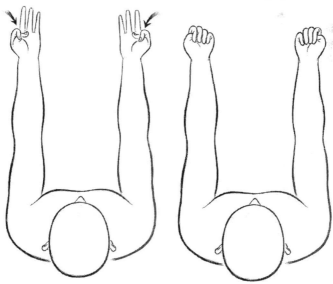

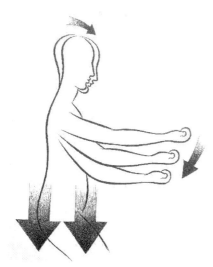

As the thumbs go to the palms, begin to bow your head into the movement, and as the fingers cover the thumbs, the head bows a bit more. When you lower your head, do not lead from the head, so much as lower it by lowering your neck. Your chin is not pressed into the chest or neck. Instead you are allowing your neck to curve outwards to enhance the rounded curve of the upper back that naturally forms when standing in this posture. You are not actually pulling your arms into your body. Instead, you are concentrating force at your center by using the neck, head and upper back to stretch outwards, letting the front of the chest stay hollow. Isometric stretches like this, using small, subtle movements that work from the inside out, are the hallmark of Daoist qigong practice.

A good way to get the full effect of this posture is to raise your head at the same time as your neck is lowering halfway down. Your head will be held so that it's more or less up but also craned forward, so that the neck stretch is complete. Let your whole body sink into a subtle C posture as you intensify this movement, to further stretch the curve of the upper back, then straighten up gently as you release. Over time, this will greatly strengthen and remove stiffness in the neck and upper back. Always remember to breathe naturally into your movements, so that they stay gentle and fluid. That is always more important than having the maximum extension in your stretch, which will develop on its own with daily practice.

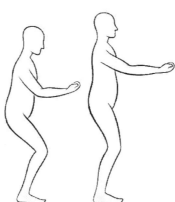

Hold this posture for a moment, then take the right arm back to your centerline, by rotating the forearm, wrist and fist around so that the fist is down again and the elbow is bent at a right angle, then lowering the arm back down to the side, bringing the forearm diagonally down from the center. Basically it's reversing the motion that brought the arm up. After the right hand is lowered to the side, gently open the hand. Return the left arm to your left side in the same way. As you bring your right arm down, raise your head slowly so that it's at a halfway rise when the arm finishes at the side.

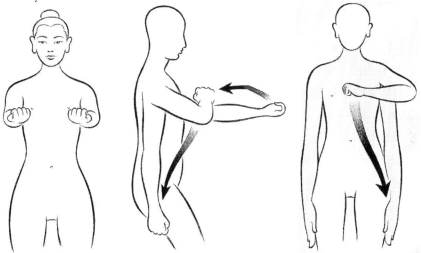

Raise the head more as your bring your left hand down, so that is it raised completely, and even facing upwards just a bit, by the time your finish. Once both arms are at the sides and the hands open, feel yourself completely relax. This is Embracing of the Sun, the final operation of welcoming qi. This is how we welcome the sun and invite it to us. Once you do this set of movements, you will capture the sun's attention and the sun will help you. It's analogous with raising the national flag every day over the capitol building, a custom of every nation and state the world over. At major political or social events, we perform the national anthem. When we practice qigong, we don't have a national anthem. Instead, this is our ceremony of identity for the nine palaces Nine-Five Maintenance of Qi qigong.

Ceremony, Art and Personal Expression

It's very important to understand the order of each movement. When welcoming qi, the three salutations, and the embracing of qi, keep your eyes closed and feel the sensations. Some parts of the practice, you need to keep your eyes open or slightly closed, and some other spots it doesn't matter whether they are open or closed. For welcoming qi, keep them closed, unless you feel you need them open to keep your balance safely. The movements' details and exact order have a strong subconscious influence. You can compare it to an experiment made on two bowls of rice.

You would sit with one bowl and tell it you wished it well and the other that you wished it ill. The rice that received the good wishes stayed fresh longer than the one that was told harmful things, which spoiled faster. Practicing the nine palaces is a ceremony, a ritual of courtesy paying respect to the sun. The monks of the White Cloud Monastery would not only practice it. They also studied the effects of practicing it versus leaving the monastery without practicing it first. Their research showed there was a big difference between those who practiced before leaving the monastery and who did not practice before they left. Practicing together as a group allowed them to stay much better connected with each other, even though they were apart. Whether you want to think of it as an emotional connection or something more, the sun will help you if you practice and pay your respect.

This is a ceremonial service, or *gongfa*, in the sense that it's a highly ritualized set of predetermined gestures but it's a personal practice of individual cultivation, as well. In the monastery, it is performed as a group practice, but on an individual level, it is more important to view your practice as a personal expression or communication. Embracing and welcoming the sun initiates your connection with the sun. It's an initiation practice in the fullest sense of the word. You have captured the sun's attention and the sun in return will benefit you.

Dr. Wu sincerely believes there is a protection that you gain from paying your respects to the sun. If you don't practice or pay respect to the sun, then the sun will not protect you. Every day you go to work and punch your work card. You have to sign in or clock in to have your work hours filed. Welcoming qi is the same. You want to say "hello, I'm here" every day to the sun. All religions of the world believe in prayer and the power of prayer to be answered by deity. Pray to Guanyin Bodhisattva in the face of hardship and adversity, pray to the Jesus for forgiveness, pray to Buddha for blessings. All traditions teach prayer and adoration of the gods as the way to let them know you are talking to them and only once you have reached out, will they give you their blessing.

To have a two-way conversation with another person, we have letters and postcards, cell phones, email, video chat, and all manner of other even newer technologies, but for our communication with the gods, there are few methods other than prayer, especially ones that send an answer directly back. Some traditions will use three sticks of incense and let the smoke rise up to heaven, or present sacrifices and offerings at an altar and observe the results. In this respect, our communication with the sun using welcoming qi stands out as uniquely effective. We follow the steps of the practice with our body, heart and mind and in turn, the sun will give us energy and messages and opportunities to face adversity and overcome hardship. The practice makes us partners with the sun, to lessen hardships and smooth the experiences for each day, while in its simplest function, minimizing the chances of getting sick or ill.

When first learning the Nine-Five Maintenance of Qi, perform welcoming qi nine times in a row, from the Three Salutes to the end of Embracing of the Sun where the hands come to the sides as one set. Simply put, you do this in front of the sun and the sun will give you energy. You can do nine sets, but don't do it more than nine. Three times is good too. At first, if you chose to do it nine times every day, you will train yourself very thoroughly, but as you build up your ability, it's not necessary to practice nine times every time. If you are truly a master or have been repeating daily for a long time, then you could do the practice once and that would be good enough to capture the sun's rays. But normally, do nine sets. The number nine has its special ability to contact the sun, just as three sticks of incense are traditionally used in ceremonial offerings to the gods.

Although welcoming qi and the Nine-Five Maintenance of Qi were developed as ceremonial rites in the White Cloud Monastery, it's important to view it as something more than a Daoist religious ritual. On a deeper level, it isn't just a ceremony. It's also an art form that you perform creatively with your own personal voice. Every pianist plays a Beethoven sonata with the same notes, and yet no two pianists will interpret it exactly alike. To face the sun with dedication and sincerity, you will have your own highly personal experiences. It will help you in whatever way you need. This is one of the beautiful and powerful aspects of qigong. By nature, it is a highly self-regulating practice and a person gets whatever they need out of it based on what they put into it. It benefits body, mind and spirit at exactly the level they require. This is why although we practice to gain assistance from the sun and the forces of nature, there is no need to ask particular questions or even visualize particular imagery at any point. Just follow the steps of the form with genuine intention.

How is one set of steps capable of fitting the needs of each man or woman who follows them? The form is a pattern. Making its movements creates a sign, like a talisman is painted on a scroll and then hung for protection. Think of welcoming qi as something you do to the sun. Do it, and the sun will know of your existence. Then the sun will know that it is allowed to give you energy. When you align your qi with the sun's qi then you will both mutually benefit. This is the concept of same qi, matching like with like. To give a fengshui example, if you live on a property where there are buried many dead rats, that might sound very unsanitary. However, if you are born in the Year of the Rat, those rats will actually help you to reach your goals and this property is perfect for you just the way it is.

When people clap at the end of a lecture, the applause is a polite ceremony. The audience shows its appreciation, that it's been paying attention, as a sign of respect. It's important to go further with welcoming qi. It isn't just a formality. Each movement has deeper meanings and knowing them is what inspires you to bring your personal feelings into the practice. Think of the first of the Three Salutations, where the fist fits into the flat palm. These layers of meaning are why a martial artist of Bruce Lee's stature was able to learn so much just from this sign. It is said his master only taught him this move. He didn't really need teach him anything else.

Your fist is hitting the other hand. The deeper understanding is that your fist is very hard and your palm is very soft. With much practice, you learn the power of a soft palm, as much as the power of a hard fist. Knowing how to throw a punch is not the highest fighting ability. Above that, you learn to cover a striking fist with your flexible, sensitive palm. It holds onto the fist, bending and twisting it back on itself until the direction of the punch is unbalanced and taken off course. Any way the opponent was to turn, you are able to counteract his force and hurt him with the momentum of his own force. It's an application of force. So you are taught with one simple practice movement, but to learn its fullest application, you really must take time and make it your own practice, your own cultivation, to discover the true meaning in it. This is the way we learn qigong. Simple movements, practiced with a clear mind and personal connection, until the understanding flows in naturally.

This is why we have to break down each element of welcoming qi in such detail, to really understand the meaning behind it. When we curl the thumb into the palm, with the fingers over it to form the fist, it symbolizes the five elements and also you and your parents, family and friends. The movement itself intensifies the focus. The first of the three salutes is in a sense, enacting the birth of the human principle. It is initiation. It is your first contact as a human entity reaching out to the universe.

The second salute, with the hands in prayer position, means sincerity. Then as the hands separate and come to the third salute, the movement reflects yin and yang. The vertical hand is yang and the horizontal hand is yin. Separating the two energies allows you to put them back together again to form new energy in the Embracing of the Sun. Its movements come from the center. When your arms are outstretch and you curl your thumbs into the center of the open palms and wrap the fingers over them, while bowing into the motion, it's like you are turning yourself into a magnifying glass, converging the all the sun's rays into a single focal point. The midline of your body absorbs them all and becomes the conduit for communication with the sun, just as Confucius stressed the concept of the centered way. Even so, all it takes is sincere intention, gentle breathing and a commitment to daily practice to uncover the profound significance of welcoming qi. Welcome the sun and the sun will be there to help you in every way.

Chapter Four

Intake of Qi

Basics

After welcoming qi, the next step is intake of qi (*fuqi*) or absorbing, gathering or collecting qi (*caiqi*). We have developed many strategies over the years to regulate and refine our intake of food and drink, while our intake of qi has been left to one side, underestimated in its importance. Never forget, qi is air. If you think about it, you may be able to live for up to a month if you stopped eating and drinking. Some people might even be able to live longer than a month, depending on their metabolism.

A person can live for up to two months without food, if they still have water. But if you stop breathing, in other words, halt your intake of qi, then you will die in a matter of minutes. Without air, your body would be unable to sustain itself for more than a few minutes. When we talk about air, we usually mean oxygen, its most essential element. Studies have shown that along with chemotherapy, oxygen therapy using pure O2 can also kill cancer cells.

By breathing well and filling ourselves with the ideal amount of oxygen, we can prevent cancer, as well as many other illnesses caused by poor oxygen circulation in the body and brain. Qigong is the art of working with qi and there are many methods of using it to enhance our health. The Nine-Five Maintenance of Qi cultivates a unique method to not only intake an optimal amount of breath for health, but teaches us how to refine this intake to strengthen and protect us under special circumstances, in times of hardship.

The Tree

After embracing the qi, we are going intake, or swallow, the qi. Begin by visualizing yourself as a huge, ancient tree. Normally, in qigong practice, visualizations are uncommon. Usually, you want to keep a clear mind and focus on feeling the sensations in your body. If images or colors come into your mind as you practice, it isn't uncommon, but you want to move on and continue your practice without fixating on these thoughts. Just as we've talked about se, or the colorful world, this imagery is by nature changeable and fleeting. It's the sign you are processes sing emotions and memories that have been lodged within you. Many times students would come to Dr. Wu after starting to practice qigong and tell him about the amazing things they saw. He would usually laugh and tell them to just keep practicing. Visual imagery when practicing qigong is a phase, but when your body and mind get past it, there are much deeper levels of meditative experience that will occur that involve your entire body in a fresh, new way.

Nevertheless, the Nine-Five Maintenance of Qi practice is quite unique, when compared to other Nine Palaces Qigong forms. In this instance, we specifically want to use the visualization of a tall tree to help position our bodies perfectly while taking qi in. Trees have many levels of significance for qigong practice, but on the most fundamental level, a visualization such as what follows is used as a message to your body, to push it to straighten into the flawless posture that is more than we normally allow ourselves. We finished welcoming the qi with our arms down loosely at our sides. Take a moment to check that your posture is still stable, with toes turned in and comfortably balanced on your "tripod." Adjust your breathing too, as needed, so that it's still soft and natural. Welcoming the qi can be an intense practice, so take the time to rebalance before continuing.

First stand solidly. Now think of yourself as a huge tree, growing from your feet up. There's a Chinese saying, "stretching to the sky, standing on the ground" (*dingtian lidi*). It is used to describe people of indomitable spirit, who have guts and a sense of responsibility, who can handle anything that comes their way. It is with this spirit, that you want to visualize yourself as the tree, so tall you touch the heavens and the earth. Our feet are like the roots of a tree, and the internal organ that corresponds to them are the kidneys, so we are working on a continuum of tree roots, feet and kidney energy.

Now focus on the qi. The qi originates in the earth. Suck the qi up from the soles of your feet. Do this with intention, because your mind is what makes the qi travel where you want it to go. It's common to have blockages and imbalances in the body due to health or emotional reasons and they can become particularly noticeable when you first start to practice qigong. If you always maintain gentle breathing that is paced with your pulse rate and let your mind tell the qi where it is going, this is the way you can bypass the kinks in your body. This is why straining to open these pathways slows your progress. That way, you have to fight your body and its obstructions. Instead, just go very lightly.

It might feel like you're imagining the qi move more than you feel a huge current passing through you, but this actually will override your blockages within a few short days of practice. You are experiencing your ideal flow first, and your body will follow, rather than dealing with a constant battle against your initial limitations. Gentleness, emptiness, and not struggling with the things you desire are as always, the key to perfect qigong practice.

Suck the qi up through the soles of your feet and have it travel up the back of the body, all the way up to the top of your head, at the Baihui point. The Baihui is the vertex of the head. If you trace a line from the peaks of your earlobes and another line crossing it from the center of the base of the skull up and around to the tip of the nose, the highest point where both lines meet is the Baihui. This is another point that might be more or less open for different people, due to muscle tension, congestion in the cranial cavities, and so on, so just guide the qi to this ideal spot, allowing it's current to flow as delicately as you need. Once the qi has arrived at the Baihui, you want to try and grow it up further, as high as possible, carrying the qi up to the point you feel you can't push it any higher. Remember, the whole time you are doing this, you are envisioning yourself as a towering tree, growing and growing.

As soon as you've thrust the qi to its peak and you can't push it any higher, allow it to pour down the front of the body, branching in two at the lower *dantian* so it flows all the way down the fronts of the legs and out the soles of the feet. Repeat from the beginning, sucking the qi up through the soles of your feet, for a total of nine sets.

When you visualize yourself as a tree, pick any kind that you feel an affinity to, but it must be enormous, as huge as possible. Daoists believe that as tall and wide as a tree's canopy grows, that's also how deep and wide its roots spread within the earth. Growing from the soles of your feet up mirrors the growth of a tree, which starts out as yin, deep in the earth, and becoming yang, as it grows higher and touches the sky. You need to try and raise up the qi, before returning it after, back to the earth. Your tree remains tall, even when the energy comes down and splits at the lower *dantian*. Then, in the next repetition, growing as the tree, try to push it even taller.

Continue at all times to breathe slowly and very lightly in rhythm with your pulse, rather than holding your breath. You are growing your tree up by guiding the qi with your mind, not with your breath. Push the qi up from the Baihui point. On your first try, it doesn't have to go very high. Eight to ten inches above the head is fine. Just hold on to that sensation of height as you bring the qi down again and try to grow it higher on the next repeat. To maintain this upward sensation of growth without jamming yourself by inhaling too much and then holding your breath is the challenge of this exercise, but this challenge is the physical training.

It will push through any muscular or energetic blockages and in particular, relaxes and trains the diaphragm muscles from the inside. This is why we use the image of the tree to help us as we slowly push through. In Daoism, all forms of life have a place on a continuum that is connected in a perfect circle, without a beginning or an end. At the very top of the circle, right next to each other, are the human and the tree. Our humanity is in tight accord with the life force of the tree. We learn from and help each other constantly, as two connected segments in the cycle of life. Imagining yourself as a majestic tree not only will keep you standing straight and tall, it sparks creativity and emotional inspiration in your practice. The tree is our first teacher as we train our bodies to take in qi.

Water

On the ninth repetition, instead of guiding the qi down to the lower *dantian* then splitting it to the legs, you are going to melt into water. Imagine yourself as water, liquefying, completely dissolving, and sinking down into the center of the earth. You stand as one with nature, a colossal tree. Instead of guiding the qi down through your body and out the soles of your feet into the ground, you release all ties to your sense of solidity and spatial awareness. You are only flowing liquid, pouring endlessly into the soil. As usual, continue to breathe lightly and steadily, even as your awareness is on melting further and deeper, rather than exhaling too far and then holding your breath. This is a very important visualization.

When you practice on a daily basis, you will come to understand its great magnitude. You begin standing, unified with nature, but still one presence. Maintain the height of your tree, even when you melt away, dissolving from that height. When you've dissolved into water, you will see you have nothing left inside of your body, that you have relinquished your form. You will gain the perception that nothing in the world belongs to you except for your health. All the rest of it, the money, the lovers, none of it belongs to you. Your health and life force is all that you possess. The tree growing and the dissolving as water is the cycle of life. You are experiencing the process of birth and death, rising from and returning to the earth. Water can seep into the smallest crevasse and wear through the mightiest rock, but always stays limpidly soft and tranquil. Visualizing your body melting as water will make you very relaxed and resolve your frustrations and difficulties. It brings a sense of absolution, all problems dissolved away like water.

The Sprout

After you have dissolved into water, grow the tree again as before, sucking the qi up through the soles of the feet, up the back, then out and up as far as possible, and when you can't grow higher, dissolve again. Repeat this cycle one last time, for a total of three melting's. For the last visualization of intake qi, instantly, as soon as you've finished your last dissolve, imagine yourself as a bean planted deep in the ground. Grow a sprout up from that buried bean, pushing up through the soil and sprouting from the ground into a plant that grows to the size of your body. Once the plant reaches your size and height, inhale deeply from the top of the head at the Baihui point down into the body, while also thinly but steadily inhaling through the nose, connecting the growth of your plant with the heavens. In essence, with this plant, you have grown yourself anew, and bounded yourself on both ends by the qi of heaven and earth.

Keep inhaling, filling the front and back of your chest with qi, and continue to inhale until your whole body is filled with qi. Mainly the front and back of chest will expand, but keep inhaling steadily and you will feel this expansion down to the base of your torso. As much as you have created a new sense of the space and shape of your body by growing the sprout, that entire area will be filled with qi, if you breath slowly and keep yourself, particularly your diaphragm, relaxed. This muscle control is built up over time with practice, but you will make the steadiest progress filling yourself gently, without strain or holding on to the breath as you inhale, letting your mind do lightly what your muscles can't do with force.

When you feel full, do not pause and hold your breath, even for an instant. Immediately exhale very gently and slowly, out through the mouth and down the arms and legs and out the ends of the four limbs, fingers and toes, dissolving again like water as you exhale. Relax the mouth and lips, and the anus and the urethra as completely as possible as you exhale and dissolve. Repeat this set of growing and dissolving three times. As soon as you have completely dissolved into the earth, instantly start the next set, growing the sprout again.

Growing the sprout is connecting your growth to the qi of earth and heaven. The bean sprouts from deep in the earth, pushing up slowly but surely. Once it breaks through to the surface, it redoubles its efforts and speeds its way up to the sky. First you are growing as a bean sprout, higher and higher. Then you want to connect the heavenly qi with your own growth, which is the inhaling through the Baihui point. At the end, you fill yourself with qi then dissolve it away, exhaling out the limbs and relaxing the anus and urethra.

When Dr. Wu first discussed this exercise with us, he used some interesting hand gestures to illustrate the discussion. He formed the fingers of one hand into a sword-shaped mudra, with the first and middle fingers stretched straight up and held together, while the other fingers close and touch the thumb. To indicate the sprout growing through the ground from the seed, he quickly pointed down at the earth where the bean is located, then flipped the mudra fingers pointing up and drew it steadily in a focused movement up the center of the body, slowly but with some force. To demonstrate the plant growing above ground to the size and height of the body, he gestured again with both hands, first opened down to the earth as if grabbing some qi then both going into sword mudra together, flipping over and drawing solidly and decisively up the center line of the body until coming to the head, where his hands opened up, facing the body, and gently passed them over his brow and back over the hair to the Baihui point.

To enact connecting one's growth with the qi of the heavens, he used the right hand in the sword mudra doing the same flip he used demonstrating the bean sprout in the ground, then brought it up and held it between the lower and middle *dantian*. At the same time, he lowered his left hand from above to form a Taiji ball with the right, which had opened palm up, to demonstrate a sense of energies meeting and concentrating. He then placed the upper hand representing heaven over his upper *dantian*, indicating the line at the brow, above which your own Heaven is located in your body.

When discussing filling the chest and trunk with qi, Dr. Wu's gesture was to stand with his right palm down and his left palm up, which he then both opened downwards to the sides, making fists and then reopening them, one finger at a time starting with the pinkie, to illustrate allowing yourself to dissolve, release through the fingers and toes and open and relax the anus and urethra. These movements aren't part of the form, but it is worthwhile to think about them, as they perfectly convey the force, direction and sensations of growing the sprout.

This is how a master teaches, partially with words and partially with gestures and movements to help guide both the theories and the internal effects of the form. For some movements, it's enough for teacher and student to demonstrate them and then practice. For the intake of qi, you are growing a force from within that needs this deeper demonstration. With them, we learn how we grow from a seed, meet the energy of heaven and bring it in, so that our self is now newly defined with the qi of the earth and the qi of the heavens.

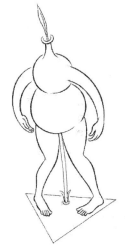

The seed is the essence of a plant. Of all the parts of a plant, the seed often has the highest nutritive value. In the White Cloud Monastery, broth made from cooking beans the colors of the five elements was a diet staple. A heavy emphasis was also put on including all manner of seeds in the daily meal plan. Eating broth made from long cooked seeds and beans is considered the ideal food for longevity and renewal, for its concentrated nutrition. This concentrated essence is what we prize when we practice growing the sprout.

If you were to hold a magnifying glass over a piece of paper and let the sun hit the glass at just the right angle, you are concentrating the essence of the sun. All the light converges into one focal point, it reflects on that on tiny pinpoint on the paper, and it will get so hot, the paper will start to burn. This same theory is the reason why Daoist fengshui advises that your house should not be too large, especially if you live by yourself. Its size needs to be in proportion to the number of people living there.

You are the focal point of your property. You want to gather qi rather than have your qi disperse. At the least, if your house if very large and you live alone, choose a bedroom that's on the smaller side, rather than the master suite. It's a matter of harnessing the qi to optimize your environment. Have you ever wondered why large dogs normally live around ten years but small dogs can live fifteen or even twenty years? Daoists would say it is because their qi is more concentrated. With intake of qi, we are further concentrating and refining the qi we have reached out for with welcoming the qi. We have much to learn from the power inside one tiny seed.

Swallowing the Qi

After you have grown the sprout and then dissolved three times, it is time to harvest the fruits of our effort. After dissolving, stand relaxed. Clench your teeth and rotate your tongue clockwise, from top right to left and around, nine times, behind the clenched teeth. Use as much of your tongue as you can to feel every part of the back of the teeth and upper and lower palates as you rotate. Try to use the upper and undersides of the tongue as well as the tip as you circle, just as long as you keep your teeth firmly pressed together. Continue clenching the teeth and rotate the tongue nine times counterclockwise, from left to right, around the back of the teeth. A lot of saliva will start to form. Do not swallow it. Instead open your jaws, without opening your lips or mouth and bite together, knocking your teeth together, twenty four times, at a medium speed. Take all the saliva that has by now formed, and swallow it all the way down to the lower *dantian*. This is the completion of the Intake of qi.

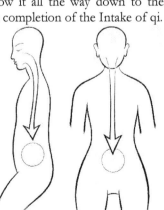

The twenty four bite downs represent the twenty four seasonal phases of the Chinese calendar. As we said in chapter one, the line that divides the yin and yang in the Taiji symbol also represents the varying changes of these twenty four seasons. With the stages of the intake of qi, we have reenacted the formation of "yang rising out of yin," or "yang originating from yin," by growing the tree. We have experienced the cycle of life and death, by dissolving into water. From this water, the sprout is given life from the seed and grows to connect with heaven's qi. We bring the qi of the earth and the heavens into our new self and generate a concentrated essence of these natural forces by circling the tongue. Biting the teeth together refines this essence with the seasons of the year, the timeline along which yin and yang are constantly in motion, balancing and rebalancing. We then swallow down this harmonized fluid to nourish the field inside the body where all new life can grow, the lower *dantian*.

Pay attention to the direct connection and relationship between trees and people, the two neighbors on the circle of life forms. A tree's rings show its age, new rings forming outwards at every growing season of its life. The rings also show signs of activity from outside of the tree, such as earthquakes and other seismic movement within the earth, which make their lasting mark.

So it is for humans as well. Daoists observe and record special marks on the tips of the fingers, almost imperceptible white spots, that they consider the human rings. Our body makes these marks appear, and they can disappear as well. *Book of Changes* diviners will use them in conjunction with the person's birth date and time information to foretell their personality and opportunities. Of course, external events also shape our bodies and minds, as much or more than is apparent in a tree. Performing the intake of qi is designed to work with the differing facets of kidney energy, the essence or jing that we are born with from the womb, and the qi, which we are able to tonify and add back into the body. Dissolving into the earth is the cycle of life and death. A tree grows up, yang rising up from the yin of the earth. Water pours back down and returns to earth. From that water, a seed is nourished and sprouts up, and after it too has dissolved, a concentrated essence is formed and swallowed down into the body to create a brand new energy.

When beginning this practice, it might seem a bit slow and repetitive, or even boring for people who are more action oriented, but there is an important aspect to this seeming lack of activity. There are martial arts that are very pleasing to perform, with beautiful *dance*-like movements, but internal practices such as the intake of qi, are not as obvious. The artistry of the performance comes from within and is something you will feel very strongly. Regular practice will definitely benefit your health, and it can also play a factor in changing your opportunities. Don't underestimate the small subtleties of each step. There is a certain *Book of Changes* calculation and resulting significance behind every movement and every small adjustment in breathing or imagery that is asked of you. Not everything can be explained at all, much less presented in the context of the Nine-Five

Maintenance of Qi. Just know that everything counts, every tiny detail, so practice well.

The intake of qi practice is a way of letting go of old thoughts and emotions and creating a new perspective. First you stand tall like the tree, stretched between heaven and earth, feeling ready to confront any challenge. Then as liquid, you dissolve and disappear as you sink into the earth. The seed is always there inside you. It just needs the water to sprout again. This is what we mean by transforming yourself. You shed your old self and become a new individual. You are born, you die, and then you live again, reborn.

When eagles reach a certain age, they molt their feathers and shed their claws, growing fresh new replacements. This full molt occurs at an age equivalent to forty or fifty in human years. People are not that much different. By practicing the intake of qi, it's as if you become the eagle, so when you reach the same age, you will be able to shed your own feathers, grow something new and then be able to soar again. When Dr. Wu talked about this, he demonstrates this physically, extending his arms up over his head and springing up off the ground.

When people are going through menopause or midlife crisis, which is the period in life when we're trying to reinvent ourselves. That's the struggle we are going through. We are trying to shed our feathers, shed everything that has burdened us from our past and grow something new. After menopause or midlife crisis, there will come a time when you realize you are now a wholly different person than you were. Practicing the intake of qi before and especially during this time in one's life facilitates the change. For women, it assists the process of menopause, reducing the need for reliance on medication. Not only women go through these changes, as new research is beginning to show, so it has equal possibilities for middle aged men. In fact, the intake of qi practice benefits any gender or age, for it smooths your reaction to change. It enhances your ability to navigate the ups and downs of life, let go and move on to something new, because every day as you practice, you are re-experiencing the cycle of life, death and rebirth.

After you practice intake of qi just a few times, you will gain a deeper awareness and understanding of the changing world around you. You will be able to let go of things you were unable to let go of before. You will gain the realization that ultimately, when it comes right down to it, nothing really belongs to you except your own health. No treasure, fame or emotional attachment is yours to keep. The only thing you can maintain is your own health. This is why monks living in temples and monasteries are able to let go of things. They're human too. They have human emotions. There's nothing psychologically off about them. They're normal people just like us, but after they practice this art form, their hearts turn into water and just dissolve. This is why monasteries are located in isolated areas, to eliminate as many external influences as possible, but it's never enough.

The Dragon Gate lineage of the Complete Reality school is primarily an ascetic order. Many environmental controls are placed on the young, cloistered, monks so they will be less inclined to arousal. The young monks sleep on small circular mats, almost like baskets. Sleeping curled up in this way prevents arousal while they sleep and upon awakening. During the day, they are taught to practice the intake of qi to counter any immediate feelings of arousal. Afterwards, they are able to calm their spirit and their heart.

Of course, there's a story behind this. The legend recounts that Daoist immortal Lü Dongbin, instructed his males students not to become aroused in the presence of women. He told him "Women are tigers; they will argue and fight." Little did his students know, he would tell the younger nuns the same thing: men were tigers and would argue and fight. Needless to say, they avoided each other. After always being taught this, Wang Chongyang was tasked to take up the beggar's bowl and collect food from all over the town. As he interacted with many people while begging, he realized woman weren't so bad. In fact, they would often give him an extra portion of food and treat him with special kindness. He returned to his teacher and rebuked him, insisting that women were kind and helpful and couldn't possibly be tigers.

After this, Lü Dongbin had to change his philosophy, as he saw that teaching fear of the opposite sex did not work as a method of control. He recognized that it was the teachings of Laozi, of Wu and emptiness that were the true path to clearing the mind and freeing the heart. After he studied the words of Laozi and practiced his qigong forms, he came to a realization that, while the beauty of a woman is deserving of admiration, it was no matter because his path is as a monk and his home is in the monastery, seeking another beauty within contemplation. Instead of teaching that the opposite sex was a tiger, he taught this form instead. Subsequently, he wrote poetic tracts on his experience, which were recorded and passed down in the Daoist Cannon, which is how we know this story today.

So often, we begin by practicing one discipline or art, with a certain set of intentions, but from the many hours of study, we gain an awareness, or a new understanding of something else, quite different from what we set out to learn. For Immortal Lü Dongbin, through the intake of qi he gained a new acceptance of the sexual impulse, found his way to rise beyond its ties and wrote mystical poetry of great nobility that generations have been enriched by. After you practice this form, you too will gain a new understanding. Simply put, you gain a greater appreciation of yourself. And through that appreciation of your selfhood, you will do harm no longer to others. An old self is relinquished, and a new vision is attained. This is the intake of qi.

Chapter Five

Adjustment of Qi

Balancing

First we welcomed the sun and embraced its qi. Next was the intake of the energy given by the sun. Now we come to the third stage in the total integration of solar qi into our being, adjustment of qi (*tiaoqi*). After we swallow down the qi we have obtained from the outside, we must allow our body to adjust to it. We are going to balance the qi that we have pulled from the sun, utilizing the principle of same qi.

Tiao is an interesting word: it means adjusting, balancing and harmonizing all in one. Since "same qi" is the concept of putting like with like, what pattern are we adjusting it to match? We are matching the qi to the fourteen main meridians that exist in every person. These are the lung and large intestine, stomach and spleen, kidney and bladder, heart and small intestine, liver and gallbladder, pericardium and triple burner (*sanjiao*), plus the Conception Vessel (*renmai*) and Governing Vessel (*dumai*). By balancing qi we adjust and attune the qi in accord-ance with these meridians.

For as intricate as this might sound, there are only two exercises in the adjustment of qi and they are simple and straightforward movements without a complicated number of steps. They take a moderate amount of physical exertion at first, but it won't take many days to build up the necessary strength to perform them with ease. By the end of adjustment of qi, you will have essentially filled your body with qi.

73

Of course, keep in mind that we continue to stand facing the direction of the sun, which due to the time of day we are practicing, will be east. If you can't practice between 7a.m. and 9 a.m., just face the sun in whatever direction is needed. Another thing to note is that while welcoming the qi and intake of qi were both heavily ritualized and conceptual exercises, with many layers of meaning, we are moving to a stage that is more of a straightforward physical exercise. Dr. Wu presents less philosophical theory along with them, but they have no less of a profound impact on your physical health, emotions and cognitive perceptions. There are always much meaning to uncover in the Nine-Five Maintenance of Qi practice.

Circling

To quickly describe this exercise, we are going to clasp the hands and starting from the right, circle them up the right ear, across the back of head, down the other ear, then drop the arms to hit the lower *dantian*. All the while, we use a circular momentum to propel our arms up and around, down and then up again. We do fifty repetitions from right to left and then another fifty starting from the left.

This exercise is done in one smooth motion, around and around. You want to let momentum and gravity do as much of the work for you as possible, to give you the stamina to do the required number of repetitions. There are key points in the circling that you want to be aware of, so we will break down the movement into its components, for clarity. However, when you practice, you want to smooth all these points into one movement without pauses or irregular speeding up or slowing down.

As usual, you want a firm, tripod-like stance. It might be helpful to keep your knees slightly bent, to create a solid foundation, but since the goal is to stretch and open up the upper body, don't bend so much that it gets in the way of a good upward stretch for your torso. You will find a good balance of how low of a stance you need if you remind yourself to always stay completely loose and unrestricted through your ribcage, spine and midriff or core. Daoists always keep their bellies soft, rather than sucked in, to maintain equilibrium between the upper and lower body, so that shoulders balance and mirror the hips and arms balance and mirror the legs. A soft abdomen also will promote gentle, steady breathing, which is always the number one priority above any other aspect of the exercise.

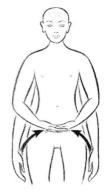

To begin, clasp your hands, solidly interlacing the fingers with the palms but keep the wrists and finger joints flexible. The only spot that is really holding on is right at the juncture where the bases of the fingers meet and every other joint is free to adjust as needed within the entire arc of the circle we will make.

Clasp the hands like this at the bottom of your circular path, just barely making contact with the center of the lower *dantian*. You can give the *dantian* a slight tap with edge of your hands that is facing it, as if to wake it up for duty.

After this, raise up the arms by giving them a good rocking swing out and up to the right. You want to generate momentum beginning from the bottom of this arc, to put as little emphasis or strain on the shoulders as possible. This exercise is a strong workout for the shoulders and shoulder blades, but the point is to build them up indirectly by using momentum and letting its trajectory do the follow through rather than leading with the shoulders. Like this, you are working around the key points, which strengthens them at their root, while also stretching the muscle tissue and underlying tendons and fascia radiating out from center of the shoulder blades along the upper back.

It's quite normal to have tension in the neck and shoulders as part of daily life. With this swing upwards, we are trying to bypass engaging the areas that are normally tense. The more fluid momentum you put into the start of your swing up, the more the vertebrae in the neck and the all the connecting muscles through the shoulders will be able to float free. Not only will you strengthen the entire area, you will also relax it and increase circulation. Your body will fall into alignment by choosing momentum over muscular effort. Think of it as massaging your muscles using momentum, up, across and down. It's an interesting isometric moving stretch, as opposed to the usual static stretches we normally see in the West. It will loosen you up in a very short time.

Please note that although there are times women start from right to left and men from left to right when practicing qigong, in this exercise everyone uses the same direction, moving to the right. When the arms swing up, bring them up in a circle with the fingers always interlaced. The thumbs don't have to touch, but it's good if they can. Twist just enough as you swing up and around that the palms face the body and pass up along the side of the head, barely brushing but not touching, up the right ear. The top of the ear is as high as the hands go. Keep your arms as rounded at the elbows as you can and twist at the wrists to let the palms still face the back of the head at the top of the circle. You are now leading from the wrists in this movement, and the wrist twist not

only positions the hands correctly, it also passes along the momentum of your upswing, so you can change direction without breaking the flow of the motion.

Pass the interlaced hands around the middle back of the skull, where it swells out at its fullest. The movement is horizontal, as this is the top of the circle you are describing. Again, without touching, but just very barely brushing the back of the head. Once your palms begin to reach the opposite ear, it's time for them to connect, touch the ear and rub all the way down the ear. Note that just like when the hands are shifting from going up the ear to passing along the back of the head, the motion here is involving the wrists. Keep them loose so the wrists bend quite fully into right angles when passing up over or rubbing down the ears. Rubbing down this ear with firmness, letting the palms tug down is the most crucial part of the entire movement. Make sure every part of both palms contact the ear. Your ear will certainly get warm or even hot while rubbing it this way. This is your proof you are doing the exercise correctly.

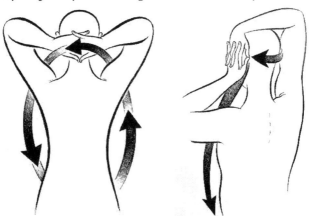

Once you have rubbed down the entire ear, keep your arms nice and rounded and just drop them down, letting gravity do all the work. Drop them so that they have swung around completely with palms up, so that the edge of the palms hit the lower *dantian* with a light but sharp force, as if you are striking a drum. There's no need to use force. Gravity will position your hands in just the spot and the momentum will let you strike this spot with just the right impact. Just drop the hands down very naturally. The natural, effortless drop is the most important part of this portion of the circle.

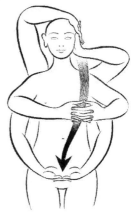

This movement has been taught in other forms of Nine Palaces Qigong, but for our purpose in the Nine-Five Maintenance of Qi, the most important part of the circling is rubbing the ear down firmly. It's our main focus. Dropping the arms to strike the lower *dantian* is the second prime focus. It's not necessary to bang the *dantian* or hit it really hard. The *dantian* will be stimulated enough because we are going to do plenty of circles. As you finish the entire circling around, don't pause. Just go right into another revolution. Do a total of fifty circles from right to left and then without missing a beat, switch directions and do another fifty circles from left to right, rubbing down the right ear.

To discuss breathing, you want to breathe normally. It is very easy to hold your breath on this exercise. The more you do, the harder the movements will be and the less of a nice stretch you're going to get. Smooth easy breathing is the foundation of the movement. Making that your awareness's first priority. The more you are breathing smoothly, the more of a stretch you will get all through the front of your chest, as well as through the back and shoulders, and even the waist and lower abdomen.

Count to fifty in your mind as you circle around. Not only do you want to make sure you're actually doing fifty revolutions, the act of counting is a good way to focus the mind and not get lost in the movement. You want to stay focused and stay connected to your body and the rhythm of your trajectory. One last thing keeping your breathing steady and gentle is helpful with is it will minimize any discomfort you might feel when first practicing. This is a real workout and it's using small muscles that don't always see a lot of activity. Also your ears are going to get very hot and maybe even a little painful. The same may also be said for the lower *dantian* after it has been struck so many times. Light breathing will mitigate any discomfort here too. Just remember that qi flows to where there is this kind of heat. You are improving your circulation in an extremely targeted and effective way. Start from the right fifty times, then start from the left fifty time, for a total of one hundred times.

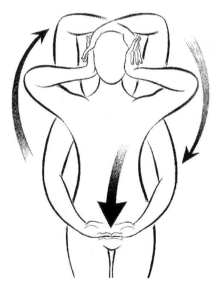

As we have talked about before, the world is square and the heavens are round. We enact the concept of the square inside of the circle with the circling of the arms. "The world is square" is represented by the arms, chest and shoulders. They form a square. "The heavens are round." The motion you are making is circular. This exercise is for combining heaven and earth together as one. Even though you want to keep your arms as loose and rounded as possible, the interlaced fingers and the positioning of the hands isolates your chest, upper back and shoulders into a very solid cube, from the inside out.

The circular momentum going around and around forms a spherical energy that surrounds this cube. It also opens up the ribcage and gives an excellent low impact cardiovascular workout. It's better exercise than running for opening up your chest cavity from the inside out. Also unlike running, you don't have the impact the joints. You're not putting strain on the muscles, even ones that are already stiff, since you are using momentum to fulcrum your arms around a very small central point, rather than actively engaging large muscle groups. It's like doing calisthenics, stretching and massaging at the same time.

As you form the circle around the square, you generate a lot of concentrated energy. Rubbing the ears with their myriad acupuncture points and striking the lower *dantian* disperses this energy throughout the body in waves, like dropping a pebble into a still lake. You clasp the hands, and with the palms facing the body, start with palms up at lower *dantian* level, then circle up and around the back of the head then down the side of the ear, keeping the arms rounded. It is worth observing that the bending and twisting of the wrists appears to facilitate a squared shape and also helps to firmly drop the arms to the lower *dantian* with the proper looseness.

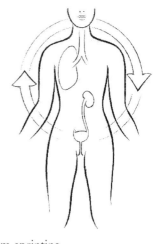

The circular arm swing reflects that the heavens are round and the earth is square. You can massage the internal organs with this exercise as you get looser with practice and go deeper into the layers of muscle and fascia. As your arms rise and fall, you are stretching then compressing the internal organs and stretching the heart and lungs. This is the same workout benefit as a four hundred meter dash, but it's good for older people who can't do that sort of running anymore. One hundred revolutions total is exactly equivalent in its effects. If you measure the metabolism, the breathing and heart rate after completion, they are about the same. Obviously, even younger people can obtain certain advantages from this exercise that aren't gained as directly from sprinting.

Because you are stretching from the inside out and using enough momentum to get movement into the internal viscera and organs, you are activating the positioning of the heart, opening up any potential blockages in the arteries or veins. Normally you would have surgery to unblock an artery, which can lead to complications such as blockages in arteries of the brain. If you have hardening of the arteries, you can do the arm circling exercise intensively for three months, while also eating black fungus (*mu'er*) and white fungus (*yin'er*) together every day. After three months of this regimen, you may be able to avoid the need for surgery. Dr. Wu prescribes this course of therapy for anyone who has heart problems or arterial blockage. He has them do arm cycling plus eat the two funguses daily for three months. His patients have reported an excellent success rate and prevented surgery to a great extent.

This exercise also works out the shoulder and over time you will have increased flexibility. Upper back pain and frozen shoulders go away. It also leads to increased mobility and opening of the joints. This exercise was originally developed by Wang Chongyang as a martial arts training. The arms will have more strength and longer endurance to continue boxing. It's a very simple exercise but it protects the shoulder and elbow joints, correcting the movement of the joints. For example, nowadays people do yoga for stretching out the joints and muscles. It's good, but it can also lead to overextension. For the most protection of the joints, you want to flex and contract the arm first, then extend. This is what's done when setting a dislocated knee, for example. You have to flex the leg before you can pop the joint back in. Once you flex, afterwards the muscle and joint can realign properly. If you only extend without a flexion first, eventually you will tear a ligament. You have to practice well to understand the full implications of this. Retraction before extension is an underlying physical principle throughout Daoist qigong and comes into play in many ways.

As you come down when circling, you want to sweep down the side of your ear and hair. You want make pronounced contact with them. Why is this rubbing so important? As people age, the wrinkles and folds in the brain become shallower. Brushing the hair and ear increases circulation very dramatically in the head, radiating inwards due to the openings of the ear canals. The ears are also the external organ connected to the kidney meridian, which governs the endocrine system and brain, as well as the kidneys. Stimulating the ears will deepen brain's creases, as well as helping the ears themselves. You need to make contact with the ear and press it down firmly as you sweep down. This also indirectly helps any skin problems.

Thirdly, as you come down, the arms must reach the lower *dantian*, dropping on the *dantian* very naturally. *Tian* means rice field. For the body, it means right here you can plant a rice field of growing new energy. Out of the three *dan*, only within the lower one can you plant a field. Therefore, the function in the area of the lower *dantian* is very important for reproduction, and not only for women.

The fourth point on the Conception Vessel meridian is Guanyuan. You can locate it two fingers above the top of the pubic bone in line with the navel. This is a very important point. In Traditional Chinese Medicine, moxibustion, burning prepared sticks of mugwort next to an acupuncture point to bathe it in the smoke, is performed on this point to gain longevity. In Daoism, we don't often use moxa. We just hit the point directly. It's the weakest point in the body. This is why you always want to strengthen it. Hitting this point will strengthen the bladder. As you get older, the legs get weak, there is frequent urination, menstrual problems, listlessness, bladder problems and lower back pain. Hitting this point helps all of these symptoms and will also postpone them if you are younger and have not experienced the aging process yet. Just allow the arms to drop and hit the point as you go downwards on your sweep.

Dried bladder ground into powder form contains progesterone analogs that can be used to regenerate tissue. The famous patent medicine Yunnan Baiyao is used to stop bleeding and also helps the blood to circulate. It is famous as a battlefront treatment to quickly stop bleeding throughout Asia and around the world. It's also used to stop post-operative bleeding. Its formula is a closely guarded secret, but it contains Sanqi (*Panax notoginseng*) and also powdered bladder, among other herbs. Some research has suggested it may be possible to regenerate tissue and even body parts using this formula, although this is not proven yet. It's also good for the skin, as well as stopping bleeding and increasing circulation.

Qu Huanzhang was the herbalist who invented this medicine in the early 20th Century. In China, Yunnan Baiyao is renown to the same degree as penicillin is in the West. The bladders that are used are primarily from chickens, since they only have one orifice for excretion and reproduction. We discuss this as a means of illustrating the importance of striking the lower *dantian*. We are making our body's own medicine with this practice.

When you circle your arms around you need to sweep over the ear and then hit the lower *dantian* to make the practice effective. The ear sweep is yang, in part since the head is yang, and hitting the lower *dantian* is yin. Where these two stimulated sensations collide is where the effectiveness occurs. You can swing your arms up slowly, but as soon as you press against the ear, you want to drop them down quickly, letting gravity take its course. After one hundred repetitions, the lower *dantian* will feel a little painful. This is what we want.

As part of the Daoist traditions of internal alchemy and longevity cultivation, strengthening the lower *dantian* has been a cornerstone for many generations. It will increase your sex drive and sexual performance. If you are sexually potent, it means you are strong, male or female. You can be celibate, and still be sexually vigorous. It's like the forceful triangular energy of the pyramid.

When you strengthen the lower *dantian*, you are strengthening the base of the pyramid and also its apex, at the very top. Both male and female genitalia are pyramidical. There is much theory and study behind this in the Daoist body of knowledge. After one hundred revolutions, your back pain will subside and you will have more energy and improved sex drive, based on the individual needs of your body and lifestyle. There is one caveat to be aware of. Lower *dantian* training strengthens your body, not your fortune. This is why it's only a part of adjustment of qi, rather than its focus.

Although we only need to do fifty circles on each side for the adjustment of qi, if you build yourself up and are able to do one hundred on each, you will have gone deep enough to completely open your ribcage on each side of your body. It can enhance the lung capacity, which in turn increases the blood supply to the heart. It will help irregular heartbeat. It will be a great help for martial arts practice. Once you attack, you will be able to keep punching without tiring, even past five or six punches in a row. You can also attack much faster, not giving your opponent a chance to breath. When you do the circling, it should not be tiring. It connects the lungs and the heart, bringing out the lung capacity and blood flow of the heart. If you feel tired while you practice, remember to breathe gently and never hold your breath and you will see a very rapid change in your ability.

Chinese characters are often made up of root characters called radicals. The radicals are the most ancient pictographs and the ancestors of the written language, although they are not always words themselves. The radical *chuò* means walking and is found as part of many characters that describe different kinds of movement. The radical *shǒu* is made in nine strokes and variously means head. If you put the radical *shǒu* ("head") next to *chuò* ("walk"), it forms the character for Dao. So moving around the head is the Dao. The heavens are round, the earth is square. That's why the circling exercise of adjustment of qi is based on this principle. By practicing the circling we are practicing the roundness of heaven, the square of the earth, and merging the energies together to find the Dao, which is the way, as well as the journey, as well as the truth. Don't overlook this circling.

After you have circled, you want to feel some heat and a light sheen of sweat on your skin. Sweat is the body fluid related to our limited quantity of pre-natal jing, the essence we were born with, so the Daoists don't recommend sweating profusely, as a means of preserving the jing. On the other hand, the light sweat that is brought up from just the right amount and kind of exertion can act as a barrier against pathogens.

This practice not only benefits heart and lung, it also strengthens the trachea and the respiratory system. It is a great help for asthma. If you have a minor cough or cold, circle one hundred or two hundred times. When you lift the arms, you are lifting the shoulder blades and surrounding area, which makes contact with the lung points. The Guanyuan point is related to the bladder and kidney, which has its own association with breathing. Exhaling is governed by the lungs, and inhaling is governed by the kidneys. As your lift up in the swing, you are exercising the lungs. As you lower down on the opposite side, it's exercising the kidney. So this one exercise is taking care of the entire breathing system. It's especially good for the elderly or those with chronic coughs. If you have a cold, circle for as many times as you need to feel a sensation of heat. You will feel better afterwards.

The act of hitting the bladder at the lower *dantian* and rubbing down the ears, disperses the energy we generate with the circling, so that the organs that need the stimulus will get it. The Yanglao and Guanyuan form a pair of related acupressure points. We have already discussed the Guanyuan, two fingers above the pubic bone. The Yanglao point name means "nourishing the aged." It was named this, so that people would never forget it significance of this point for prevention of old age. This is taken very literally. Just as the points at the sides of the nostrils are called "smell fragrance" because pressing them immediately increases and maintains the sense of smell that is how efficient the Yanglao point is for slowing the aging process.

The Yanglao point is the sixth point on the small intestine channel. Find it by locating the soft spot next to outer wrist bone on the back of the hand. It's in the hollow at the base of the ulna, where it meets the hand. You will feel a little soreness when you press into it. The Yanglao point being related to the Guanyuan now explains the reason we want to always keep the wrists loose and rotate them as needed to pass up the side of the head, across the back of the head and then down the opposite ear. We are helping to engage and stimulate the entire area around this point. Not only do we let the wrists carry our momentum up and around the head and ears, when we drop our arms to strike the lower *dantian*, the Yanglao will naturally meet the Guanyuan as it hits. There is no need to forcibly position these points to meet each other. The natural momentum of the circling is enough to ensure they carry youth-giving energy and vitality throughout the rest of the body.

It is acceptable to pause slightly on the lower *dantian* when you strike it. There's a lot of meaning involved in this. The sun rises from the eastern horizon, then circles around the earth. This is the motion of the arms coming up in an arc, and passing along the back of the head. Then the circle of the sun's trajectory meets and becomes the square of the earth. The point right before the palms start to touch the opposite ear is this same point. After the circle has become the square, then you want to rub against the side of the ear as you're descending, and then after you rub you drop the arms to the lower *dantian*.

Your ears are the external representatives of your kidneys. The older you are, the bigger your ears are. If you observe a person of advanced age, all their features will have shrunk and sunken with the exception of the ears. When you get to the age of ninety, you will see that your ears are actually much bigger than they were when you were twenty. All of the systems within the body shrink with age, with the exception of the ears. In this sense, the ears are just like the rings of a tree trunk, which also continue to grow outwards as long as the tree lives.

If you've adopted a dog and don't know how old it is, you open its mouth and count the teeth, looking at their condition and then you will have a good idea of its age. The same thing applies with horses. You check their mouths and see how many teeth they still have. In the same way, the ears are usually a good indicator of a person's age. This is especially true after the age of eighty. An eighty or ninety year old person will have special development of the ear. The point to remember is our ears are just like the rings of a tree's trunk.

So as you come up and go down in the circling exercise, you want to be mindful of touching or not touching the ear. You do not touch the ear when you're coming up, although your hands are close, and as you're coming down, you want to be touching the ear, with a firm hand. Why make such a careful distinction? Remember, as you were coming up, it's like the sun rising in the east. You will be carrying enough qi in your palms that the qi will be touching your ear, even though your hands are not. When you are coming down the other side, the circle of the sun has ended and the square of the earth has begun. This is when it is time to touch the ear firmly with your palms and pull down well, before dropping the arms.

The circling is done in one simple fluid movement, but you are really regulating the qi you are spreading through your body to a very fine-tuned degree, with many subtle adjustments in each detail. Then you'll be touching that ear as you're coming down. Dropping the arms to the lower *dantian*, you are moving from one representation of your kidneys, the ears, to another, the lower *dantian*, which is another expression of the kidney essence or jing. Going from rubbing the ear to hitting the *dantian*, you are hitting two interconnected kidney points.

The entire circle is demonstrating the cycle from yang to yin. Yang starts to rise at daybreak, as your arms come up, then reaches its peak of nourishing force at noon, as the palms pass the ear without needing to touch it. Yang now begins to decrease, while yin starts to rise as well. They mix across the back of your head until the western horizon is reached, and the circle of the sun dissolves into the square planes of the earth. At this moment of perfect blending, this new cargo of energy is rubbed firmly into the second ear, and the first yin of the evening, the kidney point of the ear, is dropped away from effortlessly, through the period of deepest yin, finally to meet the second kidney point of the lower *dantian*, in the perfect blending of decreasing yin and yang just about to rise to meet another new day. This is a beautiful process, filled with the poetry and drama of the cycles of the sun and moon, the heavens and the earth, all meeting at their proper places and times to bring the best mixture of yin and yang for nourishing your body. You must practice it correctly and with deep sincerity.

The simple question asking if there should be a pause once you've hit the lower *dantian*, now reveals its answer. Don't do the circling too fast. There is much to savor and sense as you move through the motion. To pause once the hands have come down is a moment to acknowledge that one full cycle has completed. However, do not pause for more than a moment, because the cycles of life are unceasing. The momentum you need for the next journey around comes from the nourishing energy you brought in at the end of the last rotation. The meaning is ultimately in the movement.

There are many other ways to conceptualize the movements of the circling. You can correlate the movements with the seasons, for example. Coming up is spring, circling round the back of the head is summer, touching the ear going down is fall, and hitting the *dantian* is winter. This exercise also enacts your relationship with the nine stars. These are the seven visible stars of the Big Dipper constellation, joined by two assistant stars, one that is invisible, but near the Big Dipper's handle and one that is a part of the Ursa Minor constellation. Each star has its own Daoist name and relates to one of the nine openings of the body that we are concerned with in Nine Palaces Qigong.

Sometimes Dr. Wu will give a very detailed description of the interconnected meanings of a form, and sometimes he will make mention of a subject such as this with only one comment; that you must practice to understand.

Qigong is always a combination of rigorous detail and complete open-ended interpretation, for as much as you can learn from the teacher, it is always up to you to be diligent in your practice and uncover the insights that have the most personal meaning just for you. Despite all this, just as circling the arms can be seen as an allegory of the day and night upon the earth, it is valuable to recognize that is also an interpretation of the movements of the heavenly bodies across the universe.

As always, it is very important to rub the ear coming down. In this representation raising the arms with the fingers interconnected is still round, but now it depicts the moon. Rotating around the head is like the moon revolving around the earth, and as the energy transforms, the whole body becomes the star system rotating around the sun. When you come up, you are opening up the muscles and the ribcage, massaging the organs. You will feel the discomforts in body, especially digestive problems, fading away. You can understand it like the moon orbiting the earth or the earth orbiting the sun or the sun orbiting around the center of the galaxy. The exercise is simple as always, but the meaning behind it is very profound.

As we said, practicing the lower *dantian* alone strengthens the body, but does not address changing one's fate. The circling works with the *dantian*, but is also carefully connecting various elements from the cycle of our fate, both from the pre-heaven and post-heaven cycles of the eight trigrams. On our bodies, from the top of the head to under the chin represents our first sixty years. It's yang energy that moves down from top of the head to underside of the chin and is pre-heaven. The next sixty years of our life is yin and moves from feet up to under the chin, rising up and is post-heaven.

When you rotate around and then hit the bladder area, you want to create a vibration that will ripple through your body. As discussed, it's not a question of striking with strong force. Natural force will have just the right impact. When you hit the bladder, you are also exercising the lung and stomach too. Exercising the kidney is pre-heaven, spleen and stomach is post-heaven, so in this exercise you are connecting pre- and post-heaven. You are enhancing the spleen and stomach functions. After you finish, the whole upper body will feel very relaxed. You'll almost feel like a whole new person, because in a sense, now you are.

Connecting the Triple Burner

Circling the arms can be a difficult workout when you first begin practicing. Our feet and legs get a lot of exercise just from the average amount of walking we do during the day. We don't have nearly as many opportunities to fully exercise our arms. Breathing gently and smoothly is the key to easing the exertion of circling one hundred times. After you have finished, you should feel very relaxed. The second half of adjustment of qi will help to relax you further, while also continuing to train the arms.

Like circling, it is a very simple exercise, but highly effective on many different levels. Take your time with the adjustment of qi and your body will reap permanent results over time. To explain the exercise in brief, when your hands drop for their last beat on the lower *dantian*, your fingers are still interlaced with the palms up. Bring them up slowly to chest level, palms up, exhaling through mouth very thinly, gently and slowly. As soon as the hands reach chest height, flip the palms over, keeping them interlaced and lower the hands back down to the lower *dantian*, inhaling thinly and continuously through nose. Repeat for a total of fifty to one hundred times. These are the steps in brief.

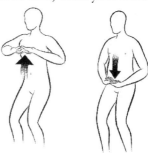

First let's break down the hand and arm movements. Your fingers are interlaced as in the circling, but there is one difference. Now you want to pay more attention that the thumbs are also kept interlaced. You can keep the left thumb laid over and touching the right thumb as part of this clasp, but it doesn't matter which finger you keep on top. You do need to have your fingers wedged together quite well to accomplish this, which will keep your palms slightly cupped. Keeping your hands clasped and cupped in this way will greatly add to the sensations you feel as you do this exercise, so it is worth it to be attentive to their positioning.

Then raise the interlaced palms straight up the centerline of the body. If you recall, you can locate the middle *dan* by placing your hands in a triangle pointing up, with its center at the center point midway between the two nipples. Raise up your hands until they reach the point at the top of the middle *dan*, which will be above the center point between the breasts. As soon as they reach this point, you want to flip the hands over very lightly and gracefully using the wrists, so the fingers stay interlaced and cupped, but the palms are facing down. Then lower the arms back down to the lowest point of the lower *dantian*. To start your next repeat, rotate your wrists to turn the palms back over, lightly but with a bit of a scooping effort as well.

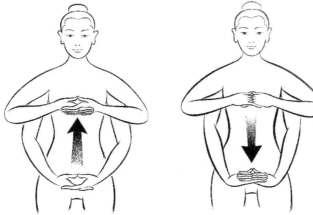

When you raise your arms, bring them up to the center of the middle chest region, between the breasts. You are exhaling through the mouth the entire time you are lifting your arms and hands to this point. From Traditional Chinese Medicine theory, the lungs are shaped like an open umbrella. From the umbrella representing your lungs, you start descending the arms down, inhaling through the nose the entire time. It is very important to inhale and exhale continuously, without a break or holding your breath. When you exhale, use the opportunity to release and relax as much as possible.

A thin, completely silent stream of air is ideal. If you're feeling troubled emotionally or under stress, you can change your breathing to help release more. In this case, blow the air out faster, and move your arms faster to keep up, so that you never run out of breath. If you are feeling particularly unhappy, not only blow out, but lift your chin up so your head is thrown back, and blow upwards, sending your breath out as far as it can go. This posture is the most releasing of them all, both psychologically as well as physically, since it helps open tightness in the chest.

No matter how you choose to breathe that day, it is important to understand that we want to empty ourselves. This is because when you flip the hands over and start inhaling, the goal of this inhale is to fill the kidneys and your lower *dantian* with qi. With some practice, the diaphragm will relax. You will be able to do a very controlled inhale far down into your lower abdominal area, filling it up so that the whole band around your midsection from the navel and hips all the way to the back over the kidneys expands from the inside out. You want to deposit the qi there, in a measured way, so that you have a complete isometric stretch the circumference of your core down into the hips and lower abdomen. If you exhale thoroughly when bringing the arms up, your internal muscles will be prepared for this very deep inhale. The breathing in itself relaxes the organs.

Breathing so that you expand from within with the depth of your breath creates the effect of an internal massage. Never use muscular force or inhale harshly, loudly or too quickly or you will block this stretch, rather than increase it. The more forcefully you try to inhale, the more you just trap the breath in the upper chest, with nowhere for it to you. Let your lungs expand softly to lead off your inhale rather than sucking air through the nose like a vacuum cleaner, to give the air you are inhaling somewhere to go. Start off gently and your body will expand more and more with regular practice, without the need to force your breathing. Understanding the purpose and pace of your inhale and exhale is the key to understanding this exercise.

Our objective is to connect the triple burner. The torso is divided into three sections or burners (*jiao*). The heart and lungs are in the upper, spleen and stomach are in the middle, and the kidneys are in the lower burner. The key to opening communication between the three is to exhale first. This is due to exhalation being controlled by the lungs, which are there in the upper burner. Inhaling is governed by the kidneys. Coughing and wheezing is related to the kidneys. Perform this breathing one hundred times and you will feel the energy intermingling between the burners.

Although we have already spoken about the importance of calm breathing, it is worth it to explore a little further, in the context of transforming the self. The exhaling up and inhaling down has to done slowly. Be scrupulous in this effort and match the speed of your arm movements to the speed of your breathing. Readjust yourself if you catch yourself holding on to your breath, or running out of inhalation or exhalation before your arms have gotten to position. Both the physical act and the mental state must be relaxed and unlabored. You should feel grand and serene. Placing yourself into this state of mind, you cultivate your ability to feel calm, broad and open. This expansiveness is a special state of awareness that both physical and emotional. When you enjoy a fine liqueur or a perfect cup of rare tea, you savor it little by little, sipping it slowly in contemplation. Approach this practice with the same attitude of refinement. Exhale slowly then immediately inhale when you get to the top. There should be no break in the cycle of the breathing at all, or it could harm you. The breathing must feel like a complete cycle. It's the circle of Taiji.

This is a very good example of using a psychological or emotional state to assist your body in a strictly physical exercise. The proper mindset aligns your posture in subtle ways, and also helps you direct the qi to otherwise difficult to reach locations. And you're still interlacing your palms and you exhale as you bring up and you inhale as you lower it. A refined and expansive awareness is the perfect state of mind to help you breath properly down through the diaphragm and deep into the lower *dantian*. Normally that's how it's supposed to be done, but if you're distraught, have stress, if you're frustrated or depressed, it's difficult to clear your mind to this point.

This is where we can reverse our effort. If before, we used a mental state to improve our breathing, now we can change the breathing to bring our emotions back to peace. Daoists wisely understood the connection between difficult emotions and muscular tension and misalignment and did not judge one to be more or less easy to retrain. The circling exercise and others we will encounter are loosening up areas of the body that normally store all our bad memories and troubled feelings. Opening up these constrictions can happen very suddenly and many emotions might come out on their own as they are being released. So it wouldn't be unusual to start your qigong practice feeling perfectly fine, then hitting a point where suddenly you feel very sad or very tense.

An old memory could come back, or it could be an inexplicable mood that abruptly washes over you. It's important to be aware in advance that this is natural and nothing to be afraid or ashamed of. In fact, it's best to just keep going with your practice, because the form itself has tools to help you through an emotional moment. After you have practiced for a while, it becomes easy to see how the steps of the practice are arranged to give you release and then give you a moment of calm to rebalance yourself.

The standard exhale is done imperceptibly. The mouth is supple but not particularly opened or shaped in any way and the air comes out so thinly, it's almost more of a mist than a stream. If this is not possible, there is some tension in your body or mind that needs to be cared for. Then the breathing converts to blowing the air out quietly with the lips very rounded. Inhalation through the nose down into the lower *dantian* is always the same, with just one form of inhale, but there are six levels of exhaling force. So, if you're stressed out or frustrated, instead of simply exhaling, you want to blow the air out. We mentioned earlier that if you're angry on the verge of exploding, you want to blow upwards, diagonally up and forward above your head, with the head tilted back. Exhaling is more like letting the air rolling out slowly, naturally, without much movement in the chest or diaphragm. For blowing, you want to feel the movement upwards and out of the body. When blowing out, the air and movement carries a lot of your stress and frustration out of your body.

To go over the six different intensities of exhaling and blowing, the first is the simple exhale. Next is just blow with rounded lips so that there's a perceptible stream of air coming out, but no active pushing it up and out of the body. The next levels involve adding tones to your blowing, sometimes a sigh-like *aaa* or more of a hiss like *sss*. Shaping the exhale with either of these tones will automatically start to involve actively pushing the air out. Next is blowing up and out as we have discussed in a thin stream and lastly would be blowing up and out forcefully in a bigger, shorter rush.

The most all-purpose forms are the simple exhale or blowing out and very slightly up in the slow stream, without making sounds or tilting the head back. You will need to bear in mind that different levels of exhale might take less time for you to reach the point where you run out of air. You must move your arms up faster to match this so that you are never, ever holding your breath, waiting for your hands to catch up. There has to be an instantaneous flip from exhale to inhale, the hands flipping and the exhale flipping to inhale without missing a beat. Even a tiny moment of holding your breath or being out of breath means you are doing this practice incorrectly and even potentially with negative consequences, so you need to be mindful. The simple exhale will naturally make you go a little slower. If you're stressed or tense, you will naturally want to go a little faster. Think of the pacing as an exhale taking about two or three beats to bring the arms all the way up, while the blowing out could be as short as 1 beat, with a fast lifting of the arms and even a fast lowering down/inhale, the exhale and inhale are more of a pumping action.

Please do not feel that going slower is automatically better. What will feel the best will be what also is the best for your mood and will also be the level of training that will relax you fastest and develop your overall breathing capacity in the shortest amount of time. That's the important thing. It's accepting the natural needs of your body. It's the same as checking your tongue when you wake up and using that as your guide for how slow or fast you should do your practice for the day. As we said before, you are savoring the experience of breathing, paying attention to your needs. Vigorous breathing can be just as relaxing and pleasurable as slow breathing, if this is what your body needs. Just knowing that there isn't some outside ideal you need to conform to will help you lift your mood up and feel calmer. Repeat fifty to one hundred times and you will see how different you feel. This is the adjustment of qi. Adjust the qi in your body precisely the way you require.

When you lift up your arms while exhaling, pay attention to immediately shift to the inhale and synchronize it with the flipping over of the hands. The breathing, hands, and muscular activity within the torso all go together as one. It is a very light, subtle shift, but the sensation is noticeable. You want to make sure to drop your arms down, as if gravity is pulling them down. It's as if you are pressing down when you come down, pressing all the way down so that you can't press down any more. Your arms can finish very straight, but just make sure to keep your fingers interlaced and your hands clasped securely. The emphasis here is not on speed. It's on focus. If you are feeling tense, you will go a little faster, but the focus and sensation of inhaling down will be the same. If you are going slower, you don't need to raise your hands too high. They should not be higher than the middle *dan*. Going slowly to this height is a good practice for controlling high blood pressure. For other issues, you could raise your hands a little higher, but never higher than the eyebrows. If you lift your arms above your eyebrows, it will increase your blood pressure, so be careful never to lift up too high.

Generally, for normal people with no health issues, just raise the arms up to the chest, with the hands centered between the breasts or pectoral muscles. To find this perfect height grab your breasts or pectorals with both hands and while still holding onto them, form your hands into the interlaced, palm up clasp. This will show you the perfect height for your arms. If you have insomnia you would like to treat, you can raise the arms a little higher, right beneath the brows. To find the correct height for insomnia treatment, raise the arms to just below the eyes, so when you flip the clasped it's as if they are cupping the as they flip over and once they're flipped over the tops of the hands are level with the brows. Don't go above the eyebrows, because the area above the eyebrows represents heaven, while the area below the brow is still representing you. As we have said, bringing the arms up too high will also cause hypertension, aside from the esoteric explanation.

A professor who is friends with Dr. Wu arranged for a well-known taijiquan practitioner to come speak and teach at his college, and he brought him over to visit Dr. Wu. Dr. Wu asked the taijiquan artist to show him how he does the "cloud hands," which is a primary movement of taijiquan, when lifting your arm up with the palm facing your body. When the practitioner lifted his arms, he raised them too high, his palms were at the level of the eyebrows. That was a red flag. Dr. Wu figured he just didn't understand, that his understanding of theory was not sound. Because in taijiquan, cloud hands needs to be at eye level or lower than the eye. You need to perform cloud hands with the palms at a level so that you have to look down into them as you pass the hand along.

To lower your blood pressure, you need to keep your hands lower than your eyes, and the eyes focused on the lower *dantian*. Raising your hands above eye level, you're actually increasing your blood pressure. And also if the hand is excessively high, by raising your blood pressure it might also affect your sleep patterns. Sometimes people try to resolve insomnia by counting. In Daoism, we ask you to lie down flat and try to look below you as you're lying on the bed. Lowering the eyes allows them to relax within their sockets and the rest of your body adjusts from there. You will fall asleep very quickly.

The eyes play an integral role in the cranial nervous system, because of the nerve bundle they are connected to. Out of the twelve pairs of cranial nerves, we have eight pairs at the base of the skull where the neck meets the back of the skull. So when you consider the movement of cloud hand, as you're moving and following your hands, you're actually adjusting the eight pairs of cranial nerves that are there between the neck and the head, the brain stem. Keeping your eyes looking down, relaxed in the sockets, keeps their nerve bundles out of the picture, so to speak. If your hands were higher, you would have to look up to see your hands, instantly activating the muscles and nerves of the eye, which take precedence with your brain. You would be defeating the purpose of adjusting the nerves at the base of the skull.

There is a common western style neck stretch where people bring their heads down to the chest and then up, leaning the head and neck forward and back. Sometimes you might feel a temporary relaxation after you do this stretch, but it actually is bad for cervical spine problems. The Daoist theory is to help spinal issues in the neck, you must press downwards in order to alleviate the pain. You can never bring your head up to alleviate neck pain because it's not in accordance with the Taiji symbol. Another way to put this is, stretching the head back is fighting against the natural curvature of the spine in that area. So if you have cervical pain, to help alleviate it you want to press down, rather than raising your neck.

A good way to do this is by clasping the hands and pressing down with them over the base of the neck. Generally speaking with any form of qigong or martial arts or other kinds of stretching, whenever it involves you looking up, it's not recommended. As we age, high blood pressure can lead to a lack of blood supply to the brain, so we need to be more careful about the kinds of exercise we do as we get older. Even though cloud hands is a very simple movement of just bringing the hands up, it can adjust you an exceptional amount. When doing the adjustment of qi exercises, keep your eyelids lowered but open and your eyes relaxed and focused downwards, for maximum relaxation. If you are feeling stressed and need to do the breathing blowing out where you tilt your head back, keep your eyes down, rather than tilting them back with your head. You will notice the difference in sensation. Exhaling up cleanses you internally. Doing one hundred repetitions can get rid of bad temper and help the stomach.

The Elixir Pill

When you have finished connecting the triple burner, there will be extra saliva in your mouth. Swallow it all the way down to the lower *dantian* or bladder. At first when you do this you might feel a slight chill as the yin is brought out from the kidney, while on your chest you will feel heat where it's been brought out from lungs. This is forming the internal medicine, the Elixir Pill. You are training the Li and Kan trigrams, fire and water. Inhale towards the kidneys or lower *dantian* to effect this transformation. Together with circling the arms, you have completed the adjustment of qi. Although they are simple exercises, they perfectly illustrate how the Nine-Five Maintenance of Qi form allows you to align your practice to the needs of your body. You not only adjust the qi with the important meridians, you allow your body and emotions to tell you how to practice. To harmonize with the rhythms of nature, you must listen to the rhythms inside of yourself. This is an important lesson to learn along the journey of qigong.

Chapter Six

Tonification of Qi

Enhancement

The next phase of Nine-Five Maintenance of Qi is known as tonification of qi (*yangqi*). The term *yang* here is an interesting word with a variety of meanings. It means "raising," as in raising a child, tending livestock, keeping a pet, or nourishing life. All the processes of caring for another being are referenced. It means to support and nourish a creature that needs this help to grow strong. The qi that we have brought into our bodies in the last three phases of the practice is inside of us. How do we insure that it grows well? How do we nourish ourselves with this qi, so that it feeds our whole body? This is why we chose to translate the term as tonification of qi.

In Traditional Chinese Medicine, tonification is the treatment method used to nourish and replenish qi, particularly in the blood. To define it as nourishing qi is accurate, but it doesn't convey the systematic and thorough method we use in its practice. An alternate term for the process is "guiding qi" or "leading qi" (*lingqi*. The practice allows qi to flow to every place within your body, filling it on the deepest level.

Tonification of qi is one of the most challenging and unusual qigong practices that Dr. Wu has ever taught, but results in huge gains for the body and for qigong practice as a whole. It's hard to consider any individual part of the Nine-Five Maintenance of Qi to be the centerpiece of the practice, as each step is integral to the whole and flows one into the next. However, mastering its operations will open your eyes to the true power of qigong. It is an elevated practice, a flawless expression of internal alchemy in its highest form. It's all the more fascinating because the exercise itself goes against the grain of the essential guide-lines of most qigong practice. In this training, we are going to break every rule to accomplish a physical goal, that when mastered brings a state of consciousness that could easily become one of the peak experiences in a lifetime of practice. There is nothing like it.

Normally, for the most effective qigong training, we don't hold the breath or use strength or force, but here we specifically are doing both. Remember that qi means energy or life force, but it also means air and breath. Qi permeates everything around us, so to get qi into the body, we breathe it in. Tonification focuses on breath training to maximize the body's capacity to stretch open and let the respiratory system expand to its fullest. Here we intentionally hold our breath, but it's not simply to train lung capacity. It's to train the body to stimulate qi and air to flow through the energetic pathways and the circulatory system at an enhanced velocity.

Just as in all practice, you should not hold your breath to the point of gasp-ing for air. There is still a natural breathing process, but one that works on an-other level of efficiency and body control. We uncharacteristically use our full muscle strength to pull qi into position in the body, but we stop using force as soon as the energy is in place to pump it through body. Continuously using force makes the practice unnecessarily difficult and gets in the way of experiencing the accumulation and flow of the qi as it expands through the system. The practice demands but also develops a higher order of breathing and a higher order of muscular strength. We go against the grain, but only to push our qigong perfor-mance ideals to the next level. We will present the steps to practice and encourage the reader to accept a gradual and steady process of transformation that requires great effort, discipline and self-awareness.

Stance

After completing the adjustment of qi, take a moment to readjust your stance if necessary. The feet are shoulder width, toes pointed inwards. Place the tongue lightly and naturally on the upper palate. Keep the knees slightly bent. We are going to form a two-handed, clasped fist at the middle *dan*, with the elbows pointed out to the sides. To form the fist, the left hand is on the outside, palm facing the body and thumb facing up and the right hand fits inside, thumb facing down, so that rest of the fingers hook together in a very solid clasp. We will go into more detail on this, but for now, once you have formed this hand posture, point the tips of your feet inwards a little more.

You're forming an extremely stable pyramid with your body. This stance will open the hips. The hips open wider than when normally standing because of the clasped hands acting as a solid cross brace giving more support to the usual tripod stance. The usual tripod stance is formed from the two legs and a column of energy coming down from the end of the spine as the third support. Recognize that tripods are more stable than humans, that three legs are more stable than two legs. Now we not only have the three legs of the tripod, but we have widened it and braced it enough to accentuate the central column of energy that runs down the middle of this triangular stance, down the centerline of your body. This practice will be using the pyramid, circle and square to a great degree, turning the entire body into all of them merged as one.

Hand Position

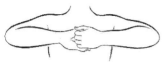

The hands clasp with the fingers hooked with the left back of the hand facing out with thumb on top and the right back of the hand facing the chest with the thumb on the bottom. The way to form this hand gesture is to bring the left arm up to the middle *dan* in a loose fist facing the body, so that the thumb is at the top, and the forearm is parallel to the chest. Now bring your right arm up also in a fist, but this time the thumb is down. The forearm is also parallel but the fist and forearm are turned facing out. Bring the two fists together so that the left fist is on the outside and the right fist is on the inside.

Then just very lightly open your four fingers and the tips of the right hand fingers will naturally go towards the base of the left hand's fingers. From here, just hook both sets of fingers together, the fingers clasped together, rather than interwoven. The knuckles of the right hand are basically in the left hand's palm.

Lay the left thumb at the top and keep the right thumb up against the bottom of the left hand. This forms a very solid connection so that if you try to pull out, you feel it in your forearms and chest, but the hands don't budge and just hold even tighter.

Once clasped, see to it that the forearms form a straight line all the way to the elbows. This will keep the clasped hands at just the right distance from the centerline of the body. When your hands are in the proper position, this is when you want to check your stance to see that it is very stable and you feel the sensation of the pyramid, with the three spokes of the tripod, the fourth central column running from the pyramid's apex down

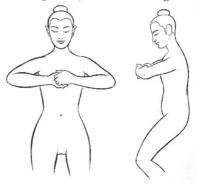

the centerline of the body, and the two equidistant cross braces of the arms and the hips.

If you think about it, the arms form a triangle of their own, and so do the hips, each pointing in the opposite direction. We are going to use these two cross braces not only to shore up the pyramid, but also to form the square with the rest of our torso when we begin the active portion of the exercise. The tongue is naturally resting on the upper palate in a comfortable manner, not curling back or tense. This will be our final link point in our stance of perfect stability and energy flow.

Upper Back, Ribcage, Lower Dantian

Now that you have taken this extremely stable stance, it is time to begin the first of three stations of tonification practice. We are going to be inhaling while pulling the clasped hands outwards with force three times, each time focusing on a different part of the body. Start to inhale. Inhale through the nose. Your tongue should naturally touch the upper palate. As you inhale, you want to pull outwards from where the hands are linked. The hands do not separate because they are joined in a natural fastening. The more force you apply, the tighter the clasp becomes.

You want to apply force, put some effort into it as you pull. You want to pull apart using strength, while you are inhaling. As you are pulling and inhaling, you want to crouch a little bit, lowering down a bit at the knees, and also bringing your shoulders and upper chest forward, and in your mind, concentrate on your back, particularly focusing on the upper back in the area between and above the shoulder blades. When lowering down and bringing your shoulders forward, you want to cave the front of your body in, allowing the chest to be hollow and the back, particularly the upper back become more rounded. You can slightly tuck your chin into your neck a bit to maintain a neutral position, but you want to keep your head up, not drooping or craning, integrated with your forward lean.

This curved posture is very important. It is going to help accentuate the pathway of the qi into your body as you inhale. It is the vertical line of energy down the centerline of your body that the qi from your inhale is passing down through. Dr. Wu demonstrated this concept by lowering his knees a bit, sticking out the pelvis so that the torso caves in and taking his right hand in a prayer mudra, fingers up and together, thumb side edge of the hand facing the body, down the center front of his body down to the lower *dantian* area in one decisive motion. It's very important to have your shoulders and upper chest leaning forward slightly. It takes pressure off the arms and shoulders and helps keep the back rounded. It relaxes the chest completely so that any personal tension in the chest and diaphragm is minimized and released, whether physical or emotional.

Lowering from the knees, curving out the pelvis and hollowing the front of the chest, combined lets the internal organs hang freely so the body can balance itself on the inside. The interior planes of the muscles and tendons will also be free to relax and realign. The more relaxed it is, the less your body is blocking the flow of the qi. Subsequently, you will experience its movement through the body clearly and with control.

Inhale steadily through nose while pulling out with the clasped fingers until you can't inhale any more, then count within your heart up to two hundred, while holding your breath. Focus on your upper back while doing all of this. You are pulling with your hands, but you are also opening along the upper back just by thinking about it. Keep pulling out with force for as long as you are inhaling. You want to use as much strength as you have, even to the point of shaking with the exertion, but understand that you will build up the ability to pull apart completely over time. When first starting out, you will need to strike a balance between using all your strength to pull apart and being able to inhale deeply and slowly, especially bearing in mind what comes next.

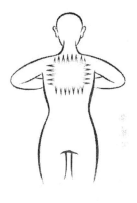

When you feel completely full and expanded and can't inhale any more, continue to focus on your upper back. Now you are going to hold your breath, holding in all the air you've inhaled, and start counting off numbers inside of your heart. You can stop using all your strength to pull outwards with the hands once you're filled with breath and start counting, but don't let go of your hands. Don't let go of your fully extended and activated stance. You are still stretched open and holding there at the peak of your extension, just not applying any further outward force.

The ideal is being able to count to two hundred at a measured pace while holding your breath and standing in this posture, still leaning forward at the shoulders with a rounded upper back, hands clasped tightly. Then, relax all your muscles, while still keeping in your position and exhale gently through the mouth.

Counting to two hundred is something you want to build up to. At first you may only be able to count to twenty or thirty. It is crucial that when you exhale, you do so very slowly, very thinly and with perfect control, feeling all your internal muscles helping to push the air up through the torso, throat and out the mouth in one integrated current. If you've held your breath too long, you will exhale in one big rush and will have sorely diminished the quality of your practice. You've already put a good effort in with your inhale, so why waste all that work by pushing yourself too far while you hold your breath?

It is better to hold and count for a shorter time so that you save enough time to really do a proper exhale. It might take a little practice to get the timing right for your level of ability and it's all right to push harder on getting a fuller count, but overall, you will make better progress to gradually increase your count over days and weeks. Once you've developed a high level of muscle relaxation and breath control, both on the inhale and the exhale, you will have permanently improved your body's capacity to absorb and manage qi for your health and longevity.

After exhaling fully, repeat the inhale and pull, focusing on the sides of the ribcage. You want to be in the same stance as before. Lowering yourself down as you inhale down and pull with great force, focus your mind on the lateral surface of the ribs, the full length of curved outer portion between front and back. When we inhale, the intercostal muscles between the ribs naturally contract and expand up and out, to make even more room. By inhaling and pulling, we are greatly increasing this automatic muscle behavior.

When you inhale, breath is flowing down into you and as you pull, you are pulling the qi in the breath into all the fine capillaries that bring oxygen to the vein into the heart. When we hold the breath and count, we are pressurizing the circulatory system and energy channels and when we exhale and relax, qi pumps through with enough force to reach the finest and furthest reaches of the body, unblocking clogs and congestion on the way. It can be a very strong sensation, but the Nine-Five Maintenance of Qi exercises that have come before have prepared us to fully absorb its intensity.

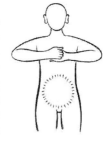

For the third inhale and pull, focus in your mind on the lower *dantian*. Just as your ribcage naturally expands during a normal inhale, the diaphragm also moves downwards to make room for the lungs to expand. We focus on the lower *dantian* as we inhale and pull, because it's the spot in the body to strengthen and open in order to support the diaphragm going deeper and becoming very relaxed. Pull while you inhale until you can't fill yourself any further and then as before, stop and count while holding your breath. Hold it as long as you can while still leaving time to comfortably exhale through the mouth slowly, letting the air come up in one smooth column up the center of the torso, throat and out the mouth.

To recap, the first time, put your mind's focus on the upper back, the second time on the sides of the ribcage and armpit area, then the third time, think about the lower *dantian*. If you feel covered in a light sweat, you have practiced with the correct intensity. It's not a passive grasp where you place your hands together. The fingers are always being gripped by each other, in a rock-hard lock. Even when you start to relax and exhale, they stay well clasped, although softened. It's not as simple as you might think. You have to make a serious physical and mental effort when you practice.

While practicing each stage of tonification, do not tighten the perineum, anus or pelvic floor. If you were to contract those muscles, you would change the natural pattern of the qi flow. Some qigong exercises do employ this type of muscle tightening, but for the purpose of our practice, always keep the area loose unless specifically mentioned.

We are trying to harmonize with heaven and earth. The ebb and flow of the qi as it circulates into and out of the body are a large portion of Nine-Five Maintenance of Qi training. We can make a comparison to the concept of qigong practices that use different kinds of trees that we've discussed earlier. To practice with a younger tree or older tree is different. For instance, if you're forty years old, you need to find a tree that's younger than you so that you can practice and grow together. But if you're over seventy, then you need to find a tree that's older than seventy, a tree that could possibly live two hundred or even one thousand years.

In the White Cloud Monastery there is a ginkgo tree that is over a thousand years old. When Dr. Wu was young, his master told him to practice in front of it. A year from the day he was told to start practicing, his master instructed him to immediately stop and find a smaller, younger tree to practice with instead. Shortly before he was about to leave the monastery with many of the other departing monks, the master directed them to start practicing in front of that old tree again. There are rising and falling changes always in flux along our timeline. There is a reason. Many axioms, philosophies and theories lie behind the master's instructions.

Daoists observe that elderly people, over the age of one hundred usually will have a young partner or helper of the opposite sex in their lives. They are either married to them or working as a close aide, taking care of them. Usually this caregiver is very young, a counterpart to the aged person. That's the yin-yang balance for this set of circumstances. It's something to think about. However, we are using a different combination of yin and yang in the nine palaces practice, since we are training to maintain ourselves on our own with nature to help us.

Inhaling and Pulling

The purpose of the tonification of qi is to spread the qi out to all the channels and collaterals of the meridian system. You supply your qi to every channel and also as air, to the circulatory system as well. This is the feeding and nourishing process. It is a dynamic method that intakes qi through the breath and then amplifies its natural movement to pressure-pump it to every corner of the body, to the farthest reaches of the meridians and blood vessels. The key here is using the opposing forces of your inhale and you're pulling to energize and stimulate these systems.

When you inhale, the qi enters your body vertically. During inhalation, you suck the qi through the nose and then it shoots straight down without impediment, due to the specific details of the posture we assume. This is why it is very important to have the pyramid shaped stance, forward lean and the hollowed torso emphasizing a rounded back. However even though the qi enters the body vertically, you're pulling horizontally. So you are creating two pathways of qi at the same time that form a cross inside the body, the qi going straight down from inhaling through the nose and the puling which is horizontal and stretching out laterally from both sides. This pattern of energy flow is enough to protect you on its own, even without the rest of the practice.

When you are pulling, your chest will lean forward a little bit more. You need to be pulling as you're inhaling. Lower down a bit, with a bend in the knees while you pull and inhale for extra balance and power. In your mind, you want to be concentrating on your back, ribcage or lower *dantian*. You don't have to physically stretch the back or these other areas, especially when you're first starting out. Just thinking about the spot is going to direct qi to it. This is another important concept that comes into play constantly in qigong practice.

The mind directs the qi. Your focus guides it to where you intend it to go. This is particularly relevant when you consider all the aches, pains, stiffness and blockages we accumulate in the body. Daoists had the brilliantly simple insight that if the flesh was getting in the way, using breath along with the mind is enough to engage the fine neural triggers in the intended area. The gross muscular level might need strengthening, stretching or aligning, but at its root are the subtle neuro-muscular controls. Bypass your blocks by connecting to your body at more refined meta-level. Make the brain-body connection first and the muscles will start doing what you want with a little regular practice.

As in many other qigong exercises, you want to expand and stretch your body from the inside out by filling it with breath. Letting your mind, not your muscles do the work is the best path towards a highly integrated musculoskeletal and neuromuscular system. Of course, if you are pulling and inhaling and feel like you are filling yourself with so much breath that your back, ribs or lower abdomen are expanding from the inside out, you are definitely advancing in your ability, but you only need to use real muscle strength in the hands and arms as you pull. Pulling and thinking of the three locations is enough.

After you've inhaled to your maximum, hold your breath and start to count in your head. Stop pulling but stay in that completely expanded position, rather than relaxing the hands, arms or torso. After you have counted, relax your hands and exhale slowly up and out of the mouth. This is the point where you will feel the true power of forming the cross with your breath. It might take some practice to get to this point, but you should feel a sensation within your body of the qi rushing outwards to fill and energize the rest of the body. It might be subtle or it might be very powerful, but this is the nourishment of the practice.

We use force to create a pathway of qi within the body. It might seem like an isometric exercise, using muscle against muscle, pulling the hands, stretching the body from inside with the inhale and holding of breath. But isometrics is only a partial explanation of what we are doing. The muscular force and stretching is only done as a means to an end, which is to facilitate an amplified thrust to the qi's movement in the body.

Let's start with a simple concept, two cars travelling in opposite directions, on a collision course. Every event has a vertical and horizontal force. Vertical velocity is yang and horizontal motion is yin. Yang movement in the body is considered as accelerating from north, from your head, to south, down to the toes. It has a quality of strong acceleration. The horizontal planes of the body are yin, the direction east to west. They act as a straightaway, a steady current, but without much force. This is easy to picture when you remember we are much taller than we are wide. There is just more room in the body for a downward force to pick up speed than any side-to-side internal movements can. In addition to this, the Daoists conceptualize the internal organs as clock bells, hanging down vertically within the body. It is true that our organs do hang down in this way when we stand.

To go back to the metaphor of the two cars, one is travelling east to west and the other is traveling north to south. And instantaneously when they collide, if the car that's going north to south has the greater force of impact, that momentum will carry the other car off course, diagonally off its horizontal route. If however the size and speed of the car going east to west is greater, it will push the other car off its course instead. This is Newton's second law of motion in a nutshell – velocity changes as force is applied, and force is determined by the acceleration of an object multiplied by its mass. To put it in slightly simpler terms, the direction, rate of speed and size, shape and density of an object will determine its force, and the stronger force will push the weaker force off course.

From both TCM and Daoist internal alchemy theory, when you become sick, the sickness is actually hanging vertically within the body, as the organs themselves do. The twelve primary meridians (*zhengjing*) are always vertical. There are also the eight extraordinary vessels (*qijing bamai*) that branch diagonally from the twelve primary meridians with a slight horizontal bias. Included in these eight is the Belt Vessel (*daimai*), which is completely horizontal, as well.

The eight extraordinary vessels supply the twelve primary meridians with qi and blood as needed, so that they can circulate them to all the organs in the body. During the tonification of qi, when we are pulling, we are pulling these eight extraordinary vessels. We are pulling sicknesses apart in the body using its counter flow. It's like an arm wrestling match against sickness. The opponent is the disease, the clasped hands of the two wrestlers represent the disease as it is manifesting in the body and you are your immune system, which is not strong enough to fight the opponent back and forth down to the table. You can't pin him that way if you are not strong enough. Instead of wrestling back and forth, pull your arm back in towards your body, cave your chest inwards just slightly and it will be enough to counter his force and change the force vector to your advantage. Now you have unbalanced him enough to win the match and halt the onset of the disease.

Since we have established that disease is vertical, if we can't counter it vertically, we need to counter it some other way. By moving horizontally, the force vector will be totally changed, pushed off into a diagonal. This is our winning move. Now we can disperse illness and bring more healthful nourishment past any blockages to where it needs to go. It's a matter of physics.

The tonificaiton of qi is based on very simple application of force. All you need to do is practice to understand it. Qi flows into the body vertically, but pulling horizontally forces it past the standard vertical columns of energy down the center of the body and main vertical meridians. Inhaling in vertically and pulling with force horizontally is turning the standard qi flow inside of us into a cross shape. Using the cross-shaped pathway enables detection of blockage and disease in the body. This is why the pulling is especially important and requires focus and force.

You are thinking about the back, the ribs or the lower *dantian*. You are counting as high as you can, up to two hundred as your ultimate goal. And as you're pulling, you need to envision yourself as a cross, a cross of colliding energies. We've used examples of horizontal and vertical, the two cars and which one of their forces is greater. But what do we do about the sickness in our body? The organs hang vertically, but what about cancer, a tumor, hardening, swelling or other irregularity? How do we know if our disease is vertical or horizontal, so we know what opposing force we will need to use to break it up?

The pectoral muscle has fibers that lie horizontally, but there are other muscle fibers, such as in the thigh, which connect vertically to the structure underneath, rather than transversely. In the field of massage, you want to massage the muscle tissue in the direction that muscle travels. If the muscle is horizontal, you don't want to be massaging up and down, on a vertical line. It's just like a boat floating on a river. You don't want to force your way against the current, if you can help it. You want to go downstream for the fastest, easiest travel. Birds don't fly against the wind. Following the air currents conserves energy for their travels.

All natural beings know how to utilize nature. Swallows find a natural spiral of rising air to lift them up high. They wheel around and around in ascending circulars until they are high enough to find the jet stream, hundreds of meters up. Once they have found their air current, they stop flying all together and just glide. Swallows will wait for that specific day of that specific month of that specific season, to find the exact current they need to begin their long journey of migration. The right current is the starting point of their migration pattern. Instead of flying where they want to go, they use the natural current to help them begin their travels. Instinctively, they know the current that will take them where they need to go, passed from generation to generation within the genetic knowledge of the flock. Even as weather patterns shift, the birds find a way to adjust their flight path season by season, to insure their survival.

Unlike the birds, for human health and survival, we have to attune ourselves to internal currents. We don't know exactly where our illnesses are, deep within the body, so this is why we pull across. We pull horizontally across with our hands and arms, with physical force, but we visualize our breath and body locations vertically, so there is our cross. So when you breathe in, and cave the front of your body in a bit as we inhale, both the breathing and the posture are all in the category of vertical. Your imagination and visualization of the back, the lateral aspect of the ribcage, are all vertical as well. Even the lower *dantian* is a vertical visualization as well. Just remember the triangle you form over the lower *dantian* with your hands to see its size. The triangle is an expression of vertical form. All these elements are vertical, however as you're pulling with strength and force, that is horizontal.

You might have blockages in your blood vessels, arteries or veins, or in the meridians, but through the combination of horizontal effort and vertical focus, you can actually clear these obstructions. As you slowly exhale after holding your breath and counting, you will feel the pulsations of blood and qi as you become empty and relaxed again. The collision of these two forces creates an impact that shoots the blood and qi through to where it needs to go, stagnant no longer.

Daoist theory does not explain tonification using a Newtonian physics model, of course. The way the Daoists understand it, it's as if you are turning your body into a giant magnifying glass. Sunlight shines onto the lens, converging all its rays into one focal point, which is powerful enough to light a piece of paper on fire with its intensity. How is this so? It is because the clasped hands are the exact midpoint of your body when practicing. The hands are your focal point of your lens, concentrating both your horizontal pulling force and your vertical inhalation and mind body focus. You're pulling, which is horizontal, but you're also visualizing, which is vertical, to take the form of a cross.

The yangqi practice creates a body-mind transformation, with which, you can reduce or alleviate any pain, clear any sicknesses that you might have. After practicing a full nine sets of the three inhales and pulls, you will feel that your body has generated noticeable energy. If you have any minor colds or allergy symptoms, after you practice and have worked up a sweat, you will get better.

Keeping the hands and arms in the clasped position is more than just a conceptual center point of two energies. Their grip helps stabilize the rest of your posture from two directions. When pulling, they work in tandem with the hips to brace the torso into a solid cube within the pyramid of your stance. When they start to relax while exhaling up and out of the mouth, they stabilize the spherical space that has been developing front to back with the hollowed out chest and rounded shoulders.

While you're holding your breath, the cubic and the spherical volumes you are carving from the inside out within the torso are merging and blending within the pyramid. Then when you have exhaled completely, the qi is expressed out to all the subtle channels of the body, filling the pyramid and being guided upwards by its apex. When you practice, don't try to visualize any of this. Just pull hard, focus on the upper back, ribs and *dantian* as indicated, hold your breath with deep concentration, and then exhale with perfect control.

As found in the traditions of the great Chinese thinkers, Laozi, Confucius, and Sunzi, we never work directly on the spots we are trying to expand, because we want them to be soft, comfortable and natural, not just strong and powerful. Focusing on upper back, ribcage and lower *dantian* is all that is needed.

We unconsciously use the paradigms of square, circle and pyramid to help position the body and keep it open as we breathe. As we have already seen, there are many layers of archetypes we incarnate as we practice Nine-Five Maintenance of Qi. Because they are natural patterns of the universe, it is useful to know the theory, but it is with your body that you actually practice.

The rhythms of the universe will flow along with you as you practice with sincerity. This is why the actual exercises are basically very simple movements, without an emphasis on visualizations unless they are being used to help target a part of the body or an ideal posture. Keep your mind clear and instead, feel your body as you cultivate. You must become one with yourself to become one with the universe, but it's a gradual process and you are working together with heaven and earth at all times, rather than struggling alone in your mind.

With practice, the archetypes will be an experience as your musculature becomes strong, open and integrated. At high levels of development, practicing tonification when your interior muscles are strong enough to stay fully expanded but relaxed enough to not require effort, you will easily be able to count to two hundred and exhale so slowly you barely feel the stream of your breath. It will feel like your body has found a new way to breath by circulating the qi inside of it, rather than worrying about breathing in and out. This is tonification of qi, the ultimate in nourishing and caring for the qi.

Counting

Counting is an integral part of this process. You want to count consecutive numbers "one, two, three, four" and on, as many as you can up to two hundred. Verbalize each number in your mind, one by one, using a steady pace. You might only be able to count to twenty at first, but it's more important to really concentrate on each number clearly and not rush through, than get to two hundred without the right mindset. Counting creates focus.

Careful counting with a steady beat increases the involvement of the brain in this exercise. Just as stretching widens the pathway of qi in the torso, counting stimulates a part of the brain in a rhythmic way, to allow the qi to flow easily through this pathway. Your brain is helping to pump the flow of qi through you just the same way squeezing your fist helps a vein to stand out when you're having blood drawn. The pace of your counting subliminally regulates and enhances your pulse as you hold your breath, to strengthen yourself as you make the effort to control yourself so intensely. By extension, it strengthens your entire body, the muscles, the posture, the mind and the physical sensations, as it trains in tonification.

How important is it to be counting numbers in your mind? Can't you just concentrate deeply and not count? Counting is a steadying force. Of course, you don't want to lose track of yourself while holding your breath, just for safety purposes. You want to be grounded in your body and not be distracted or spaced out. More than that, counting steadies you in the physical sense. There is a lot of energy that is passing into the body and pulsing within it as you inhale, pull, then hold your breath. These pulsations will be held in check and calmed to a steady, even level if you use the counting as a mental net to keep them contained.

It's is a matter of timing, as well. The length of time it takes to count to two hundred is a specifically designed measure. It's the ideal amount of time to take to enter the next level state of body control and awareness that this practice is capable of. Don't run the numbers together so fast that you're up to one hundred in a few seconds. The proper pace is moderately quick but even, each number counted in roughly half-second intervals. You can adjust this to be a little quicker or a little slower depending on the speed of your entire practice for that day, but when you practice, get used to this general pace and as your ability grows, you will see that it's a natural rhythm that suits the body's functions during this exercise. Don't count off as "ten, twenty, thirty and so on…" Just count each number in order, one at a time, not in intervals of fives or tens.

If the pace is so important, would it be better to use a ticking clock or a metronome to get the speed perfectly timed? While that isn't unacceptable, it also isn't recommended. You should start off right by getting in the habit of making the count from within. The ancient people who first devised this training didn't have external devices at their disposal. They used what they had at hand, the capabilities of their own mind and body.

This is similar to the question of practicing qigong with shoes on or off. Traditionally, the Daoist monks wore shoes made out of woven plant fiber. Dr. Wu's personal experience is you should try not to wear plastic shoes or shoes with plastic bottoms when practicing. Plastic dampens the subtle sensations coming up from the earth. The same thing holds to a lesser degree with leather as well. It's best to wear a pair of thick socks instead of shoes. This way you can effectively ground any static electricity present in the body. This is why we often take off our shoes and socks entirely and walk barefoot on grass, before various qigong practices. If we have any static charges built up within the body, we can discharge it into the ground when we walk around.

From a Daoist perspective, that typical American homes and neighbor-hoods have plenty of green grass, is actually very good. You will be able to easily release static into these lawns. An environment without a lot of grasses is un-healthy. If there's no place to walk around barefoot with all the static noise and static electricity buildup all around us and accumulating inside of us, it can be-come trapped and eventually have a negative influence on our health. We've got to release this build up and grass is the natural way to ground ourselves. We always want to keep naturally balanced, using the simplest means at our disposal.

For this same reason, we count in our minds. It will make us more aware of our body's rhythms as we practice. We will be able to answer our natural rhythms with a natural controlling force, steadying the mind as we steady the body. Two hundred is the highest count to achieve. The important points are to pull and inhale at the same time and think about back, ribs and lower *dantian* as you hold your breath. We thoroughly nourish the body with qi, but after you reach the point of being able to count to two hundred, you begin to develop your body on an even more heightened level.

The goal is to enhance the body internally, so that it becomes strong and hard like steel. Another old proverb describes this target: "Golden bell helmet and iron cloth shirt" (*jin zhongzhou tie bushan*). This is the martial arts application of tonification, as practiced in the monastery. You're trying to turn your body into steel. At very high levels of accomplishment, if someone tried to cut you with a knife, they could not pierce the skin. The practitioner's skill would be tested by withstanding being struck on the back with a wooden stick until it broke, all while doing the pulling, inhaling and counting. Even metal rods would be employed, hitting the trainees at key points during their efforts. The idea was to make the body so hard with qi that nothing could cause pain, or penetrate the skin. Just pulling and breathing will develop the body to this level, if done with serious intention. Note that this is not just an "iron shirt" practice, but a "golden helmet" practice as well. You are using the mind in tandem with the body, and strengthening them both. This is the importance of counting.

Martial Arts, Medicine, and Advanced Practice

Pulling is tied to inhaling. If you inhale without pulling you will not create the cross within your body, which is the source of tonification power and strength building. Holding the breath is tied to focus counting. If you do one without the other, you will not modulate the energy generated by the cross so that it can be dispersed through the body to make it powerful and strong.

If you practice correctly for a long period, you will train your body to be-come steel and when other people are hitting you while you're in this posture you won't feel much. Their punches will be repelled by the qi that is generated in your body. You pull as you're inhaling and the muscles and the bones will create their own force to repel external forces. This is the line where internal qigong meets martial arts. This is real gongfu. It requires resolute practice. When you're able to reach a two hundred count, someone could hit you over the back with a chair and it would not register. The primary goal is to protect your body, however, not feats of strength. If you're able to achieve that level of control, you will be able to sustain your body and enhance your immune system greatly.

Focusing the mind on the back, ribs and lower *dantian* is very important, as we've already stressed. Dr. Wu has done the hitting training on me as I was practicing. I was already on my third set of nine, at the lower *dantian* pull, concentrating deeply. I wasn't even aware that he had approached me or what sort of stick he was using. The strikes were sharp but not lingering, landing around the upper back, shoulder blades and on the ribcage area. As Dr. Wu explained to the rest of the class, doing this to my back and sides was actually helping me to excel even more. In the White Cloud Monastery, they would use steel rods, but the intention is never to hurt but to help.

Normally we rarely discuss individual experiences, so as not to influence others' experiences, but it's worthwhile to describe what being hit while deeply practicing tonification was like for me. First of all, I was in a totally relaxed state, in a state of concentration where there was only focus on the qi. Basically I was not paying attention to anything in my physical body, just experiencing the qi flow in a non-defined space. I was holding my breath and counting and feeling pulsations of blood and qi beating within. When he hit me, it didn't take me by surprise or make me flinch. I was in too deep of a meditative state for that. Instead, each strike greatly increased the sensation of energy pulsing through me, as if I was a big bell being rung.

This sort of strong vibration coursing through the body is so important. It's what allows healing energy to get into every tiny vessel and fiber and shake free any blockages. Far from being painful, it was a highly pleasurable sensation. A good comparison to it would be taking your arm and gently jiggling it right after the muscles have been massaged to bring motion back in and relax any residual tension, the gentle shaking letting the last fiber release. Practicing qigong lets your body and breath make vibrations such as these penetrate your entire system, a fine muscle stimulation from a combination of breath, your nervous system and your viscera working in harmony. This is why learning to stay completely relaxed is so important. It lets you help your body allow itself to shake off muscular tension at a very deep internal level.

In the White Cloud Monastery, during tonification practice, they normally have someone there to hit the trainees on the back or the side, but only when practiced as a martial art. When performed as part of the Nine-Five Maintenance of Qi ritual, striking does not take place. Will it help to have a friend hit you on the back as you're doing the pulling? If you're practicing to help yourself, to increase your immunity or as a preventative to sickness, it's not necessary to be hit on the back or the sides. Striking during tonification of qi targets points of blockage or areas that need increased circulation, so that the pumping action can send the qi to every part of the body, past these blocks. Only someone who has already passed this level of training personally and understands Traditional Chinese Medicine principles is going to understand how to properly strike you, where on the body and with what sort of force.

Even Dr. Wu will not employ these techniques on his patients, unless in very specific circumstances. He has a humorous story about a patient who was a very successful individual, prominent in his industry. Even so, his health was poor. He came to Dr. Wu as a patient, wanting to improve his immune system so he wouldn't be struck constantly with common colds. He also wanted to improve his sex life. He had a high sensitivity to medication and eschewed herbal treatment, along with any other kinds of drugs.

At first, Dr. Wu treated his condition in the standard manner, how he usually would for patients with the same complaints. The results were not very decisive, and Dr. Wu was wondering what was obstructing the treatment. One day, the patient brought in his very glamorous and beautiful wife and Dr. Wu immediately saw what the problem was. After this, he taught his patient to do tonification of qi while having a treatment and would use the hitting technique on him while he practiced. After a month, all of a sudden anyone could tell he was much improved and stronger than he had been originally. In most cases Dr. Wu would not consider this as a patient treatment, because people's personal space needs to be respected, and it's a physically grueling practice that is very demanding, since it does involve blows, not just patting people down.

After he had gotten better, his wife told Dr. Wu their sex life was great now, but joked around that her husband must like to be abused. Dr. Wu told her to just go home and enjoy how things were going in the bedroom. Even with the joking around, it was obvious her husband was doing much better for the both of them. He was motivated to put in the work on his end and was completely open to the massaging effect of striking combining with his own efforts. This attitude was what gave Dr. Wu the confidence to teach him and work along with him in this way, when normally he would not publically employ tonification in a medical context.

The first thing it requires is sincerity, but with serious intention, it's the most effective way to boost your immunity and reinforce your health in the shortest amount of time. Striking speeds the process up and helps those who may already have illness or tissue damage, but steady practice must be made on your own to benefit long term. For our purposes, solo practice will boost the immune system, preventing frequent common colds. First you will have to believe in the practice's value. We are teaching every aspect of the process, but you have to practice with genuine trust and sincerity to reap all its rewards. To understand tonification of qi, you have to practice it. This is the one fact to remember.

What happens when you can count to two hundred while holding your breath? There is a stage of development where you pass the point of a normal sensation of holding the breath and needing to exhale and take a new breath.

You may feel as if your body is beginning to breathe through the skin or at least is circulating the breath you have already taken in so efficiently that you have no immediate need to take a new breath. It can feel like a heightened state of awareness you could stay centered within indefinitely. You can stop counting, but you may continue holding your posture and breath as long as you feel comfortable, allowing whatever time you need for a slow, measured exhale, as usual.

Remember that a properly controlled exhale allows all the qi that was taken in and down into the body to come back up and out the way it came in. The sensation of energy in the body while holding the breath can become very strong. Exhaling slowly with control helps contain and modulate the sensations in the body, which in turn allows the qi to penetrate more deeply and unblock any resistance. Never skimp on this, no matter how much control you have while pulling and inhaling or holding the breath.

If you train to this point past counting to two hundred, you will definitely know it. It's an experience of the perfectly balanced, volumetric space within the body. It's worth describing a personal experience, for this is truly an exceptional state. If you practice with sincerity and attention to detail, at some point your body will be able to completely relax, including the diaphragm and all internal viscera. Suddenly there is no longer any constriction to the flow of qi, neither in the downward intake as you inhale and pull or the spreading circulation as you hold your breath. In fact, it stops feeling as if you are using any effort to hold your breath at all. Your body is a bouncy balloon filled with a cushion of qi. Your intake of air and qi is perfectly efficient and you feel as if you could sit in this state for as long as you want, as if your body is breathing in a brand new way, from inside an endless sea of qi.

Obviously, if you can fill your body to this extent with air, with perfect relaxation in the physical structure, you will certainly be more resilient, the way a baby can take a fall and be perfectly fine. This is where the martial applications come in, and also the regenerative state of life force evolution, or internal alchemy. Although this is a physical experience, it is also a state of perception. It is created and reinforced by the counting. You may find that one day you reach this state but the next day you can only count to twenty. Don't be discouraged. It takes a lot of time to consolidate your efforts to this point, especially considering all the daily stresses and strains we all deal with. Just stay sincere and practice regularly and over time, your body will adjust.

As we've said, the goal is preserving your body. From a martial arts perspective, if you can go past counting to two hundred, you will be able to handle a strong blow to the body, but there is another training that you can add, that is strictly for esoteric health and life extension. This visualization is added when you can consistently count to two hundred and beyond. When you're pulling and inhaling, think about back, ribs, lower *dantian* as normal for that point in the practice, but then immediately after you think about that location, you want to think about your five main organs as if they are five clocks, five clocks hanging in your body. You are going to hold your breath after the inhale and pull, but there is no longer any need to count. Again, you will know when you are at this level, when you recall that the counting is partly to help you get a feel for the amount of time you need to fully develop the qi that you inhaled and also for steadying any pulsations you feel as the qi is trying to squeeze through your body. With practice, you will know when you don't need support of this kind any longer.

What are these clocks? The Chinese word is *zhong*, which is one word that means both the ancient resonant clapper-less bell and also the old form of clock, usually a water clock that had a similar shape. It's fine to visualize a regular clock as we know it today, because the idea of a clock is more important in this exercise than the image of a clock, so we use the shape that we associate with the our definition of "clock."

The five organs we are going to focus on are the lungs, heart, liver, spleen and kidneys, each with their own associated color. Liver is green, heart is red, spleen is yellow, lungs are white, and kidneys are black. Place the clocks for each organ in the body at roughly the same location as the organs' anatomical positions.

So, inhale and pull, think of the back, ribs or lower *dantian* for just a moment to activate their mind-body connection, then immediately see your lungs as a white clock, hanging in the chest above the pectoral muscles and then pull. This is practicing the lungs.

To practice the heart, pull and as you pull, visualize your heart as a red clock hanging right under the left breast. If you make a downward pointing triangle with your hands beneath the left breast, this is the area to place your heart clock.

The stomach and spleen is one yellow clock hanging right below the heart clock. Again, forming your hands into a loose triangle and placing it below the triangle you made to find the heart clock position will give you the spleen clock location.

The liver is a green clock at same height as the spleen, but on the right and on the side of the body over the sides of the ribs.

The clock for your kidneys is on the back, over the kidneys below the waist.

When you are in the pulling posture, you want to guide the qi you are inhaling to the respective organs, thinking of their corresponding colors. When the Daoists consider each organ as a clock, it is a specific image intentionally chosen to accomplish the alchemical goal of the elixir pill, the medicine of longevity and elevated consciousness. When you see the term nei*dan*, referring to Daoist internal alchemy, *dan* means pill or medicinal pellet.

For the ancient alchemists, there is an external elixir pill. Traditionally, it is a big brown pill, blended from many substances then baked and boiled in a special pot over many years. Internally, we have this same elixir pill as well, but developed through our own cultivation. We use qi and the efforts of the body. We employ the clocks to effect this process, instead of fire and external materials. The clock has the correct shape and significance to stimulate the alchemical changes within. To make a physical pill requires season after season through many years for its formation. This is true on the internal level as well, and the clock symbolizes this in a powerful way. It is a concept to be reflected upon.

Particularly if you have an illness you want to address, pull with force, visualize the corresponding color and think about that organ as a clock hanging in its place. Then as you pull and then hold your breath, make the clock disappear, as if you have pulled apart its mass until it has ceased to exist. Dr. Wu has had excellent results using this conception of pulling apart a mass as an addition to his cancer patients' clinical treatments. He will apply the usual series of acupuncture needles and as the patient lies there, Dr. Wu performs this qigong practice on them, trying to pull the masses of their cancer apart. Of course if the patient is also able to do this clock practice along with Dr. Wu during the treatment, then the effects are even better. After you accomplish this practice, you will feel that your body is much stronger than before, very firm, supported from within and solid. The clock and its color combined with the pulling and holding is a highly effective meditation, derived as it is from deep natural laws.

We focus on five organs in the clock practice. What if you have an illness in another organ that is not one of these five? Traditional Chinese Medicine separates the organs into two interrelated sets. There are the five inner organs (wuzang), which are related to yin, and primarily store qi and blood. The viscera or transforming organs total six (liufu) and are considered the organs associated with the digestive functions of the gastrointestinal tract. These yang organs are the stomach, the gall bladder, the small intestine, large intestine and bladder, as well as the triple burner.

We use the five inner organs in the clock visualization, since tonification of qi works specifically on the qi and the blood. Since in general, each of the organs is related to a viscera, all that's necessary is to know the correlation and then think of the appropriate organ's color and clock when practicing. For instance, the heart is directly in correlation to the small intestine. They share a special relationship. Your liver is specially connected to your gall bladder. The spleen is related to the stomach. The lungs are related to the large intestine and the kidneys are related to the bladder. The sixth viscera is the triple burner, which we already opened and cleared during the adjustment of qi exercise.

We will go into it at greater length, but this is a good example of why it is very important to practice the entire Nine-Five Maintenance of Qi form from beginning to end, rather than simply picking and choosing individual parts of the process to practice. The male and female reproductive organs, the brain and the various glands of the endocrine system also belong to the kidneys and the color black, in their own special relationship, outside the framework of the organs and viscera. You can look at it this way: the five inner organs are the clocks, and the pendulums are the six viscera functions of the digestive system. They are different parts of the same whole, separate but equal.

Dr. Wu has an elderly patient who was referred to him by another doctor. She has cancer that spread through her brain. The western doctors felt there was nothing left to do for her, at her advanced age and late stage of the cancer. They told her to go home, get her affairs in order and make peace with her fate. She wasn't going to go out without a fight, so she came to Dr. Wu, and he taught her tonification of qi. He had students who had practiced with him for decades who he had never taught the practice to, but he taught her. In a little more than a month, her condition stabilized and she felt much better. Her friends and neighbors could barely believe her improvement was possible. You have to keep inhaling, pulling, visualizing, holding and releasing. The effects are significant. You just need to do it. The proof is in the practice.

When Dr. Wu is treating a patient and teaches him or her tonification of qi, he may ask the subject to do it on its own, separate from the other parts of the Nine-Five Maintenance of Qi practice. This is because Dr. Wu is treating the patient at the same time with qigong, herbs and acupuncture tailored to his or her illness. Whether he uses the hitting techniques along with it, or just the mind practice of the clocks, it is in addition to a full course of treatment. First and foremost, the patient needs to practice at home as well. If you or someone you know has a serious illness, it is not advisable to practice tonification by itself without the presence of a doctor. As long as you are practicing the Nine-Five Maintenance of Qi practice from the very beginning to the very end, from step one all the way through, the presence of a doctor or a master is not necessary.

Dr. Wu is trying to accelerate the healing process for his patients. They come for clinical treatment and he can't always have them doing the full qigong form, for time reasons or sometimes because the rest of the office treatment precludes it. In this context, Dr. Wu would rather the patient only practices tonification and he will do his part to help them speed their progress. However if you would like to teach your friends or relatives to help their health, teach them the full Nine-Five Maintenance of Qi. Make sure you're not confused with the order. If you teach someone else, you need to teach it exactly the way Dr. Wu presents it here. You do have to teach them all of it, from A to Z, because only if you go through this process in order, will you gain or even notice the effects.

It's the same metaphor we used before, of a nation that must raise its flag every morning to be saluted. It's just like cooking a meal. You cook a Chinese meal in a wok. Without a fire, how do you start? Simply put, if you only do tonification of qi, it won't help you much. If you practice the Nine-Five Maintenance of Qi, however, you will gain a great deal of benefit for your health, particularly from its advanced stages of training. If you practice the entire form from beginning to end, you don't need the facilitations of others, even if you have health challenges you are trying to overcome. Just be sure to work up to being able to count to two hundred before moving on to the clock practice, so that your body is fully prepared for it in advance.

Don't forget that tonification splits into three parts, focusing on back, ribs and lower *dantian*. Even when you are advanced enough to do the clock meditation, you always still take a moment to make the mind-body connection with each of those three areas, as part of your inhale pulling, holding and exhaling. These three stages or cycles count as one full set. Always practice this set three to nine times. The three cycle set counts as one time, so repeat for a minimum of three times or a maximum of nine times. Practice until you have built up a light sweat. If you haven't exerted yourself to that point after three sets, keep going for the full nine if possible. It is true that Nine-Five Maintenance of Qi can be a rather time consuming practice, especially when first starting out, but the time investment pays back your efforts with abundant returns.

Dr. Wu has taught publically for over thirty years, and never introduced this deep level of qigong to his students before now. Right now we are in a crisis, financially, politically and also individually speaking. These stressors weaken our health on the most basic levels. Viral diseases are multiplying and mutating, bacterial diseases are becoming resistant faster than we can develop new medications to treat them. At the very least, practicing tonification of qi within the context of the nine palaces Nine-Five Maintenance of Qi qigong, you can boost your immunity to the point that you won't catch many colds and won't be easily infected by the growing list of untreatable illnesses that are spreading globally without halt.

We are teaching tonification of qi, so that you can better yourself. It is helpful to everybody who practices it. Dr. Wu earnestly believes it is beneficial to so great a degree, that with enough people practicing worldwide, it would lower global infection rates. It has the ability to transform the human body into a stronger vessel, much better adapted to the new challenges we are faced with in this world of global pandemic and non-localized threat. On the individual scale, it boosts the immune system and fights tumors and cancers. The tonification of qi is significant for its place in the White Cloud Monastery's cannon of martial arts and alchemical traditions. It is equally significant in its power when practiced for health and longevity. We hope that you take away an understanding of its meaning and a desire to go forward and sincerely practice it.

Chapter 7

Utilization of Qi

Application

We have come to the last of the five stages in the art of working with qi. This is the utilization of qi (*yongqi*). Normally, these stages are only taught up to the fourth step, tonification of qi. The latter is a high enough level to attain in its own right, as it is enough to boost your immunity and ability to fight off disease. Your body develops its innate strength and automatic health maintenance capability. Proper utilization takes this one step further, as it teaches you how to intentionally maintain your body's health, using your will. Rather than just perfecting your body's autonomic health preservation systems, utilizing the qi builds the mind and body skills needed for direct, hands on healing, guided by your will. Utilization of qi brings out your ability to purposefully direct healing power into the organs you wish to maintain.

It is a simple, two-part process, if you have practiced the other steps of Nine-Five Maintenance of Qi with sincerity. First you use a light tapping massage around each of the nine openings of the body. As each opening is activated, then focus energy into your hands and send it into these nine palaces and their corresponding internal organs, to heal them on a profound level while they are in their newly opened state. It's like smoothly sliding a key into a lock to easily turn it, rather than jimmying it open. One by one, you are opening each organ network then healing it with pure, focused energy. Just like a key fits perfectly and turns easily in one direction, the utilization massage is performed with a very specific type of force and always in one correct, opening direction.

Again, we are going to use a particular count for each massage, to align with cycles of nature, as determined by the *Book of Changes*. Utilizing the qi practice teaches us how to focus healing heat into the palms of the hands, as we work with each opening and organ in turn. Once each opening is treated, you may treat any other organs that need it. The form completes by gathering all the extra heat and mind power you have generated to suffuse yourself with radiant energy in any way you most deeply wish.

Tapping is the Key

We begin with tapping. Tapping is the key we put in the lock to open the nine palaces. It is a very subtle movement that bears some explaining. We are going to use the tips of all five fingers, including the thumbs, to tap all around each of the nine openings of the body. If you recall, in the yangqi practice, sticks or rods are used by the master to hit the pupil as he or she inhales, pulls, then holds the qi within the body. This striking is used to stimulate blocked or sluggish points in the patient's circulatory and energetic systems, so that the qi can better disperse throughout the body. The student is not hit all over, just in one or two key spots, as needed. You could compare it to hitting an old fashioned television to get the picture to come in clearly, or to a gong or Tibetan singing bowl that needs another minor tap to continue to resonate after its initial note has been sounded. As we mentioned before, it's something that a doctor or teacher might do to speed your own progress, but without this hitting, you will still be able to unblock yourself on your own over time, with consistent training. Your body will strengthen and open itself automatically with daily practice.

In the utilization of qi, we move to a new phase, where we are actively and directly unblocking, opening and assisting the circulation. Rather than stretching from the inside out to eventually open and release, as we do during tonification, now we are going to tap directly around each of the nine openings of the body, working from the outside in to open them immediately and intentionally. Even our hands, which clasped together in a static, forceful grip during tonification, are now going to do the opposite, and lightly but vigorously tap with the fingertips, just using the momentum that comes from the wrists.

To properly tap in the first movement of utilization, you want to gently and softly hold the hands in a loose and rounded form, not quite cupped, but naturally positioned so that each fingertip, including the thumb, will be able to tap and make contact all at the same time. The actual tapping motion mostly comes from the wrists, with very little movement coming from any other part of the arms or shoulders. Do keep the shoulder and elbow joints very loose, along with your wrists, which are extremely loose. Remember that qi flows from the joints.

As we have already done in other movements, such as the arm circling in adjustment of qi, we keep the joints loose, so that we can transfer momentum through them for our motions with the least amount of physical exertion. We are not tapping to pound our bodies like hitting a stiff piece of meat with a mallet. Instead, we aim to strike sharply but so lightly and quickly that we set up a current or vibration around the area, like skipping a stone across a pond and watching the water as it ripples outwards in concentric circles. To accomplish this, we keep our hands facing each opening, with the fingertips very close to the skin, just a quarter of an inch or less, just far enough away to get enough play from the wrists and backs of the hands to make this slight strike. This way you will greatly increase the circulation at the surface of the skin, with enough of an attack to resonate deeper down into the muscles below, but gently enough to leave the skin unmarked.

We start with the ears, as we so commonly do in other qigong and martial arts practices. Why start here? Because our ears are a microcosm of our entire body. There are points all along the ears that correspond to every acupuncture point and pathway in the body. As we've mentioned before, the ears continue to grow as we get older and take on special levels of growth after we reach our eighties and beyond. Just like trees grow their rings outwards every year, we grow our rings here on the ears.

On the other side of the same coin, the ear looks like a fetus head down, as it grows in the womb. From these two facets alone, we can see how the ears represent our birth, our growth, our longevity and our revitalization, renewal and rebirth. From a Chinese medical perspective, the ears are the external organ that connects with the kidneys. They are two ends of the same pipeline. Our goal is to put the key into the lock that can open this conduit up so that the healing qi of the universe can flow in. This is always the primary goal of Nine Palaces Qigong, but unlike other levels of its practice, where we simply open ourselves and let qi come in naturally in its own way, in Nine-Five Maintenance of Qi, we learn to concentrate this flow and consciously direct it in.

Bring the hands up so the fingertips are just barely touching the surface of

the ear and without tensing any muscles, put just enough of a loose flip in the wrists and backs of the hands so that all five fingertips tap the ears with a short, sharp and light force. Your ears will immediately feel hot and perhaps a little painful with the impact. Tap at a rapid pace, with roughly two or three taps per second, working all around the upper, outer and lower portions of the ear, contacting the rims and lobes, as well as all the cartilage around the ear openings themselves.

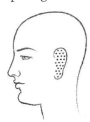

Work in a circular motion up from the inside close to the temples, up, outwards, down and then around. Your fingers are just open enough that the entire ear plus the muscles around the temples and jaw where the ear connects are all going to be in contact with them while you tap. At first, you may not be used to the sensation, which can definitely feel hot and painful. Just remember to always make breathing gently your first priority, and keeping your chest, shoulders, arms, wrists and hands as loose as possible your next priority. With these two elements prioritized, you will minimize any discomfort or tiredness while you tap. This is particularly important because we want to tap all around the ear no less than fifty times. By this we mean fifty full circles, which will be made up of multiple taps each. There is no need to count each individual tap. Just count each full path around the ear. Make no mistake about it, this is an exercise that takes strength and flexibility and the ability to stay very calm and natural.

Now it becomes very clear why we have taken our bodies step by step through the different stages of the welcoming, intaking, adjusting, and tonifying to come to this point. Qigong is a physical training, first and foremost, where we use our breath and our mind in service of strength, flexibility, relaxation and improved circulation within the body as a whole.

Opening the Lock

Once you have tapped out fifty circles around the ears, place the palms directly over the ears to cover their surface, centering the middle of the palms over the openings of the ears. While keeping the palms solidly in contact with the ears, rub them in a circular motion "counterclockwise," up, outwards and around from the jaw line. Rub fifty times in this manner. As before, the ears will feel very  hot and you are definitely working the upper body with this motion, so pay attention to your breathing and don't hesitate to pause for a moment if your shoulders or arms are feeling tired or starting to stiffen. With practice, it will get much easier.

The critical element is to massage outwards or counterclockwise at all times. From the Daoist perspective, the image of the clock face is constantly used as a reference for orienting movements on the body. We are the clock and our motions are viewed as going clockwise, with the hands of the clock, or counterclockwise, in the opposite direction. Going with the clock means closing, concentrating and calming. Going counterclockwise means opening up what is normally closed, dispersing, stimulating. This is a tricky concept to discuss, because what is "clockwise" for the left hand and left side of the body is reversed for the right.

There are also underlying Chinese medical factors influencing the understanding of the directions, as some of the channels move upwards and others move downwards within the body, plus other yin and yang factors based on gender and time of day. For this reason, in utilizing the qi massage, consider the center-line running down the middle of the body and the circling motions you make with your hands as going up and outwards from this center line. This will give you the correct opening motion for both ears, both eyes, etc., and also direct you in the correct motion if you are rubbing an individual organ such as the heart, which is only on one side of this center line. When you rotate outwards, that is the de facto counterclockwise motion.

The fundamental intent is by massaging outwards, we want to push out the sickness, creating a stimulating movement to get rid of it.

Rubbing fifty times has a significant meaning in this context of counterclockwise movement. According to the *Book of Changes*, the number 5 represents wind. All the sickness you have and will ever encounter comes under the category of water. The wind will dry up the water by blowing on it. If the bathroom is damp after a shower, what do we do to speed up the evaporation of the moisture? We open the window and have the wind carry it out. That will make it evaporate much quicker.

Number 5 in the *Book of Changes* is wind, Xun, the fifth trigram and 6 is water, Kan, the sixth trigram. The wind trigram on top of the water trigram forms the fifty-ninth *Book of Changes* hexagram, Huan, which means "dispersing." So when we rub counterclockwise fifty times, we're using the wind principle to disperse illness in our organs. Another idea to remember is that one complete natural cycle in the *Book of Changes* is the sixty year sequence of the Jiazi, the pattern of the ten heavenly stems, which are the yin and yang pairs of each of the five elements, in combination with the twelve earthly branches, corresponding to the twelve animals of the Chinese zodiac. We want to rub fifty times and never more than sixty, in reference to this sixty-year cycle.

The Satellite Dish

After rubbing the ears up and outwards with the flats of the palms for fifty circles, the next step is to focus energy into them. The ears will feel very hot after the circling. Lift the palms away from the surface of the ears. Cup the hands to emphasize the center points of

the palms then place them over but not touching the ears and hold there until the ears feel warm and clean. When you cup your hands, you make a concave hand shape, like a satellite dish. The hands are not soft. It is a strongly concave shape, accentuating the sensation in the centers of the palms at the Laogong acupoint.

Think of a satellite dish. Frequencies are absorbed into its center, concentrated, and then transmitted back out in a newly narrow, focused band. Place the palms over the ears, very close, but not touching, about half inch or less away, emphasizing the concave area right over the ear opening. You can tilt the angle of the fingertips a little more upwards or a little more pointed towards the back,

whatever feels comfortable. It's all right to just barely touch the fingertips to the hair or ears, but the central focal point of the palms must not touch body. The main thing is positioning the concave palm right over the ear. When you cup your satellite dish hands over the ears, you will feel warmth. Hold your hands in this position until you feel the heat concentrating and your ears feel very comfortable.

It's important to remember that the point in the center of the palm has another point connected to it, directly opposite on the back of the hand. While the concave palm is focusing heat that was generated from the tapping and circling then reflecting it back towards the ear, the back of the hand is at the same time operating like a convex lens, with rays converging at its peak, concentrating and diffusing out the other side, to inside the center of the palm. Again we use the concept of a magnifying glass or mirror, fusing all this energy through it into one point hot enough to spark a flame. We start with the gentle dispersal of wind, but we complete with the healing ignition of the sun's fire.

After your ears feel hot, clear and balanced, bring your arms down to your sides, closing the palms into loose fists, thumbs not tucked in, as if collecting up the leftover energy. As soon as you have made fists like this, flick them open again, using a very slight gesture. Your ears will feel very clear, energized and open. This is the process of maintaining yourself with the utilization of qi. All the exercises you've done up to this point are for preparing yourself to be able to cup your hands and send in the heat. It has a very powerful effect. You are giving yourself a treatment; healing yourself using vital force you have gathered through the five stages of nine-five utilization of qi.

The Nine Openings

The 9 in Nine Palaces Qigong represents the nine openings of the body, but we don't always think about the word "palaces." Why this term in particular? Because it is a practice designed for preserving the body, maintaining yourself optimally through your own efforts. "Your body is a temple" is a saying that is overused to the point of cliché, but the Daoist scholars understood its truth at the most literal level. We build a palace for each of our senses and organs, to treasure them and keep them safe.

After performing utilization of qi on the ears, we will continue to the eyes, the nose, the mouth, the anus and the genital openings. Each area uses the same basic sequence of tapping, rubbing counterclockwise and then cupping the hands and focusing heat back in.

For the eyes, tap lightly around the periphery of the eyes, using the same quick wrist motion and five fingertip strikes, using both hands at the same time, one for each eye. Without rushing, tap gently along the orbital ridge, starting at the brow, then going out, around and underneath, then returning again to the ridge of the brow. It looks like you are forming a circle, but you are lifting your hands up after striking the bottom edge of the eye socket and bringing them back to the brow, rather than trying to hit the inside corners along the nose. The sensation will feel like a complete circle, even though you are not striking the inner points. Tap for fifty of these transits of the eye sockets. Again, each circling will be made of multiple taps, but we count fifty as fifty full orbits. Keep your elbows down and let your wrists and hands do most of the movement, with your fingers held close to the eye area, less than a quarter inch away.

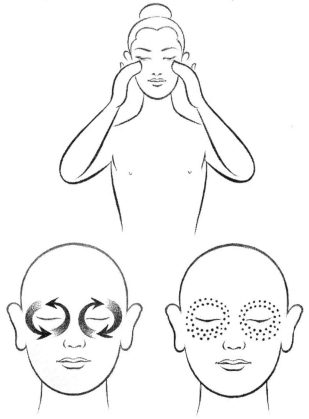

Afterwards, again place your palms over your eyes, with the center of your palms lined up over the eyes. There is no need to press in so that the palms actually press the eyeballs. Just let the rest of the palms make a solid contact, then rotate counterclockwise fifty times. With the palms flat over eyes, go up, out and around with both hands at the same time, rubbing outwards. Don't be confused by the term "counterclockwise." Your hands rub outwards from each other, rather than in the exact same direction.

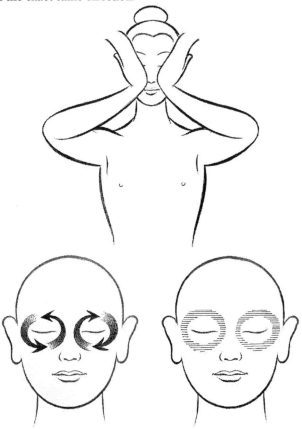

As we were saying before, if you analyze the theory behind it, our point of reference for the proper direction is tied to the individual hand, as what is counterclockwise on the left side of the body is clockwise on the right. Just keep it simple for yourself and remember the centerline dividing the two halves of the body. Know that rotating up and outwards from this line with each hand will give you the correct direction for the both of them. After fifty outward circling rubs, you will most certainly feel heat and maybe a little dull pain. Breathe gently as you rub and pause for a brief moment if you need to rest your arms to make it easy on yourself.

After you have turned the key in the lock, so to speak, hold your hands again like a satellite dish and lightly cup your eyes with the curved palms. The tips of the fingers can just barely brush the face for the proper distance between the hands and the eyes. As before, keep your elbows pointing down and the forearms quite close together. You can hold your hands steady or move them slightly to adjust the feeling of contact, but always keep the centers of the palms aligned with the center of the eyes. Take as much time as you would like to feel this sensation as it balances and adapts. It can be a very relaxing sensation. After a while, take your hands off the eyes by opening the hands up, and opening the fingers and pulling out away from face in a decisive motion. Form light fists as you do this to grab onto any extra energy, then release it by opening the hands back up as they come down to your sides. You will feel your eyes are brighter, the tissue around the eyes is lighter and your vision feels clear and lively.

After the eyes, we work on the nose. For the nose, you want to first tap up and then down the sides of the nose, from the nostril level up the sides of the nose to the bridge, and back down. You may only use mostly the middle finger and the first finger or third finger as the hands go up and down, although all the fingers are held more or less together. If you can make contact with all five fingertips, that's the best. As usual, each cycle up and down is one of fifty total.

For the counterclockwise massage, stick your index fingers directly into the nostrils. Hold your hands so only the forefingers stick out, with the rest of the fingers held together lightly. Insert the forefingers at a depth of a quarter inch to a half an inch in. Keep the elbows out slightly so that the fingers are not inserted upwards but more horizontally. They are inside the nostril openings at a slight diagonal angle upwards. To circle them counterclockwise, rotate from the lowest inward point closest to the head, up and outwards and around, or to put it another way, forward, up, around and back down. As before, circle fifty times.

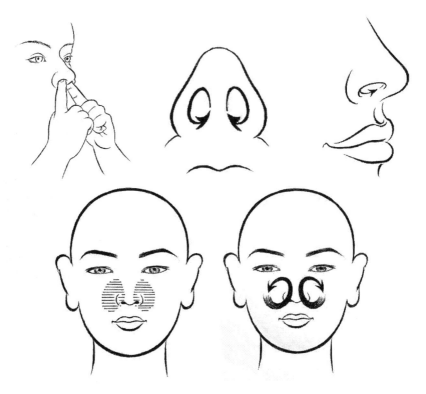

It's all right to rub the sides of the nose with the full palms moving outwards if you don't want to insert your fingers into the nostrils, but the interior of the nose is an area where excellent circulation is of great help to the respiratory system and immune response. It is well worth inserting the fingers and massaging this way, for noticeable results. After you rotate or rub, cup the center of the concave palms over the nostrils until you feel heat, elbows down. Hold approximately one to two minutes and then let go and bring the hands down as before. From other qigong practices, we are very used to exercising the ears and the eyes, but working

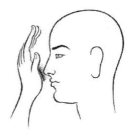

the nose, although unexpected, is very practical. You will feel an instantaneous improvement.

After the nose, we repeat utilization practice for the mouth. Different parts of the body can be read for signs of illness or general health conditions in related organs that are not as easily viewable. The ancient traditions of Daoist medicine developed many techniques to form a diagnosis of internal organs from viewing external indicators. They still have a high degree of accuracy, even though we have medical imaging and tests of all kinds that we can use today.

In their system, the condition and color of the mouth and surrounding tissues directly relate to the uterus and are used to determine a woman's fertility and reproductive health. Treating the mouth with the utilization of qi practice will also maintain the uterus, as well as the mouth itself. If you are experiencing a heavy but irregular menstrual cycle, you will see that your lips are a little purple around the edge of the lower lip. You may see a purplish line or lines in this area, indicating stagnancy. Fertility problems can be judged by observing any white lines at the corners of the mouth, where the upper and lower lips meet.

Three women came to Dr. Wu's clinic with fertility problems. All had been tested by their primary doctors, using Western medical techniques and their fertility issues were confirmed. The first woman was able to get pregnant but would have constant miscarriages. The other two women were able to be treated easily using standard TCM methodology and became pregnant very quickly after a basic course of treatment, because the whiteness around the periphery of their lips was not that conspicuous.

However, the woman experiencing chronic miscarriages had many clearly observable white vertical impressions around the edges of her lips. These lines are another human sign that tell a lot about our life, like the rings of a tree. Because her condition was chronic and she had lost many pregnancies, there were many lines that had developed.

Creases on the earlobes where they meet the head indicate heart attack and lines around the mouth are reflective of the uterus. For people with heart attack risk indicated by the earlobes, do plenty of earlobe pinching and downward pulling, to smooth out the creases. For women with lines around their mouths who have uterine issues, Dr. Wu will select acupuncture points on the face as a special addition to the standard treatments. Now she has been able to get pregnant and hold her pregnancy to term. Normally, the interior organ related to the mouth is the heart, but utilization of qi is also a great help for the reproductive system.

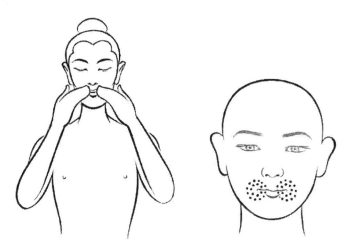

Tap around the mouth in the usual way, using both hands moving outwards and around from the midline down its center. Start at the top of mouth, go outwards then down and around under lip line, then back to the upper lip for the next cycle, just as we did with the eyes. The two hands are tapping out the two halves of the whole. The mouth is held with the lips open and relaxed while tapping. As usual, tap for fifty transits around the edges of the mouth, then place the center of the palms over the mouth and rub in two simultaneous circles fifty times, each hand going outwards from the center line, starting from the top, outwards, down, around and up in complete circles. For both tapping and rubbing, again keep the elbows down, keep the lips loose and mouth slightly parted, and breathe naturally all the while.

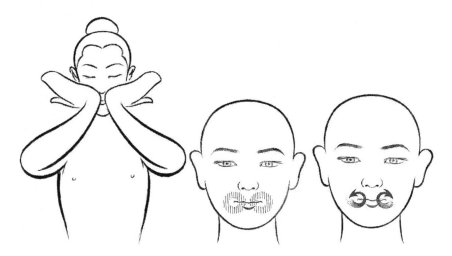

After the rubbing, cup the center of the concave palms over the mouth next to each other until you feel heat, making sure not to stick the elbows out too far. Hold approximately one to two minutes.

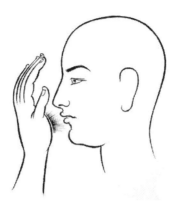

It's easy and straightforward to tap and massage the ears, eyes, nose and mouth. Now we are going to do the same for the anus and genital openings. These are very important health treatments for men and women, especially as we age. Don't feel embarrassed about performing utilization of qi over these areas. It's important to have privacy when practicing qigong just in general, but if your regular practice spot is outside in less than perfect seclusion, it is acceptable to move indoors to have privacy while doing utilization at the anus and genitals. If you have been practicing with concentration up to this point, stepping away for privacy won't break the mood or sense of energy. Of course, if you do have enough privacy and don't need to change locations, and can still stand outside facing the sun, that is ideal. It's better to feel comfortable in private so that you can properly massage the area, than to rush through outdoors where you're not comfortable. Do not skip these two steps, no matter what, though. They are absolutely integral to the practice as a whole and will make a huge difference for your health and wellbeing.

First start with the anus. You want to use the tapping to really relax the large muscles in the area, so while you still are striking with the fingertips, rather than a flat hand, you want to put your whole hands and arms into the motion for a much larger slap. Reach behind you and slap the buttocks and sides of hips firmly, with the whole hands providing momentum. Slap hard enough that you hear the sound of the slaps. Using one hand for each buttock, Strike outwards across the tops of the buttocks, down the sides by the hips, down at the bottoms of the buttocks and up the inner portion of the muscle, on either side of the center line of the body. Bend at the knees a little lower if necessary to more easily reach the full surface area. Do fifty times as usual, with enough force to soften up the muscles and get the area warmed up and tingling.

For the counterclockwise rubbing, use your left hand to form a sword mudra, with the first and middle fingers pressed together and the other fingers folded down to the palm with thumb on top of them, holding them in place. Both men and women start with the left hand. Using the first and middle "sword" fingers, run fifty times counterclockwise around the anal opening. For the correct orientation, start at the top, go towards the left, then down and around. Then switch hands and using the right hand in the same sword mudra, rub again fifty times in the same direction, but this time starting from the bottom going right, then up and around towards the left. It's basically the same direction, but starting from the bottom of the circle instead of the top.

Then cup around the anus area, using the left hand first for a minute or so, followed by the right hand for a similar amount of time. Don't be shy about doing this practice. It will prevent any anal disease or anal problems you might encounter. In fact, you have the option of very slightly inserting the tip of the middle finger just barely past the anal opening while you are circling, very gently moving the tissues right at its rim around in a circle as you lightly rub. This will prevent anal conditions such as hemorrhoids and polyps. Just be gentle when you rub, but don't hesitate to press down enough to really bring movement to the stiff muscles in the area. You may rub the area directly or rub through your clothing, if it is loose with thin enough material. You cannot underestimate the importance of maintaining muscle pliability and blood circulation around the anus for a truly healthy life.

The same thing holds true for the urogenital area. Even having an active sex life is not enough to maintain muscle tone and circulation in this region. It requires a focused effort from the utilization of qi to ensure healthy conditions in these sensitive and changeable parts. For females, you want to tap then rub on the periphery of the vagina, on the vulva and labia majora. Women want to use all five fingers to tap and have the option to use both hands at the same time or one hand at a time.

For the rubbing, use the whole palm, either with one hand at a time or both hands. Just remember that if you do use one hand at a time, you will need to do fifty taps and fifty rubs for that hand and another fifty for the other. When tapping, use enough momentum to really loosen up and relax the area. When rubbing, you are using the flat of the palm, not inserting any fingers, but do press with firmness so that you get movement into the tissues as you circle.

When cupping the hands at the end, use one hand at a time to well center the energy from the center of the palm over the vaginal opening. Males will do the tapping one hand at a time around the rim edge of the penile glans. Then for the rubbing, use one hand at a time using the same sword mudra as used for the anus. Rub in circles around the upper edge of the glans, rather than directly on the urethral opening. Use one hand at a time again when cupping the palm over the center of the glans. It is not required to tap and rub directly on bare skin for either sex, although it is acceptable if you choose. There may be some signs of physical arousal for men or women, but there is no reason to encourage a response or try to subdue one either. Your focus is on utilization of qi. It's very effective. This is the Maintenance Discipline of the Nine Palaces (*Jiugong baoyang haofa*).

Optionally, you can treat other sick parts of the body with the tapping, rubbing and cupping after you have completed the nine openings maintenance. When we practiced tonification of qi and pulled, using the image of the clock and its corresponding color, that was for treating diseases, especially diseases that involve blockages, growths and tumors. Utilization of qi, then, is used to preserve and maintain the vitality of the organs. If you had a blocked artery, you would want to practice tonification well, to reach the level where you could do the clock visualization for the heart. If instead you had a weak heart that you wanted to reinvigorate, or a healthy heart that you wanted to keep in good condition, you would focus on utilization instead. This is not practiced separately from the other four stages of Nine-Five Maintenance of Qi, and you would have to complete utilization for the nine openings first, so of course, your heart will be benefitting from these other practices too. The actual massaging and heating of the organ is the most beneficial tool for pure maintenance.

To continue with the example of the heart, after treating the nine openings, tap directly around the left chest where the heart is. You can tap using both hands at the same time or each hand separately. If using both hands, tap going up and down the side perimeters of the heart, fifty times. If you chose to do one hand at a time, you must use both hands fifty times each. For individual hands, you would tap in a full circle around the heart area with each hand. You may not only use one hand, so often it's preferable to just use both hands together to begin with. Apply a little force when tapping. There is no need to worry about damaging the organ from tapping too hard.

Afterwards you will rub counterclockwise, but when treating a specific organ, always rub with the left hand first for fifty times counterclockwise and then with the right hand for another fifty counterclockwise turns. For the heart, use the left hand first, going from the inner bottom edge of the perimeter, up and around to the outer top edge then down and around. Then the right hand circles going from the upper outside inwards then down and around, then up again.

Notice that the counterclockwise motion is coming from the elbow in both the right and left hands, while the circling itself appears to go outwards to the left when using the left hand and outwards to the right, when using the right hand. Just think of going outwards from an imaginary center line if that will make it easier to understand. After the rubbing, cup your two hands together where your heart is with the right hand on top and left hand underneath. The palms must be concaved around their center point. You will feel the warmth emitting from your hands into your heart. After you've held your palms over the heart for a short while, you realize that your heart is healed. Do you feel the warmth? That sensation is the proof you have just healed your heart.

You can do this for any organ you want to bolster. If you want to do a relatively large organ, just follow the same steps as for the heart, tapping with both hands at the same time, rubbing with individual hands starting with the left, then cupping with both hands together. If it is a small organ, like the thyroid gland for example, you will have to tap with each hand individually, fifty times each, rub with individual hands as usual, then cup with each hand individually too, left hand first, since the organ is so small and you want to properly target its perimeter with the tapping and its center with the cupping.

If you really want to maintain an organ, just tap it a little longer, one hundred times with both hands at once, or one hundred times for each hand when used individually. When tapping one hundred time or more, this tapping in itself is its own special form of treatment, which you then follow up with the usual amount of rubbing. Always remember that when cupping the hands, the center point of the hand cannot touch the body. The fingertips of the cupped hands can brush the body, but the focal point must never touch. You need that distance to set up the connection between the energy you are concentrating and the point you want to focus it onto.

The Wish Come True

There is one last step to the five stages of Nine-Five Maintenance of Qi. There is a saying in Chinese, taken from the abacus rule of old, "Nine divided by nine goes back to one" (*jiujiu guiyi*). Nine is the last single digit and one is first: it is also the symbol of the next order of counting past nine. Mathematically, it meant "nine divided by nine equals one." Idiomatically, this describes a concept where one begins with one goal or perspective, changes it over time, but eventually comes to see a renewed meaning in the original view, somewhat like saying "when it all boils right down to it" to sum up a point.

For our practice, we have treated the nine orifices, the nine openings of our body, the ears, the eyes, the nose, and so one, but there is one last treatment to be made. All you have to do is place your hands on in the triangle over your lower *dantian*, while facing the sun as you have been this entire time and ask yourself "what do I want for myself." If you want to be more beautiful, just think about your face. By concentrating on your face, you rally all the qi and blood from your body that you just harvested from the sun and gather it into your face. Eventually, you will become beautiful. The feeling of being filled with the sun's power will be the subconscious impulse you need to make the change.

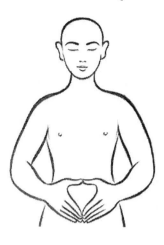

Use this thought any way you want. If you want to transfer all the qi that you've just gathered from the sun onto your hands, then you think about your hands. If there is a place in or part of your body that gives you discomfort, or you have problems with or are sick from, then you think about that part. The theory behind this is the magnifying glass shining over a piece of paper, focusing the sun's rays until the paper bursts into flame. The sun is right there up above shining down, your thoughts are the magnifying glass, and you're trying to gather all the rays of sunlight through the lens of your wishes into that problematic area, where you are focusing, to ignite it and make it catch fire. Everything that you have accumulated within yourself from the sun over the five stages of Nine-Five Maintenance of Qi, is now ready for you to harvest. You gather it up and focus it all that onto that one point on your body, that one change you want to make, that one accomplishment you want to achieve. You harness the qi and bring it where you will.

Bruce Lee was a very light fellow, the lightest of all the students, lighter than all of his opponents. When he would throw a "One inch punch," one inch away from his target, he was not just using his arm force, but applied expressive force (*fali*) of the whole body. His punch did not involve extending his elbow and then throwing a punch. The punch begins just an inch or two away from his mark. When you watch him punch, that's all he does, and yet there is enough force in that tiny movement to topple the enemy. So too do you have to use your whole body's concentration. In the same way, you must use your outward motive force to focus on that point you intensely want to place the qi that you've collected from the sun.

If you want your face to look younger, envision how young your face is and the force of your will combined with the power of the sun's qi will influence it enough for real change to occur. If you are a woman and want to get pregnant, focus on your uterus. You are instilling all these hopes and wishes within your body, using your intention. It's not just an exercise in positive thinking. These practices change how your body feels, change your perception of control over your body, and change your mental state so that a wish can now feel like a reality.

These are physical shifts that you make when you practice the Nine-Five Maintenance of Qi with sincerity, concentration and effort. This is the final component of a powerful model for change. It is the last concept that completes an entire worldview. Deep down, we all know that we can direct ourselves towards the transformations we need. It is only through diligent, steady practice, every day, day in and day out that you will get the results that you want. That's what it all boils down to in the end.

Chapter Eight

Nine Palaces Facing Heaven

The Dragon Shape Form

The Nine-Five Maintenance of Qi is made up of two parts, the five stage maintenance of qi and the actual Nine Palaces Facing Heaven qigong form that we will
cover in this chapter. Just as you had to go through each step of welcoming,
intaking, adjusting, and tonifying before you were prepared physically and mentally for the final utilization of qi, it is just as important to complete those five
stages before moving on to the central Nine Palaces form. This part of the form
is no less physically oriented than the various stages of maintenance of qi, but
the movements are less health oriented and more specifically a ritual of connecting with heaven and earth. We have gone past training the body and opening the
sense-organ networks that are termed the nine palaces. We have even gone beyond focusing one's personal will and intention. Now we merge as one with the
universe.

As we have mentioned before, there are nine levels of Nine Palaces practice,
with nine sub-levels each. It is not so much that some of these nine categories
are more basic than others. All Nine Palaces Qigong use yang energy to connect
heaven, humanity, and earth into one. It is just that different forms address this
unification from different angles, for differing purposes. This Nine Palaces form,
which completes the Nine-Five Maintenance of the Qi Nine Palaces Qigong,
also originates with Qiu Chuji.

Qiu Chuji first set out on his epic journey across Asia on the command of Genghis Khan, who demanded his presence in his court to make for him the secret elixir of immortality. When Qiu Chuji finally arrived after years of arduous travel, he told him that there was no pill he could compound for the Great Khan. In its place, he taught him instead how to practice the nine palaces form that we will learn here in this chapter. It is the Dragon Shape Form (*longxing gong*). Together with the maintenance of qi, the Dragon Shape Form exemplifies Daoist internal alchemy as it is rooted within the development and preservation of the body. It is the crown jewel in the art of protective qigong. The movements are very simple, but each gesture combines to form a sigil for safety, a call from within to the four corners of the earth and to the heavens above.

Sensitivity and Signals

We finished the last portion of utilization of qi facing the sun with our hands in a triangle at the lower *dantian*, focusing all the energy of the sun within our bodies to the place we most wished it to suffuse. This radiant state of mind is how we should begin the Dragon Shape Form. Making sure our stance is stable, with toes still pointed in and solidly rooted as a tripod, as before, open the hands out to the sides of the body, slowly and naturally. Bend the thumbs so they squarely press into the centers of the palms and close the rest of the fingers over them, just as how we began at the very start of welcoming the qi.

Fingers represent different people in our lives. As we mentioned before the thumb represents yourself, the forefinger represents your mother, the middle finger represents your father, the ring finger is family and the pinkie is friends. These same representations apply here. The fingers can send us signs about these various people in our lives. You can wave and say hello to someone you know and then test the sensations in the corresponding finger. Wave hello to an acquaintance or friend then flick your pinkie against your thumb on the same hand. If you don't have any sensations, that's good. However if you feel soreness or pain at the moment you say hello and then flick, it doesn't mean that he or she is a bad person, just a person that is not fitting for you. This might be a wonderful person, but just not right for you.

We all know someone who is smart, pleasant and well liked, but you just don't get along together, for no particular reason. It doesn't matter if they are good or bad, they might be the greatest guys or gals anyone could hope to meet, but they are not suited for you. Daoists separate people into twenty-five types. Out of these twenty-five different types of people, there is one category that you cannot afford to associate with. You cannot be nice to them. The only way you will interact with them is with meanness and cruelty, even though you yourself are not a mean person to all. This one type will always bring out the worst in you.

Another type will lack motivation and the only way you can get them to do anything is to keep pushing them constantly. Some others out of the twenty-five different types are the kind of people who like to be scolded and reprimanded by others. To them, they see scolding as the way someone shows their affection.

Different people under different circumstances will bring out these various qualities in you or you will serve these roles for others, completely unintentionally. This is the sense by which we mean a person could be individually unsuitable for you. It's quite possible you might encounter a person that has a terrible reputation, who everyone around them thinks is bad, but that person suits you and will be beneficial to your life. Don't be influenced by others, when deciding who is good and who is bad for you in your life. It's what you think of them that matters. That's the main thing, your own personal perspective, not what others say. Especially in the matters of love and the matters of marriage, it's essential. Use the technique of waving hello then flicking the pinkie with the thumb for detecting harmonious friends and romantic involvements. It's a good sign if you don't have any sensations. If you have soreness or pain or discomfort, it's bad. You can either wave hello or goodbye or check after you shake hands. Use it for these specific greeting formalities, not at random.

When Dr. Wu was at Kyoto University back in his days in Japan, he was a student and looking for weekend work. If he saw the hospital floor manager or the head of the lab, he would make sure to go up to them, shake their hand and ask if there was any work. If there was anything available, it was usual working the graveyard shift in various emergency rooms. The pay was often better in the busy central hospitals, but on the other hand, while remote hospitals outside of town paid less and took time to travel to, it was likely there would be so few patients during his shift that he could nap through the night and still get paid in the morning. Dr. Wu remembered his training from the White Cloud Monastery, so if he felt like his hand ached or had any kind of discomfort when shaking the managers' hands, he would just walk away from the job offer.

Dr. Wu actually spent time examining this phenomenon, by taking some jobs even when his hand felt the signs of discomfort after the handshake, considering he didn't want to turn down every job anyway. Like clockwork, he was bound to meet difficulties throughout the night if he had felt this sign, whether it meant a rush of too many patients or difficult patients or other emergency room complications. Eventually Dr. Wu just realized that it was always better in the event he felt painful or unpleasant sensations to just walk away. Whatever the job, if the handshake didn't leave any sensation, then he'd take it no matter the pay or the location. It's a very effective prediction technique.

In time, Dr. Wu had the opportunity to publicize this hand sign practice among his colleagues in Japan and it met with great interest. In fact, there was enough attention paid to it in influential academic circles, it wound up being implemented in certain official capacities. Even today, the hand signs are used as part of the acceptance process for pilots seeking enrollment in commercial flight school. Dr. Wu introduced the technique to them and they found it works well enough to make it part of the admissions tests. If you try it, as soon as you feel the hand sign pain with a new acquaintance, don't think maybe you should get to know the person first and see if it really works or not. You don't need to. It's been tested thoroughly already, in many modern contexts. If you really feel discomfort or soreness, no further tests are necessary. Instead, pay heed and avoid a bad situation.

It's a natural weather forecast, so to speak. If there's going to be rain tomorrow, today you will see ants laboring to plug the openings to their tunnels. You will see dragonflies flying very low and birds will be unusually flustered and noisy. Even some older people will feel back pain, or knee or leg pain as an indicator that the weather is about to change. It's the same basic concept. If you visit a farm the day before cows or sheep are to be slaughter, you will sometimes see the animals kneeling down and crying, obviously frightened and in distress. They have the capability of sensing their slaughter. This hand sign is our innate ability to sense or evaluate the people we encounter.

To be more exact, you must check for pain or soreness in the ring finger. Remember each finger corresponds to a relationship, mother, father, family friends, but as a predictor, it's only your ring finger that's accurate. This is the important point to understand. The ring finger is the one that you have to check for a sensation of pain or no sensation at all. It doesn't matter if it's a friend or a family member that you are trying to evaluate. It could be a classmate or your boss, but it will always be the ringer finger that will give you the sign.

Of course if you feel a sudden strong painful sensation around the index finger, without having any particular health condition or joint problem, that indicates your mother. But a painful sensation around this finger is uncommon, based on Daoist research, and will only occur on rare but serious occasions. This kind of pain is a bad indication that your mother is sick or there may be major car accident within the family. Severe pain in the middle finger is representative of your father or a family member or other person you care for strongly that is about to die. The sign is specifically sharp pain, not soreness, stiffness or an ache. All this is derived from generations of experience, compiled by the scholars of the White Cloud Monastery. For predicting affinities, only check the ring finger. The other pains we mention are special and infrequent exceptions.

There is a training method to build up this special perception in the fingers. It sensitizes them and also cleans them so that they can more clearly receive an accurate message. Initially when you start training the sensitivity of your fingers, practice with flowers to learn how to pick up the sensations. Wave your hand back and forth quickly over a flowering shrub or plant to see if you gain any sensations. If the flowers are budding or beginning to bloom, when you do this you probably won't feel anything, but if the flower or the plant it's on is just about to die, you might feel discomfort along your ring finger.

There are different ways of waving your hand if you are using the hand signals for diagnosing a patient. Dr. Wu often has patients in his clinic that cannot communicate. People will bring their dogs in, for example, unsure if the animal is treatable or not. For dogs, he will stand with his right hand flat, palm up with the thumb slightly contacted towards the ring finger, then run his left hand palm down, tracing along the spine of the dog from above. He does not touch the dog, just hovers the hand over the length of its spine. He will check his human patients too, to be sure that they are sick, doing better or doing worse. Sometimes he just shakes his hand at them like a normal wave of greeting. Other times he will move his hand with the palm up, swinging it gently upwards from the wrist, in a motion like trying to pat a baby's bottom. Sometime he will even use the same bottom patting motion but put much more swinging into it, as if fanning a fire. If he feels discomfort in the ring finger then that person is definitely sick.

In the White Cloud Monastery, Dr. Wu's master bade him practice in front of flowers. He would stand with knees shoulder width apart slightly leaning forward, with his hands in front reaching down but not touching the plant or shrub. From this position over the plant, he would wave with both hands at the same time in a circular outward manner, as if rippling them while plunged in a pool of water, undulating the shoulder, elbow and wrist joints as part of the motion so that the entire arm was involved in the movement. After doing this special waving in front of the flowers, he would then put his hands into a tub of water, or a pool of water, as was available and make similar but wider swimming motions with his whole arm, so that the palms were down but moving inwards until nearly facing each other, then outwards pointing all the way out to the sides. Washing in water in this way washes away all the communication debris or static on your hands. It neutralizes the hands after trying to pick up the signals.

Normally training would be practiced in front of flowers, but there were also practical daily chores to be done that would also require the same hand sensitivity. In the morning before school, Dr. Wu would have to get up early to tend to and feed the animals that were his job to take care of. The White Cloud Monastery kept animals of all kinds, for study and observation, as well as for use in various practices. For example, there was a pit of snakes that swords would be kept in. The snakes would crawl all over the swords to bring out the snakelike energy from their blades. To develop a certain power inside of a sword, it needs snakes around it, feeding it with their essence. To feed the sword with snake energy, it would be put in the pit for forty-nine days. The intention is to train the force within the sword by elevating it by the proximity of the snakes, feeding the sword with the powers of the snake. It wasn't something visible during the daytime, but at night sometimes when you would unsheathe these special swords, you would feel a kind of cold vitality (*lengguo*) emitted from the blade.

This same snake energy relates to another special way of training the sensitivity of the hands, particularly for detecting and diagnosing. Sometimes when training the sensitivity with water, afterwards the student would have to reach into the snake pit, pull out a snake and then stretch it out, holding its length up between the two hands. This isn't harmful to the snake. It's more like petting the snake. If it is willing to let you straighten it out, it is because you have the right touch, so it will relax in your hands. The snake training was rarely used, but it was designed for extra diagnosing ability going from the hands all the way down the arm.

Dr. Wu would have to use the same principle in his assigned morning duties. As a boy, his job was to feed and care for the eagles that were kept in quite a large quantity. How would he know which eagle was sick that day and might need special attention? For this, he was taught to fully extend his right arm straight up and out to the side of his body palm facing outwards and slightly forwards. Then the eagle handler would bring each eagle out, one by one, and if he would have that feeling in his ring finger, he would know that bird needed sick care for the day. The eagle can't communicate how it feels, so this was the ancient way of detecting and diagnosing any illness.

This sort of sensitivity is developed by special trainings and made use of with special hand motions, but even the regular practice of qigong contains so many sensitizing movements, that the signs can come to you when you're not expecting them. Out in the street when a dog walks by, Dr. Wu knows instantly if the dog is sick. Even if he doesn't use any hand shaking or postures, he's sensitive enough to pick it up. Passing by a building, sometimes the feeling will just come down from a particular apartment on a particular floor, very specifically, and Dr. Wu can tell someone is about to die there. Why? Because his middle finger felt the special sharp, painful sensation that signifies an imminent death. Initially, to unlock this sensitivity in the fingers, the practice is always with flowers as described, but once you know the sensation, regular Nine Palaces practice will only enhance it further.

Recently a cancer patient came to Dr. Wu to see if there was anything he could do for her. Of course, he first used the standard TCM diagnostic methodology and examined her tongue coating and pulses. He had to tell her that she probably wouldn't live very long. Just to judge by her exterior appearance, no one would ever be able to tell she was so sick. Her outwards appearance looked healthy. Even her tongue coating wasn't that bad on its own. Dr. Wu knew there was something much more serious at hand, because as he started to examine her, his middle finger started hurting with that special sign. Even from her hospital tests, her Western doctors thought she could still live for a long time. There's science on one side, but this pain comes from Dr. Wu's awareness and physical sensations. A lifetime of training and experience has left him confident of their accuracy.

If you want to train your hand sensitivity with flowers, lay your hands above a flowering plant or shrub and make the smooth outwards-circling motion with both hands at the same time over it eighty-one times. You can also train with water, if you don't have access to a proper plant. With water, circle two hundred and sixty times. Anybody can have this sensation, but to actually gain the sensitivity, you do have to do this training every day.

Some people can unlock their ability in seven days. Practice once a day for seven days, and you might gain that sensitivity by then. If you're gifted, you can easily accomplish it in seven days, but if you're not gifted with raw natural ability, you still should be able to release it with daily practice for up to forty-nine days, but you have to do it every day without missing a single practice. In some rare cases, if a person still cannot acquire the sensation after forty-nine days of steady practice, the master would usually just advise the student to forget about it and move on. There's a saying in Chinese, some people are just like ugly wood (*choumu*). No matter how you try to carve it, it will never make a sculpture.

Fortunately, from Dr. Wu's own observation, about ninety-five percent of people with normal psychological health can gain that sensation. Certain serious mental health conditions might interfere with the ability to sense the signs, but some other conditions can actually increase the sensitivity greatly, especially the vision impaired or blind. They have such special sensitivities in their hands, they frequently are singled out to be taught the most complete details of mastering this art.

During his early morning chores in the White Cloud Monastery, the young Dr. Wu would keep his eyes closed as he was trying to detect each eagle in turn. It would give him clearer and stronger sensations. Therefore, it's better to practice this training with the eyes closed. Even better is to practice eyes closed while standing waist deep in water, rather than just with water in a tub or sink. If you are fortunate to have daily conditions where you can practice while standing in water, accentuate your circling motions by leaning forward as the hands circle inwards and leaning backwards as the hands and arms open and circle out. This puts your whole body in tune with these subtle pulses of information. Even better still, practice while standing waist deep in the ocean, to feel the still, quiet messages in the water as well as the tide rushing in and pulling out beneath your feet. For everyday practice, using normal water in a tub or standing in a swimming pool will still give you a good training.

Although the flower training can balance the sensitivity in the hands as well as build it up, sometimes you have to wash away all the negative residue that can also accumulate. For this, you can wipe your hands on green grass, or wash them as we described before, in a tub or pool of water, rippling the hands back and forth in broad strokes. This is not to say that there are evil energies or spirits that attach to you. Traditionally, to check if a food had been poisoned, the court doctor would use a silver chopstick or needle to poke it. If the food was poisoned, the silver would darken from the chemical reaction between it and the poison.

Daoists see the hand sensitivity in a similar way. Practicing with flowers turns your hands into the equivalent of that silver needle. So many messages can come in from all around you, even when you're not actively trying to check for them. Sometimes there can be build up or a reaction that will tarnish their sensitivity, not because the messages were evil, but just because of their sheer quantity reacting with your hands' sensory apparatus. To wash yourself of this buildup, do the opening and closing wave motions with your arms and hands, using water, as we mentioned before.

If your fingers are receptors, is it inadvisable to wear rings on them? It doesn't make a difference if you are wearing rings made of metal. The metal won't block your sensitivity. Sometimes if you wear jade rings, it can actually improve the sensation. It has to be very good jade, though, with a living spark inside of it. The right piece of jade can be so powerful it can heal illnesses that nothing else can. If you have an animal that is so sick, you can't treat it with any other kinds of treatment any longer, you find a piece of jade and place it under the sick animal while it rests. Many times, the very next day the animal will be recovered.

Jade also works for humans. Whatever spot in the body that is uncomfortable or is making you feel sick, place a jade object on top of the area. The philosophy behind it is that the jade will suck out the sickness from that part. This is for your consideration as an example of Daoist medicine that doesn't have a clear-cut scientific correspondence. You do need a very special piece of jade. Any average mediocre piece of jade won't do. Jade of this high quality acts as an amplifier and broadcaster for the sensitivity in the hands. If you wear a ring made from this superior jade ring on your ring finger, not only will you be able to detect the signals of sickness around you as you walk about, you will also be giving the sick animals and plants that you pass a beneficial healing treatment, just by walking by. It has to be the good jade, though.

A good piece of jade is not always the most expensive kind you see made into jewelry. Just because it's expensive doesn't mean it's good in the medicinal way. To tell if you have the right kind of stone, hold the jade up in front of a light to see if there are any fragments or particles in it. Also observe its tone, texture and color. There will be a softness to the stone, smooth and soft like a baby's skin. That is a good piece of jade.

For the final test, drip one drop of sesame oil right on its center. As long as that drop of oil does not scatter on the surface of the jade, it can be used for medicinal purposes. However if that drop of oil were to break up, even if that jade is worth tens of thousands of dollars in Beverly Hills, it still is not suitable to use for healing. You might find a little piece of jade for ten or twenty dollars that doesn't disperse a drop of oil. It will be more valuable that the piece that cost thousands that could not hold the drop together. For treatment, just put that piece of good jade on the sick dog's collar and that's that. It's a preventative measure. It can keep many problems and *dan*gers at bay.

The healing jade can also protect and heal humans. If you have heart problems, wear the jade on a string so that it *dan*gles at chest level in line with the heart at the Tanzhong acupoint. If you have respiratory problems, flip the string around so the jade *dan*gles behind you on your back. If you have high blood pressure, wear a piece of good jade around your foot. Dr. Wu went with his student to a large gem convention and found one piece of jade that was good on the whole trading floor. There was only that one piece of outstanding jade in the entire show. Please don't judge the quality of the jade by how much it costs or how big it is. Only judge it with the oil test, if it scatters or not. You can only use sesame oil. Hopefully this is clear.

The color of the jade also comes into play, depending on the type of illness you want to cure. To treat liver problems, then you want to use green jade. If you have respiratory problems, use white jade. For kidney ailments, you need to use black jade formed into a belt you can wear just below the waist. Otherwise hang the jade from a regular belt at the side front of the hip right behind where the hip bone sticks out.

If you want to treat heart problems, it's Dr. Wu's professional recommendation not to use jade. Instead, use bloodstone (*jixue shi*). Its bright red veins look like blood is dripping from the stone. Of course, if you find a stone that really appeals to you and speaks to you in a special way, this will be a good stone for you to use for yourself, no matter what kind it is. Its quality is not determined by its monetary value.

When looking for excellent diagnostic medicinal jade, traditionally the best specimens came from Yunnan province. Today there is also excellent jade mined in Brazil. There is nothing wrong about using rocks instead of jade as you see with many trends in massage. Rocks are good for relaxation, but they aren't enough to act as a healing treatment. Just remember if you're going to use jade to treat a person, then you have to use the best quality that you can find. Otherwise, don't use it.

Clean your jade in water, the same way you clean a crystal ball. The best method is to let it sit submerged in the ocean surf for an hour. You can keep it inside of a net so that it won't float away. After an hour you can remove it. Alternately, you can clean it with tap water by letting it sit under a running faucet for at least an hour, or even overnight. These are the two ways to clean medicinal jade. The difference between jade and a crystal ball is you can dry crystal balls in direct sunlight. You cannot do this for jade. You can let the jade dry under a full moon, or just let it dry inside the house away from sunlight, which is perfectly acceptable. If you can find a truly superior piece of jade, its effect is much better than crystal ball. The light beams that radiate from a crystal ball cannot emanate beyond the room it's in. However if you have a really high quality piece of jade, you can be outside the house and be able to sense its radiance. You can feel it as a smooth yet malleable energy that it emits.

Jade is an extensive topic of scholarship, both for the Daoists and for connoisseurs of many other kinds. A number of years ago, a well-known Hong Kong auctioneer brought a prominent collection of jade ware to the United States and asked Dr. Wu to take a look at it. Out of the whole collection, there was one piece of jade that was just a broken fragment, but although it was broken, it still had the right tone and texture and also emanated the ideal smooth, malleable light. Dr. Wu told him it was probably worth twenty thousand dollars, but if it had been a whole piece rather than a broken fragment, it could have been worth twenty million instead. That's how wide the price gap between a broken jade antiquity and one in flawless condition.

It's very complicated and difficult to explain exactly how to judge jade. Today there is technology that can manufacture synthetic diamonds that are impossible to tell from natural stones with the eye. Even viewed through a microscope, it is getting harder to tell one from the other. At Cal Tech, they use the resonance from a piece of jade as the quickest method to separate the natural stones from the man-made. That is a perfect example of the sensitive and refined vibrational rate of fine jade.

There's a reason we have gone on at length about jade, flowers, and training the hands. Even without flower training, the Nine-Five Maintenance of Qi will sensitize you enough to read your own day's fortune. Attuning the body to receive more detailed information from its surroundings is a study with thousands of years of history. When you consider the depth of its lore and the detailed disciplines that have arisen over many generations to harness this ability, along with its many diagnostic, predictive and therapeutic applications, Nine Palaces Qigong's vast importance for broadening our human experience becomes clear. Qigong practice lets us pick up signs and messages from the world around us and the Dragon Shape Form brings us to a level of sensitivity as subtle as the finest jade.

In this spirit, we start the practice with the thumb, which is our self. We want to place our self in the center, as we place our thumbs in the centers of the palms. If you wake up in the morning feeling a sudden, unexpected discomfort in the thumb (of course, barring any joint disorders or arthritis), it can mean that you should be careful when you drive today. Maybe you will need to be more aware of your interactions with workmates or strangers. It might be an indicator that you will get into an argument with others or have some other agitation. It doesn't matter what things might specifically happen, but if you feel discomfort first thing as you awake, then you need to be careful for the day. Take it as a sign to be more cautious. This is for you to experience on your own. A lot of these feelings have to be felt for yourself to make sense. Practice and attention are the only guides you need.

Opening Signs

Just as the maintenance of qi begins with a stage of welcoming salutes, the Dragon Shape Form also begins with special signs to mark the commencement of the practice. As an aside, when Dr. Wu taught this form, he spent relatively little time discussing the meanings and physical systems involved with each motion, unlike his discussions about the five stages of maintenance of qi. He would point out the major theories or principles that inflect certain movements, but overall he always preferred to first demonstrate each movement while we would watch, then we would all stand up and practice together in silence. Afterward, he might pause to explain a few key points or have students come up to practice in front of the others while he commented or guided their movement. The sense always was at this point in the practice, it was time to concentrate and feel each movement deeply, rather than distract with intellectual discourse.

I make it a goal to not diverge from the topics and concepts as Dr. Wu presents them, but this is one occasion where I'd like to point out that after years of doing this practice, I have noticed that the Dragon Shape Form is tightly parallel to the maintenance of qi. The movements are different, but the stages of their progression have strong similarities. This is nothing important to pay mind to while practicing, but it is something interesting to think about for yourself when you have a quiet moment to reflect on your practice. The practice of Nine-Five Maintenance of Qi is an art form to be savored on many levels, both while practicing and later when remembering the special moments you have had. Nine Palaces Qigong is always with you after you have experienced it.

So, begin with readjusting your stance as needed, then firmly place the thumbs into the midpoint of the palms and close the fingers around them into fists. Bring your arms up from the sides of your body so that they rise to chest level, with the fists facing down and the elbows bent outwards. When you lift the arms, raise them in front of the body, slightly rounded outwards rather than perfectly straight forward, with the fists facing down, so that they naturally bend at right angles once they reach chest height, with one arm very slightly higher and somewhat forward from the other.

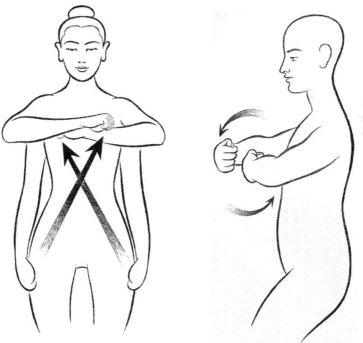

For women, the right forearm is positioned higher and in front of the left forearm. For men, the left forearm will be the one that is slightly higher and in front. If you look down at your arm position, you will see it is a good, solid, square shape. The shoulders are down and relaxed and the neck is straight with chin in just enough to straighten the spine.

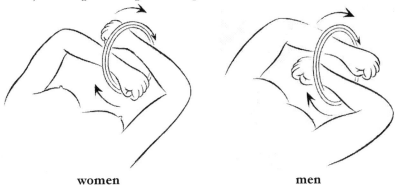

women   men

Everyone has seen images of Bruce Lee in a posture with his arms out and slightly down in front of him with his hands in fists and his wrists crossed one over the other. This is a very important stance for the Daoists. Notice how if you put your arms in this posture but then raise them so that the elbows are pointing all the way out to the sides that it has transformed into the arm position we are using here in the Dragon Shape Form. So, if the arms are down, the wrists are crossed and if you bring them up, the wrists are parallel to each other in a natural line. Sensing this line of connection between the wrists is an important factor for the next movements we make.

We are going to rotate the forearms in a circle around each other three times, using the wrists as the center point of the movement. To do this, the front arm comes down and in towards the body while back arm goes up and over at the same time. The three rotations complete with the arms, wrists and fists all back in their starting position. To rotate three times, think of it as three circling's of the wrists, as if you are winding one wrist around the other.

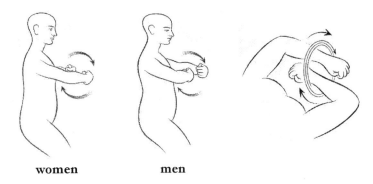

women   men

To describe this movement in extreme detail, let's use the women's positioning for the example. A woman starts with the right wrist forward and the left wrist closer to the body. The front wrist is coming down while the back wrist comes up and around over the right wrist, as if it just wrapped a covering or bandage over it. Then the right wrist continues by coming up from the back and around the left wrist like it is covering it in turn. Then the 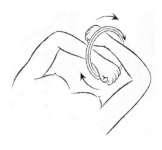 left wrist goes up and around the right wrist again as the final bit of momentum in the movement, which slows and brakes with the right wrist back in the original position. This is a somewhat subtle point.

There are three "windings." The momentum comes from the inner wrist winding over the forward wrist. It's a little complicated to discuss and not even that simple to watch another person demonstrate, but it is easy to just feel as you 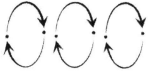 do it. If this is too difficult to follow, Dr. Wu also showed a slightly simplified version where you just consider the starting position the beginning of each cycle and count three of those, also finishing back in the starting position.

Next we do another three rotations with the fists opened out. From the starting position, open your hands and extend them so you feel the fingers and palms  stretching out. There is no need to try and stretch them with full effort. Just open the fists into flared hands, but flared so that the palms are very slightly cupped, rather than dead flat. The way to do this cup shaped palm is with hands kept very soft and the cupping only coming from the pinkie edge of the hand very slightly, not from the thumb area. On the thumb side, keep relaxed with the thumbs pointing distinctly downwards, although still on a bit of a slant. This creates a hand that is in a subtle bell shape, allowing all the fingers to stretch and separate but not get tense and also letting the palms stay relaxed.

Another thing to factor in is that the hand on the outside of the body, which is the left hand for men and the right hand for women, will be the upper hand and will have the palm subtly tilted up and diagonally outwards from the body while the inner hand that is held behind it is gently pointing down and out, but also pointed very slightly in towards the body. These subtle tilts allow the two wrists to best be aligned at their center points. This is a subtle positioning, however it's something that is very easy to feel as your hands go into the proper position.

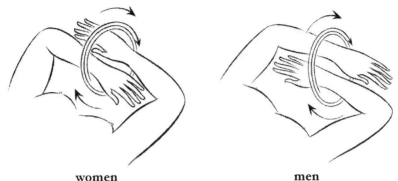

women   men

Imagine that there is one diagonal rod or line of energy connecting the centers of the two palms and passing straight through the wrists, so that hands and wrists are integrated together into one, so that they operate as one unit when winding around. Rotate around three times, as before. The rotating is the same around the wrists as with the closed fists, with one extra detail. As the back hand comes up and around the wrist, you want to also rotate the palm and point it a little more forward and out from the body than it is when it's the lower hand going down and around to the back. We have this subtle tilting of palm and wrist involved during the rotation to fully emphasize the wrapping and connected sensation around the wrists. It is very graceful.

Your motions should be slow and effortless. You should feel like your arms and hands are floating weightlessly on a cushion of air while doing these rotations. That is how light, gentle and delicate these movements are. End the last of the three open-handed wrist rotations with the front hand now even with the back hand, rather than being slightly above.

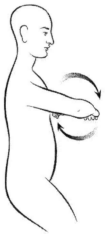

There is an important *Book of Changes* calculation to these two sets of rotations. The mathematics come from the formula "3 times 3 makes 9" (*sansan duijiu*), meaning three multiplied by three is nine. Each hand as five fingers and with these five fingers you have rotated three times. So in these movements you have combined the number nine with the number five, as befits the Nine-Five Maintenance of Qi. Make sure that you remember this calculation and perform these two signs exactly as described.

Connecting to Heaven and Earth

The next movement set of Longxing gong is connecting to heaven and earth (*tou tiandi*). You are holding up the heavens and pointing down to the earth. We ended the last three wrist rotations with the front hand now level with the inner hand. We are going to use the outer hand to push up over the head, while the inner hand lowers to flip over and point down at the genital area, all while lowering the whole body down by bringing the knees and thighs together. To repeat, the outer hand is the right hand for women and the left hand for men. Both hands are facing palm down from the end of the wrist rotations.

Allow the outer hand to float upwards. As it floats up, the elbow is soft and the open palm naturally and gradually turns to face the sky. By the end of this motion, the elbow is

still slightly bent and the palm is facing upwards, relaxed, with a sensation of being in line with the top center of the head. At the same time, the inner arm is coming down with the hand kept in its original position, palm down, until the arm is nearly straight.

At this point, the elbow is only slightly bent, so that the forearm is at a comfortable diagonal. The hand should be moving towards genital level. Before you completely have extended the arm straight, the hand twists forwards at the wrist with the palm cupping gently until the palm is held facing up, palm softly curved with fingers, and thumb out naturally. Start the rotation when the hand reaches the lower *dantian*.

This rotation from flat palm facing down to upward facing palm is a subtle transition that is going to be used to create some momentum for our final push up to the heavens and down to the earth. It starts out slowly and gently, progressively turning with increased muscle tension as the palm cups. The cupping palm and steady rotation should feel like you are carving out a sphere of energy from the lower *dantian* and genital areas, but the rotation ends all at once with a quick flipping to bring the hand into its final position, which is above the groin, palm facing the earth and totally flat now.

The lower palm's fingers are extended and squeezed together slightly, particularly the first and pinkie fingers, to create some rigor in the palm around its center point, even as it stays basically flat. Just as in the belled hands in the second set of rotations, this cupping is very subtle without much muscular force. Use just enough so that you feel the sensation in the center of the palm. To understand how and when to flip the lower hand, the sensation is that when you feel the wrist is almost at its full rotation, you release the pressure and energy in that final light, soft and quick flip. This way there is no strain on the wrist and there is momentum suddenly generated.

Use the momentum of the lower hand flip to now push up with the upper hand. All this time, the upper hand is coming up with the wrist moving as necessary, but not drastically twisting as the lower hand has to get into position. This twist begins at the upper *dan* area so that the palm is ending flat and pointing upward over the head. The elbow is bent so that the palm is soft and pointing up in a mirroring of the lower hand. The only difference is the lower hand and arm are slightly straighter.

Meanwhile, for the lower body motion, the whole time you are bringing your hands into position, you are slowly bringing your knees together. Because your legs are shoulder width apart with the toes pointing inwards, to bring your knees together means lowering down on them gradually and also bringing your upper thighs together by turning them inwards. In that last moment, when the lower hand flip generates a momentum for the whole body, drop down as completely as you can into your bended knee posture. This is a rapid drop where you also push up completely with the upper arm and extend the lower hand and arm down as much as you can too, in one last thrusting motion almost like digging a shovel into the ground.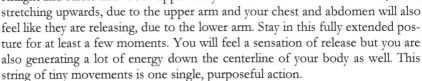

The upper hand can stretch up an inch or two more, palm flat upwards, directly over the Baihui acupoint, so that the spine is fully extended. All of this is done at once. It is a powerful sensation. The knees, upper thighs and groin will feel like they are squeezing together in a very straight and stable line. Your upper body will feel like it is stretching upwards, due to the upper arm and your chest and abdomen will also feel like they are releasing, due to the lower arm. Stay in this fully extended posture for at least a few moments. You will feel a sensation of release but you are also generating a lot of energy down the centerline of your body as well. This string of tiny movements is one single, purposeful action.

To master this act, you must use your senses to grasp its movements and how they shift and flow together. A conscious awareness of your body's sensations will allow you to fully understand and then take charge of what you are trying to accomplish with them, which after all, is the true desired end result of this entire practice. You are trying to combine the qi of heaven and earth. You can't grab heaven or hold earth, but you can go with nature and bring them together. So hold heaven up, don't try to pull it down. These opposing forces are the source of the new energy you are building within.

Forming the Taiji Ball

In the practice of qigong, mastery is attained through body awareness, noticing then understanding all the subtle shifts of sensation. We go through the arduous preparation stages of maintenance of qi, so that we can perform the Dragon Shape Form in a state of pure sensory responsiveness. It should be embraced as a great pleasure, as well as a source of power. Lofty words, it's true, but how better to use your time and effort, than to make every day's practice a peak experience?

After staying in the feeling of holding up heaven and pointing down into the earth, the next step is to take that sensation and concentrate it into the orb of Taiji. With the previous step, the focus is holding up the heavens and pointing towards the ground. The intention is to gather the yin and yang qi from heaven and earth. This is the powerful energy we feel accumulating in the center of the body. Our next step is to flip the hands over and bring them together into a ball. We let yin and yang qi flow into us and now we want to compress them together in the center of the palms.

To do this, start to gently cup the lower palm. Use the wrist to rotate the cupped palm to face up as you begin to slowly lift it up the centerline of the body. The upper hand cups right after the lower hand does and also fully rotates at the wrist so the palm is pointing down. Once the palm is pointing down, then lower the hand down the centerline at a slightly faster pace so that both hands can meet at the same time in a small ball right over the stomach/diaphragm area, just below the middle *dan*. The lower hand is actually in position before the right hand is, although negligibly so.

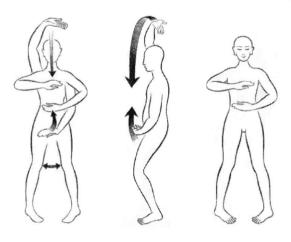

The ball you are forming is the size of the stomach and solar plexus area, and directly over the stomach, right under the breasts. The upper hand is positioned at the line separating the breast from the stomach and the lower hand is right under the physical location of stomach. The actual size of the sphere we are forming is roughly six to seven inches in diameter, the size of the human stomach and will be centered right over the physical location of the stomach, with careful positioning of the upper and lower hands. Both palms are facing each other, aligned at the centers of the palms. Both hands are distinctly cupped, empha-  sizing their centers. You want them to be almost pointy in how cupped they are, to maximize the sensation in these center points.

This is a good place to have a reminder about the proper stance. When the hands turn around and start coming together, at the same time straighten your body back up from the much lowered position you ended the last step with. As always, you want your pelvis thrust out just a bit, so that the front of your body can be very subtly caved inwards a bit. This adds to the tripod-like stability of your stance and also emphasizes the central column of energy that runs down the body.

As you lower your arms, you need to have a feeling of connection in the middle of the two hands, attracting them together. This sensation should get stronger as the hands get closer to forming the ball. Keep your internal muscles engaged as you bring the hands together. You want to feel that you are taking the yin and yang qi and squeezing it together into a Taiji ball, so let your whole body follow along if you have that degree of muscular control. It's most im- portant to feel the sensation of the hands drawing together. That sensation alone will train the rest of your body to follow along over time.

The same thing holds true for the Taiji ball. It's more important to feel the sensations that are occurring naturally in your body, rather than try to "see" the symbol of yin-yang between your hands. It's the physical sensation that counts. All the visualization and colorful imagery in the world will not change your body the way just observing every small nuance of tactile sensation will. We said before that the image is holding up heaven, pointing at the ground. You cannot grab the qi of heaven. You cannot grab the sky or raise the earth up. Those are two entities a human cannot move. As Daoists, our goal is to go along with nature, rather than change something that cannot be changed. Trying to change nature's basic laws is a wasted effort at best, and most often futile.

For instance, summer is very hot, so we wear fewer clothes. Wintertime is very cold, so we wear more. In wintertime you can't just say I want to wear a tank top today, so let's crank up the temperature outdoors a dozen degrees. Shall we pull the heavens down so the sun will be closer, just to satisfy a personal whim? The fact is, we can't pull the heavens down. It's not within our grasp.

Daoism, with all its esoteric study and ritual, is still opposed to the kinds of su-
pernatural force that attempts to impose itself above nature. Right now there are
people out there teaching who claim they have ways to literally pull the moon
towards them to face them, in a literal sense, and by extension pull the sun closer
too. Their philosophy that a person could influence the moon's orbit around the
earth or the earth's orbit around the sun, could be shown to be a theoretical
possibility, however slight, but physically it's impossible.

Even if you want to change nature, you still wind up changing it in accordance with natural laws. You can't go against nature to change it and you can't
destroy nature to put your own rules in place. And you shouldn't spread false-
hoods to the gullible. If you're a person, you're a person. You're not a god or a
spirit and you can't do things that gods or spirits can do, because you're a human
being. You can try to pretend to be god or to be a spirit or entity, but it will never
make you one and will eventually backfire in one way or another in your life. For
the Daoist philosophers, this is the central theme behind all their other principles.
There's a difference between what's real and what's fake.

We can use an image of holding up heaven, because it just supports what is
true, which is the sky is above us. When we use an image such as this, it's in
service of generating a feeling inside the body. We may not have the scientific
tools to measure yang energy, but we can definitely use the term to describe a
certain kind of sensation within the body. The sensation is what is real. So, gathering yin and yang energy into a Taiji ball is our process, but our goal is the
physical sensation and resulting changes to the body we hope to achieve. The
most important sensation we need to feel in this Taiji ball training is in the stomach area once your hands have formed the Taiji ball there. You need to have a
sensation of heat in the stomach area. This means heat in the physical stomach
and area around it, not in a *dantian* or other esoteric point.

Once you have held your position for a minute or two and you feel heat
coming into the stomach, then switch hands, so the lower hand is now on top
and the upper hand is below your sphere. To change hands, pass the lower hand
up and in front of the upper hand with the back of the
palm facing out, as if it is feeling along the outside of a
sphere. The upper hand meanwhile is rotating on the
wrist so that the back of the hand is also facing out and
then continuing to rotate until it is cupped at the bottom
of the Taiji ball. Both centers of the palms are directly
lined up at the stage in this dual movement when both
hands are completely parallel with both backs of the
hands are facing outwards completely. At this point in
the movement, which starts out nice and slow and easy,
speeds up to finish quickly in a flip. This flip is what
moves the hands right into their final position, back in
the ball with their positions reversed. It's a gentle and
quick flip that is done lightly, letting the wrists do all the work.

There is a reason for this type of flip, which we have already encountered before in this form, in the maintenance of qi. A light flip allows the sensations in the hands and body to switch over from yin to yang or vice versa. Whenever there is a swapping of energies, you want to switch into it with a light gesture, to allow your perceptions to adjust. Remember that qi collects in the joints and flows out from them when some momentum is created. You will feel differently with a light flip of the wrist than if you had moved without involving your joints.

Do this entire changing of the hand positions in a very carefully controlled manner, looking down at your hands as you move them, in order to further guide the qi. The lower hand stays in its exact position, with only the forearm doing the motion of the rotation until it reaches the top of its arc. Only then does the wrist rather quickly do the final flip so that the palm is pointing down. Meanwhile, the other hand is not really moving or rotating much and also does its ending flip rather quickly in unison with the top hand's flip. The hands soften somewhat as the rotation occurs, but once they have gotten into their finished position they are again cupped with a definite emphasis on the center of the palms, with some tension. Hold the ball again until you feel the hot sensation entering the stomach.

Don't confuse yourself by thinking about other concepts such as merging fire and water. The central theme of this exercise is Taiji. We are using it here, as we do throughout the Nine-Five Maintenance of Qi. You can think of it as conversion of fire and water, if that helps you remember it, but the original practice is Taiji, its symbol of yin and yang interconnected, and its significance in representing the ebb and flow of nature's cycles. To practice correctly, you must think of it as the Taiji ball. Even Dr. Wu also originally thought of this aspect of qigong as transforming fire into water and water into fire. But using that imagery will not help you as much as if you think of it as a Taiji ball. On the most basic level, it is the difference between a relatively abstract concept, fire and water, versus the simple, concrete and three-dimensional geometry of the sphere. Which one is closer to one's perception of his or her body?

Visualizations are only as powerful as the changes they inspire in mind and body. The ancient people, who developed the earliest qigong practices, had their certain ways and philosophies of doing it, and these actually are more accurate than the changes and innovations that were added on to them later. Some of the oldest herbal decoction formulas have only four ingredients. Over the years and especially in our current era, different people have tried to add more substances into these decoctions because they want to be innovative. They want to create something new and better, but a lot of time, it just doesn't work. The added complexity cancels out the simple efficiency of the original formula. The benefit of having those original four key ingredients that the ancestors combined is better than any other mixture we could come up with now.

It's not any different than studying cooking with an Italian chef or at a French culinary institute. They have stringent steps that must be followed to make the authentic recipes. If you follow those steps, you make the food and it tastes good. If you try to be unique and let your creative urge take over, you might add a little something here and there, or simplify the technique. The taste won't have the original flavor. Just the fact that it isn't the traditional dish may make it seem less tasty, no matter how much skill was put into it.

This now brings up the question of why we even bother to create new inventions and design new methodologies. A truly new innovation can only be based on the thorough understanding of the past as it has led all the way up to the present, and that is very rare and very difficult to achieve. In the history of humanity, there have been prolonged periods of stagnation where nothing happens, where people just study what happened in the past. This goes on for years or for generations and then after this period of prolonged repetitive study, the sheer repetition finally leads a thinker to the brink of discovering something new. On that precipice, then a little bit of ingenuity and inspiration must come into play to lead to that new invention at last. It's a very difficult, strenuous process.

You can always think about ways to be better, but you may have to practice a thousand times before you have the intuition to make a viable addition or change. Dr. Wu's take on it is it's better to go with the ancient original ways than the latest discovery, particularly when it comes to practices such as qigong that rely so heavily on physical knowledge of the body and its relationship to nature. It's not a question of being against creating innovations, but there must be full knowledge of what you do right now as part of the tradition before being capable of creating something substantial and new. If we follow the original teachings, trying not to change anything, we will gain their original benefits plus a new insight into the minds of our ancestors, as well as our own. This alone is a very valuable realization to achieve.

A person's success is a multi-faceted accomplishment. There's ambition, drive, effort, luck. It's never just one factor. But only through practice are you able to develop your personal voice. You can't simply imitate what someone else has done. You have to find your own path. But you must learn the fundamentals before you are able to propel yourself to a higher level. You have to know that taking that first step forward towards making the traditions your own is very hard, but it sets you on your journey.

Spreading the Qi

The sensation of heat is called "hot qi" (*reqi*). When holding the Taiji ball, you want to generate the hot qi on your hands and then transfer that heat into your stomach. If you can't feel it right away, hold your position for a little longer until you have it. It won't take long to come. After feeling the heat penetrating the stomach for the second time, we are going to shift the hands and build up even more sensation in them, so we can then pass the hands over the body across a special pathway used in Nine Palaces Qigong to distribute energy, enhance circulation and consolidate force.

After you feel the heat sensation, rotate your hands around the ball of Taiji so that now the palms are facing each other side to side, rather than top to bottom. Your lower hand comes out around your top hand and after that you bring your hands parallel to each other, engaging the wrists throughout the movement. As you rotate the hands, the elbows naturally come down so that they are pointed down, tucked in close to the body, with the hands only as far apart as that will allow. The palms soften out in this motion and stay softer for the next portion of the exercise.

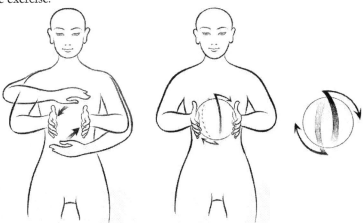

You're going to pull your hands away from each other than push them back to this ball-like distance three times. It's like pulling taffy. The taffy pulls work like this: the hands pull out then come together. When pulling out, the fingers are extended and held separated, held loose enough that they start drooping slightly downwards, rather than being held up stiff and straight. The thumb held out in its natural, relaxed position. There is no need for any muscle tension in the palms. You will be feeling a sensation building up between them without having to stiffen your muscles. As soon as the hand pushes back inwards the palms and fingers are now facing and held together in a gentle cup, rather than having the fingers spread and drooping.

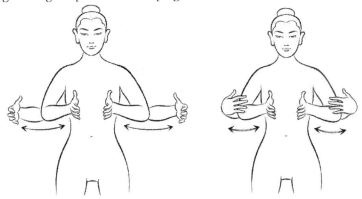

The wrists are not moving here as much as in some of our other exercises. The joints of the fingers and of course the elbows and shoulder sockets are the joints that come into play the most. Do this three times. Sense any sensation you might have. Note that when pulling out then in, the elbows will naturally flap up and then back down into the body, almost like wings.

It's useful to note what every part of the arm from shoulder to elbow to wrist and then fingers are doing, because the qi is moving along from the joints. Awareness of and involvement of the joints in qigong movements is an important concept, as we have pointed out before. This is the best way to do the movements properly, with maximum benefit. Always keep the elbows properly bent, to cause the hands to point more downward as you pull out and more parallel as you push in. One, two, and three pulls and pushes. It almost feels like holding a barrel while you're doing this, as your movements and the sensations in the hands are all very round. You must feel the sense of energy growing between the hands.

After the three pulls out then in, the hands cup close to each other, only a couple of inches apart in a very small ball. Cup like this for approximately five to ten seconds, or until you feel sensations. These sensations could be heat, tingling, heaviness, sometimes even a little soreness. Three pulls and then holding until the sensations come is one set. Do two more sets for a total of three. You must feel sensations in the hands to proceed to the next set of pulling. Yet again we are using the numbers nine, for the total number of pulls and five, for the fingers on our hand, embedded into our movements.

After the last set of pulls, you will definitely notice your hands feeling very different than normal. This is key before we move on. Hold for as long as you need to for it to register. Now we are going to run our hands across the fronts and backs of our body and then finally back to the front. Before Dr. Wu taught this form, he had never shown the hands following a pathway like this before. Since then, he has incorporated it into some other Nine Palaces forms but he has never discussed any further details about it. I think it is safe to recognize that although it might bear some connections to various acupuncture meridians and points, this is wholly a Daoist energetic pathway. It's most important to practice correctly and feel every sensation as you do.

Start by separating the hands from the ball and place them palms flat on the chest. To quickly describe the pathway, you will lower the hands down the front of the body all the way to the knees, travel around behind your knees, pass the hands up the backs of the legs to the kidneys and continue all the way up to the armpits, where the hands swing around again and end placed together into the prayer posture.

Now to describe the small details of the movement: After separating from the ball, remember that your elbows are down. Keep them down and slowly, with awareness, twist the hands around engaging the wrists, to place the palms on the upper chest on the upper portion of each pectoral muscle. The fingers are pointing up, loose hands over each pectoral muscle, fingertips an inch or two below the collar bone, as if putting the sensations in the hands from the ball into the body, in a rounded motion. The palms touch the chest, but gently and lightly. Then the wrists and hands start turning down so the fingers are pointing facing each other. We are going to pass the hands down on either side of the center line of the body, while still subtly turning the hands down until they are almost in the triangle position before reaching the lower *dantian*. When the hands come down,

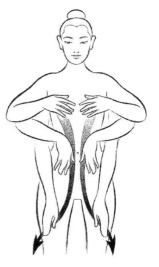

they are pushing along the lines that go down through the center of the nipples, down over the stomach channel lines on either side of the center line of the body, ending at the sides of the lower *dantian* area. Once over the lower *dantian*, you are not making a closed triangle, but by then the hands are pointed downwards enough that an open triangle is noticeable, with the hands about 2 inches apart. Then the wrists and hands turn outwards again another inch or two as the hands go below the lower *dantian*, so that the hands can be placed wide enough to pass down the fronts of the thighs. To clarify, the hands never close in a triangle around the lower *dantian*, but instead hug its sides then smoothly angle out just enough at the pelvic bone so the downward pass can continue in a line with the center of the thighs.

As the hands are passing down the center lines of the tops of the thighs, start to lower yourself by bending the knees, so that the knees are well bent once

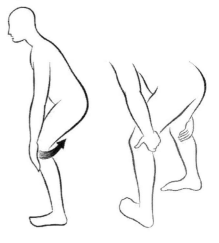

the hands have reached them after passing down the thighs. The fingers are pointing down as the hands go over the thighs. Once reaching the kneecaps, the hands briefly hold the kneecaps with fingers clutching over them lightly, then they continue around to the backs of the knees. This is the other reason you have bent down, to facilitate moving the palms around to the backs of the knees. Keep your back straight and leaned forward slightly so that the back and neck stay together in a straight line, chin in, allowing the front of the body to relax.

Pass the palms up the back centerlines of the legs while starting to straighten up. The fingertips will naturally be facing each other at this point. You are straightening back up as your hands go over the backs of the thighs and buttocks until you are mostly straightened out by the time the hands pass over the kidneys. The elbows are bent and the shoulders are rounded forward to allow the hands to be flat over the kidneys.

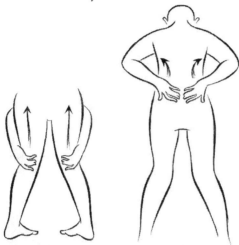

Just past the kidneys, now the hands are going to rotate up into a beak-like shape, with the palms flat and facing up with the fingers and thumbs forming a peak, without touching their tips together. The hands rotate up into this mudra while tracing along in two lines on the back, equal distances from the spine and the sides. By the time the hands reach the level of the armpits, they will be completely formed into the peak shape, pointing up.

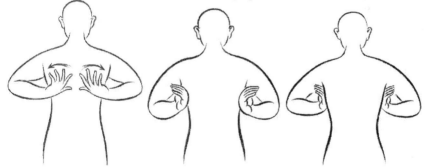

Now the wrists continue to rotate so the peaks are right under the armpits, with the elbow pointing back. Continue rotating so that the hands can exit out from the armpits to the front of the body, thumbs first. Keep the elbows back and the wrists and backs of the hands touching the body in the armpit while doing this. The thumbs are pointing up forward from the armpits while the wrists are twisting so that the rest of the fingers can move forward from the armpits too, so that by the time they have revolved completely, the palms are up but the fingers are now just pointing up and forward rather than up in a peak, with the thumbs held close. It's like the hands are "blooming" from the armpits to a standard palms-up position, with the elbows by now pointing down and held close into the body.

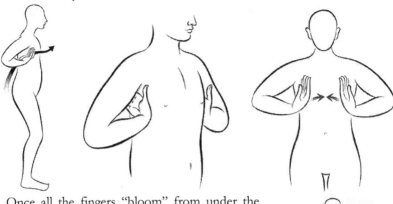

Once all the fingers "bloom" from under the armpits to the front of the body, we are going to bring them together so the backs of the hands touch, then continue to rotate them all the way around into a prayer position. When the hands come out from under the armpits, curve your upper back and cave in your chest so the shoulders are pressing in towards each other, creating some cupped space in the center of the chest in the process. The elbows, which had come all the way from behind the body to pointing down, stay held closely into the body.

The backs of the hands start to come together. The forearms twist so that the backs of the hands can face each other with the hands in a defined scoop position emphasizing the receptivity of the centers of the palms. Once the fingers have come close enough so that they are touching- pinkies first, followed by each next finger in turn, the palms transition to face up.

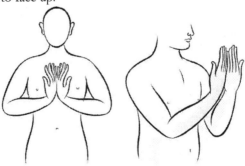

Move them forward and slanted upwards as if making an offering. The palms are not too rounded, but the pinkies' side of the hand is touching together completely. The arms push the offering hands forward and out from the body in the process, so that the forearms connect together completely as well along the same edge.

Finally, the motion is completed by rotating the hands and forearms together to touch, making the prayer hands posture. Pull the prayer hands back into the body towards the center of the chest, allowing the forearms to open again and the elbows point down loosely and naturally. The prayer hands are held at the upper chest level when finished, with the head slightly bowed. Throughout this entire process, keep your eyes open but looking downwards through hooded lids. This downwards positioning of the eyes will re-  lax you and allow you to follow the flow of the qi as you pass your hands across your body. This completes the first half of the Dragon Shape Form.

Chapter Nine

Pushing the Prayer Wheel

There are two points in the Nine-Five Maintenance of Qi where we clasp the hands in a tight solid lock, when we pull the hands during the tonification of qi and now in this last portion of the Dragon Shape Form, that completes the entire process. Before we clasped the hands and pulled outwards. Now we clasp the hands together to push. We are going to clasp our hands in a symbolic posture and push around us, forming the shape of a square. It is a simple movement, but goes deep to the roots of why we practice qigong in the first place. There are layers of philosophical significance, and layers of sensations to be experienced, but we stand in the middle of them all, forming them around us with our two clasped hands.

When we pull during the tonification of qi, it is symbolized by the Chinese character for the number ten, which looks like a cross, which is of course the shape that we are making for the qi with our bodies. Now when we push and form the square, the movement is symbolized by the root character *wéi*, which means an enclosure, and is shaped like a square. We are indeed building a square energy around us when we do this practice. It can be a very powerful feeling. But there is something more than just the simple path that we trace with our hands.

Put the cross of the character for ten inside of the square character *wéi*, and together they make the character *tian*, "field," that is, the fertile rice field we have spoken of at length. This character *wei* isn't just a square. It has a roundness to the way it is drawn, and has a volume inside of it. There is a circle inside of its square, although that is only hinted at by its slightly bulging strokes. That's what makes it an enclosure, worthy of turning into a field, where crops may grow.

You can only produce crops in a field, not from stone or concrete. Only in a field can you produce something substantial. It is a square, given volume by a circle, bisected by a cross. The very center of the cross in the center of the square is its midpoint, its strongest place of power. And where is the midpoint within us? It is the umbilicus, the point where the umbilical cord entered us when we were fetuses in the womb. It is the source of all nourishment, what made us who we are today, living on our planet earth. To practice this Nine Palaces form is to come to understand the true meaning of these words.

Mantras and Movements

We finished our last section standing solidly with hands in the prayer position at the center of the chest. First we bring our hands into the special grip that we will use to push. In the prayer position, both hands are pressed together flat, palms and fingers touching. For both men and women, take your right hand and turn it horizontally so that centers of the palms are still touching, but the hands now form a cross. The fingers of the right hand are pointing outwards. Now slide the left hand down so that you can grip the top of the right hand with all four fingers, while the thumb grips the right hand from underneath.

The right hand is wedged in the crook between the thumb and the rest of the left hand and it grips onto it with the fingers folded over the outer edge of the hand, covering the pinkie and any fingers next to it that they can reach. The thumb on the right hand falls over the second knuckles of the left hand, although it is not necessary to grip them hard with the thumb. The firm grip from both hands come from the fingers, not the thumbs.

If you look at this hand posture, we have a vertical hand and a horizontal hand. The vertical hand is yang and the horizontal hand is yin. We are going to push with the horizontal hand, which means we are going to start our pushing going towards the left. Why do we press the hands together in this way? This posture confers a running force, like a horse galloping. It gives you stored energy and helps you to be motivated. As we get older, we don't have as much drive to get things done. We put things off for the next day. This practice tries to remind us that we have to keep working to store up our reserves.

We've already wished for the qi to flow where we need it to grant us our desires in the utilization of qi. This helps us to remember the drive that we need inside of us to make these wishes a reality. You need to have the two forces of yin and yang, desire and drive, awakened in the hands when you start to turn. We use the word "turn," because we are doing more than just pushing out in the shape of a square. We are going to use our whole body to form a strong central core, as well as provide another layer of opposing force. We aren't just pushing. We are turning a prayer wheel. In Tibet, the prayer wheels symbolize the wheel of reincarnation. With this movement, we become our own prayer wheel. Instead of spinning a prayer wheel in a temple, this is your prayer wheel to turn.

As you're pushing, male or female, you always want to push to the left first. If you're a woman, you do have the option to reverse hands, and make your left hand the horizontal axis of the grasp and then push to the right with the left, horizontal hand. There is a reason for this, based on the requirements for the monks in the White Cloud Monastery. We are all equally people but as our roles differ, our work and responsibilities change.

Even amongst the monks, there are two tiers, two different levels of service. There are monks that belong to the temple versus monks who live and work outside but go there for prayers. The temple monks are sworn to the order and live in the temple, never leaving its walls, perfectly integrated into its daily duties and chores, as well as officiating at prayer and conducting rituals for the public. The lay monks also belong to the order, but they don't belong to the temple itself. They can go home and go to work and just come for prayers and cultivation. Temple monks who belong to and are a part the temple, can be males or females but the teaching they are given have no gender differences. However the lay monks that are external to the temple, are given a gender differentiation in the ways they practice. A nun member of the laity may choose to push to the right first.

women   men

Dr. Wu's personal experience is that pushing to the left is better for everybody, because of the significance of the prayer wheel. Tibetan monks always rotate their prayer wheels in one direction and the prayer wheels found in other Buddhist temples that also use prayer wheels, are turned uniformly in one direction, as well. It's not like monks push them one way and nuns push them another way. The wheel itself is in service to the teachings. The prayer wheel is the symbol of the purification of prayer. You can say that for either gender, to push to the left first is a sign that you are dedicating yourself to the peace and protection of forces that are larger than you. So whether you accept that idea, or just want to make the practice simpler to remember, always push to the left first, using your right hand as the horizontal element.

Even though we push in the shape of a square, there is a circle inside of this square. To break down the movements we make, we start with the hands clasped at the center of the chest. You know it's the right height from the rest of your stance. You want to have your shoulders down and relaxed and you want to see that your upper arms and forearms are at right angles. Make sure to press your hands together so that they are gripped firmly, but the rest of your body stays loose, including the arms, shoulders and chest. As we were saying, we want to create an opposing force within the body to magnify the push to the left.

Push firmly to the left using your hand to push and sending your forearms to the left, still on the same horizontal plane. As you do this, to create the opposing force, you want to twist your chest and hips out to the right, opposite to your arms. This can be as subtle or as strong a movement as feels comfortable. You're not trying to stretch. You're trying to bring out movement from the spine.

If you are already very loose and flexible, you will naturally be able to twist your body to the right with a large range of motion. If you're just beginning or you're feeling stiff, don't force yourself. A small movement can still generate a lot of force since the force itself comes from the centerline and the center point of the body. Just getting a little twist at the waist at the navel can be enough if necessary.

The navel is the center point of this practice, as we have said. One element that assists with this body shift is the lower body, hips and knees. If you let your knees dip and switch to the right, the hips and the rest of the spine will follow. Just drop down an inch or two as you push left and sway the knees over to the right, keeping your balance from the pelvic floor. Your body will automatically move with the correct form.

Once you have pushed to the left, then push your clasped hands outwards from the left side of your body all the way forward, completely straightening the arms. Again, keep the shoulders and upper body loose. Augment this forward motion by caving in your chest and torso, as the opposite force to your forward push. The upper back will naturally round outwards from this push. Your knees are already to the left. Rather than bringing them backwards behind your body, just drop them down another couple of inches. You are lowering down, which will press more of your thighs together, creating a firm central core within your stance. By hollowing the torso, the back automatically stretches outwards to the back. This is what provides the opposite force you want for your second push.

For the third push, your arms are out in front of you on your left. Rather than using the vertical left hand to push to the right, still use your horizontal right

hand to lead the motion to swing the arms straight across to the right. For this sweep, definitely do your best to swing chest and hips to the left. It can release a lot of tension in the spine. The knees will also shift to the left, again dropping down a little more. The more you can drop down into this position, the more you are opening up your entire spine and strengthening all your muscles down the center of your body. There is no need to exaggerate the movement. Do what feels right.

The sensation of the movement will guide you to the correct amount of effort. Take that very literally, as this is quite a physically exerting exercise. If you are straining by using muscular force instead of momentum coming from the joints, you will feel every little knot and blockage in your body. What you want to be feeling is the powerful energy of the square and the cushioning force of the circle.

You want to feel that as you push in each direction, the force of your movement can carry its trajectory out to infinity. The looser you are as you push, the more you will open your body up, for very fast results. The only muscular strength to use is in your grip and your arms and that is firm, but not intense.

For the last of our four directions, pull the hands and arms back into the body, keeping the arms on the right, for the last corner of your square. Feel your muscles engage as you pull everything in. Lower down to your deepest point from the knees as you do this. Your hip will still be over to the right but the knees and thighs can come together closely. As you pull in, shift the engagement in your muscles from the back to the front of the body. You don't need to puff your chest forward to oppose the pulling in of the arms, but you want to feel like the muscles inside of the chest are filling out from back to front.

While still keeping all of your muscles engaged, firmly push the hands back to the center of the chest, while slowly straightening back up into the standard stance. This can create a very powerful sensation of release pouring down the center of your body. The stability of your stance and of all your muscles will let this energy pour through you very smoothly. It certainly makes sense why we did so many other exercises to relax and strengthen the central core of the body before we come to the four direction pushing. Allow yourself as much time as you wish resting at your return to center before making your next rotation. Let your body tell you if you would like to be fast and explosive or go slowly, savoring every move.

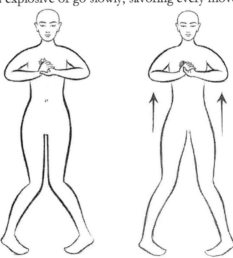

You want to make a total of nine rotations, starting with the push to the left. At the end of the ninth, twist your hands in one smooth movement out of the clasp, into a prayer position and then around so that now the left hand turns horizontal and the right becomes the vertical. Repeat the turning nine times in the other direction.

Think mechanically, if you are so inclined. The circle is your torso turning with the same motion as a ball bearing housed in a square seating, which are the braced quality of your arms locked together by your hands, your hips and the square, four directional movement. The navel point is the center of your momentum in each push and pull. Let it be loose and moving with great freedom, out to infinity. The center line of your body, and in fact your spine, pelvic floor and lower body stance, will provide a stable core from deep within the earth, all the way to the heavens. It will be at once the shaft around which you turn your prayer wheel and also by the end of the movement, as you pull back to the center, a receptacle that will fill with an overflowing fountain of energy that you have generated. This is a physical experience and a consciousness shift. Using the force within your body is the deepest principle of Nine Palaces Qigong and the foundation of Daoist rejuvenation and harmonization with heaven and earth.

Potent Words

There is one last element of this pushing practice. It acts as the final mechanism for opening yourself to the energy of the universe. When you push in each direction, there is a four word mantra you must recite out loud, one word for each direction. It is a chant arising from the *Book of Changes*. The words are *yuan, heng, lie,* and *zhen,* used like a mantra or invocation.

We all know the epic *Journey to the West* (*Xiyou ji*). In the story, the Monkey King was trapped in the Buddha's palm. Buddha flipped his palm down and a whole mountain collapsed onto the Monkey King. And while he was doing that, he was chanting *an mani bami hong,* that is, the Chinese version of the Sanskrit *om mani padme hum* that invokes the power of the *Lotus Sutra*. Because of this Buddhist chant, he was able to control and subdue the Monkey King, who was causing all kinds of chaos in heaven. When the monk, Tang Sanzang, climbed to the top of the mountain in order to save the monkey, he had to remove a talisman that was affixed to its peak. Before he was able to take off the scroll, he had to say "*yuan heng li zhen*" in order to lift the incantations that kept the Monkey King subdued.

The formula is part of the language of the universe. It consists of four words using four tones. Together with the five words and tones that were spoken by the Buddha, they form a nine-tone universal whole. These nine tones are the basis of the celestial language. You can say it out loud or you can say it from within, but you must say "*yuan heng li zhen*" when you push. Your first push to the side, say *yuan.* Your second push forward, *heng.* The third push across to the other side is *li,* and while pulling the arms back in, you say *zhen.*

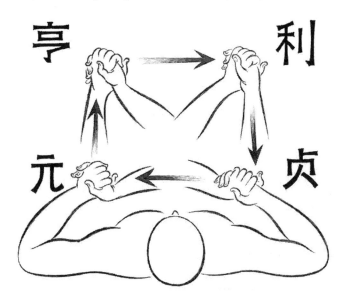

The mantra is the equivalent of *ami tuofo* in Buddhism, the name of the Amitabha Buddha of longevity and light. When you say these four words, a great deal of information from nature can come to you. You can call out these words or say them in your heart. It is a symbol from nature, in line with the tantric and shamanic practices of Tibetan Buddhism. In the celebrated Daoist alchemical engraving of the circulation of qi, *Chart of Internal Passageways*, Laozi sits at the top of the ear shaped form and the green-eyed Tibetan lama with arms outstretched, looking up, is directly beneath him in the middle above the "heart" of the ear.

Dr. Wu's teacher, Master Du Xinling, was in communication with the thirteenth Dalai Lama Thubten Gyatso (1876-1933). They talked about many different subjects. In their correspondence, Dr. Wu's master told him this story from the era of Genghis Khan, who had appointed the High Lama of his time. The fearsome warlord has already invaded a large area. Once Khan conquered the lands as far west as Hungary, Qiu Chuji sought out the Khan and told him he shouldn't invade any further and should come back to Inner Mongolia. Khan asked why he should believe him. To him, the bigger the territory, the better.

Qiu Chuji asked to allow the Great Khan's eagle come sit on his palm. He told the warlord he would stop the eagle from flying up from his hand, saying "If I can do this, you will know my qigong is strong and you will listen to my advice." He was able to perfectly counter the eagle's launching force and prevented it from flying up, so from that moment Qiu Chuji became Khan's advisor and was listened to in all matters of state. When he returned to the White Cloud Monastery, he brought Genghis Kahn's eagle back with him, a golden eagle as big as a person. To commemorate the event, this famous Daoist stone engraving was created. This is why the Daoist monk is on the top of the engraving and the lama, representing the reign of Genghis Khan is just below and above the heart.

Qiu Chuji taught the Dragon Shape Form to Genghis Khan while he served as his advisor, specifically the mantra of *yuan heng li zhen*. It is the four tone invocation of the *Book of Changes*, held sacred just as *om mani padme hum* is revered in Buddhist liturgy.

The *Book of Changes* contains the written history of this chant. According to the *Book of Changes*, there is a power of great force that is exerted when you shout out these words. There's not much explanation we can give to this based on our scientific knowledge of our world. We all know a few unbelievable sounding accounts of random impossible occurrences, alien encounters, ghosts, and a man driving his car in Europe suddenly appearing halfway across the world in Mexico with no explanation of how he got there. We might even know someone who had something inexplicable happen, or even have a few personal tales of our own, but even seeing these things firsthand, it's difficult to wrap our minds around their reality. We can't use our everyday perceptions to explain them. Because so few of us are exposed to the phenomena, it's rare to have firsthand experience of these matters. There just isn't enough data in the pool to begin a controlled study.

For the sake of the tradition or just for Dr. Wu's sake if needs be, practice the Dragon Shape Form speaking these words out loud at each push. There is a substantial amount of force and power behind them. For this whole form there are several points that have to be done absolutely correctly. One of the most important is the chant *yuan heng li zhen*. Saying them out loud is best. You don't have to say them loudly. Just let the sounds flow out of your mouth to express all the feelings and thoughts you want to release. *Yuan* represents the universe, the origin of everything. *Heng* is a relief, a sound that relieves you. *Li* is a matter of existence, it allows you to exist. And *zhen* belongs to nature, meaning whatever comes from nature ultimately goes back to nature. Practicing this exercise can increase your innate ability to fight off disease. On a deeper level it can help you to face and overcome difficulties that will arrive in your life.

Dr. Wu's personal belief is that this will help you survive the immanent disasters we face in this era of global pandemics and socio-economic turmoil. He feels the White Cloud Monastery created the practice just to prepare people for the 2010's and 20's and that this was why his own teachers adjured him to present this material publicly. This practice has stood the test of time, allowing the monastery and the country to withstand many difficulties.

At one monastery on Mount Jiuhua, where the monks practice the nine palaces, when a huge fire spread over the mountain, it only burned up to the courtyard of the monastery then abruptly stopped. This monastery also possesses a "golden body," which is a seemingly mummified human body covered in gold (*roushen*). It looks like a statue, but if you read the plate beneath it, it reveals it to be a human body, but still not the highest attainment of cultivation.

Attaining the Rainbow Body is the highest aspiration of Nine Palaces Qigong. It is a practice through which an initiate attempts to transubstantiate, or leave the material plane, rather than die in the body. For those who try but do not fully succeed, their shrunken bodies may be left behind. Even this is an esoteric feat that is past normal understanding and these remains are revered as holy relics in Daoist and Buddhist temples alike. The body left behind in the Jiuhua shrine is seated in the position of the pushing hands practice.

When you have finished nine turns in each direction, lower the hands down to form the triangle at the lower *dantian*, and step with your left foot to your right foot, to bring your legs together. Bow your head slightly, bend your knees an inch or so to relax the hips and spend that moment absorbing all of your sensations. You have completed the Dragon Shape Form and the Nine-Five Maintenance of Qi. This is the exact, original form, as taught almost eight hundred years ago by Qiu Chuji to Genghis Khan and held by his lineage of the Dragon Gate sect, in the White Cloud Monastery. Nothing has been added to the form. Nothing has been omitted. This is how it was taught. This is how it was learned. This is how it is, even its name. This is what Dr. Wu learned as a child and this is how he is teaching it to you now. It is his hope that you practice with sincerity.

Why We Practice

In the monasteries of Tibet, continuously rotating the prayer wheels is a cultivation practice. The cultivation lies in watching the turning of the wheels, never letting them stop. The message is that you are not really practicing the qigong. The qigong is practicing you. If you are the prayer wheel, than it is a qigong of you. The power of qigong practice is already there. Joining with the practice so that you identify yourself with its flow, is how the practice enhances you. Making the movements of the nine palaces a part of your inner identity allows them to give you their benefits. You need to use strength to push. It's not just the two hands together, but the entire body movement of pushing that demonstrates a vertical force versus a horizontal force. You push in the opposite direction of the rest of your body.

For a Daoist, this exemplifies how the greatest enemy one will encounter is oneself. As you press your hands together and push, you will gain an awareness of yourself in your life. Any situation possesses yang, the vertical hand, and yin, the horizontal hand. Slap your two hands together to recognize this. Vertical is yang and horizontal is yin and the unification of yang and yin is Taiji. So any situation has two different aspects, two ways of looking at it.

Clasp your hands in the start position of the pushing. If it's not success, it's failure. Those are the two ways and that is in your hands. It's for you to perceive, as your hands push to the *yuan* position. It's for you to push, hands in *yuan* position. It's for you to strive, to excel, hands at *heng* position. It's for you to be persistent and capable, hands at *Li* position. As you push and say *yuanheng lizhen*, all the way over to *zhen* position, then it's no more, no more action you can take.

Even when you get to the point of tracing the distance between *zhen* position and the return to the starting posture, the very end, where there's nothing left for you to do about the matter, and all outcome is based on the will of heaven, you still have to look at the will of heaven. With each movement, you perceive the balance of your efforts within the will of heaven, which is always present no matter how strong your efforts are. Some people can succeed and some people no matter how hard they try can't succeed. The will of heaven is a factor.

What do we mean by the will of heaven? It is a tendency in the patterns of its flow. Perceiving this tendency translates into opportunity. Sometime during a previous month you might not have been successful in your works and actions, but this month you are victorious. And just because you are successful now, does not guarantee that you will meet with the same success later on. So what does it depend on? It depends on your persistence. We are like a leaf on a tree, never knowing which way the wind will blow us. There's nothing to be done, it's beyond our control. There's nothing that can control the wind. On the other hand, what if instead of the leaf on the tree, we are the wind blowing towards the tree. Even then, we never will know which leaf might fall as a result of our gusts. All this, because of the myriad variables in the universe, too many to grasp from within their midst.

But through our own cultivation and development, we can trace our steps back and connect to our higher self, which the Daoists comprehend the half of us that splits from us at birth and resides as a star at a vantage point high in the all-knowing heavens. To be realigned with our other half, we will then truly feel and appreciate all the vagaries of heaven's will. There's a Chinese saying, "People are like the ocean" (*renhai baoma*), there are so many of us. To find a true friend is very rare, one who is sincere to you always. On the other hand, isn't accomplishing anything of value in this world just as rare and difficult, even when attempted by one's efforts alone? By practicing qigong, you can align yourself and shorten the distance between you and your other half so that you will not get lost in this world. That's the essence of why we practice this Nine Palaces Qigong.

There's a trend happening in China today, where parents try to have children so that they will be born in certain zodiac years over others. The belief is if the child is born in the animal hour that corresponds to the animal year it will be even more fortunate. With modern medical advances, families are resorting to delivery via C-section just for this purpose. The hope is to match the hour to the year so the child will be more successful. But this is not in accor*dan*ce with the beliefs of the Daoists. In Daoism, the understanding is to do everything the natural way, to go along with nature. Many people are born at the exact same time. Some will be successful in the future, some people won't. Not everyone who was born at the same moment a president was born become president. Your success also depends on your ability and your dedication towards what you do, not just the time of your birth. This is why developing yourself with the hand pushing of Longxing gong is very important.

Then there's also the question of how much of an influence one's environment has over one's success. Even if you aspire to greatness and strive to be good, do you have the right environment to succeed? Are the external factors going to help you to accomplish your goal? There has to be some natural internal aptitude. A chicken can't hatch from a stone, no matter what kind of incubator you put it in. But barring the worst extremes, external circumstances are very influential.

A chicken can't hatch from a stone, but it can hatch from an egg. Only if the egg is exposed to the right amount of heat, will it produce a chicken. If you refrigerate an egg as soon as it is laid it will never hatch. The two sets of conditions are very important, both the internal and external factors. A successful person needs to possess both characteristics, both the internal capabilities and the external opportunities. The pushing and the power of saying *yuan heng li zhen* develops a force within the body. That force allows you to merge what's inside of you with the universe. This is what brings harmony and transcends the conditions of mundane life. It is a physical training to release your power to merge into oneness.

The Dragon Shape Form goes back to Laozi. He taught his students how human life is only one small part of the journey. There are a lot of things out there we don't know. The only events we can explain through science are those that repeat themselves, but there are many things that are not repeatable and cannot be studied so scientifically. Gaining the awareness of two opposing forces helps us to see both sides of things. One generates two. Two generates three. Three is the number of the human born of the heavens and the earth.

There are always good and bad aspects to anything. When we were first born, we didn't want to leave the womb. We cry as we are suffering from entering this world. A lady has the fortunate appearance of a stalk of bamboo. Bamboo represents fortune and luck, but it's split into segments, which indicates that every seven to eight years she will have hardships in her life. What is fortune? The absence of pain is true fortune. How much money do you need when you are fast asleep? You can't take anything with you when you depart from this life. This is the Daoist way of thinking.

All in all, to remember the two opposing forces in your clasped hands as you push, gives you the most important message of the Nine-Five Maintenance of Qi. Realization is literally in your hands. Everything has a flip side, success or failure. Anything can be viewed from with perspective. When you are having your greatest luck, it means some misfortune is coming to you. When you reach the peak of success, danger will be lurking, ready to strike. When you are at your lowest, fortune has been waiting the whole time to now come to you. Practice the Nine-Five Maintenance of Qi to deal with all of these changes. It gives the strength to withstand and the insight to persevere.

Seeing both sides of matters helps us to enlarge our opportunities. There's a reason for all things, from sickness and divorce to gaining a fortune. How do we discern the reasons behind the changes in our lives? We gain two different forces through practice of qigong. It's not only that we do exercises that involve opposing forces, the practice of them trains us to be more aware of these forces as they exist in every single thing and event around us. The physical sensation becomes an intuitive awareness, which then in turn manifests as new, heightened physical sensations. This is the cycle of training in Nine-Five Maintenance of Qi.

We are able to see things more clearly by being able to see both sides, the yin and the yang that make up the event. Usually we only see the success or the failure, but success or failure is only fifty percent of any situation. There are always opportunities that run alongside the favorable or unfavorable trends we are coping with. The woman who looked like a stalk of bamboo should plant bamboo around the house, especially ones that are smaller, with low growing stalks. This will help her health. Cows and goats seek grassy lands with water. You don't have to worry about them. They roam far and wide for pastureland and then find their way back to the barn when the weather gets cold.

The Nine-Five Maintenance of Qi is designed for aligning the two halves of the body. Connecting these halves creates effortlessness and luck in opportunity. This is way, along with the emphasis on opposing force, there is such a strong emphasis on the centerline of body. At first there are exercises that open it and clear it of blockages and then at last with the hand pushing, we generate enormous force around it and within it. With Nine Palaces we are trying to align the half of our awareness that is in the heavens as a star with the half that is the awareness within our body. Sometimes you don't know why you do certain things. One word might come out of your mouth at just the right time or you might decide to go someplace on a whim which turns up a great opportunity. Once your own star is in line with you as close as possible you won't make as many mistakes.

Daoism believes in opportunity and also in luck. Some people seem to have better luck and are able to accomplish all sorts of things without difficulties. Life can feel like a long drive where you are missing or making every green light. Some people have one marriage with bronze, silver and golden anniversaries. Some people have many divorces. A patient came to see Dr. Wu with her children in tow. He could tell that she'd been through divorces. Her children were all fighting and hitting each other to such a degree, he felt they must be from different fathers. The patient then told Dr. Wu he was right. She'd had divorces and will be soon divorced again, since she still is looking for the man of her dreams.

However, Daoist research has concluded from centuries of data that marriages and divorces are life events that are pre-determined to a large degree. Dr. Wu had her practice the Nine-Five Maintenance of Qi and her marriage stabilized. When she did the practice, it would give her new thoughts in her mind about her life. She saw that she can't change others and can only change herself. She changed her body and her mind together, in the unified manner that qigong practice is so effective at, and it improved her marriage. No matter what the calculations say, a portion of our opportunities is always up to us. A shift in our perspective creates the shift in our fate. The practice of qigong aligns us with these possibilities.

According to the *Book of Changes*, it is believed that every person is a star in the sky, in the heavens. The moment you are born into your physical, mortal body, only half of that soul is yours. The other half of your soul is still held by the star that you belong to. You have to dig deeply into the ancient records of China and also ancient Egyptian texts to find the references to this esoteric concept, but there are documents from both cultures that discuss it.

The moment you were born, you were no longer fully aligned with your heavenly star. A deviation occurs that has its own trajectory and momentum. As one ages or becomes ill, the alignment can go even further off course. Death occurs at the point where the so far off that the connection between them can no longer be maintained. The compass was invented to help navigate the sea and now we have global positioning systems everywhere, from our cars to our phones, all to coordinate where we are in relation to our surroundings. We use GPS to prevent us from getting lost. We have a GPS for our soul as well. Its observations have been chronicled in the annals of Chinese historical documents for thousands of years. The study of *Book of Changes* and qigong both explore the methods to strengthen and reroute this alignment back, for the sake of our physical life.

We have parallels that can be understood with modern technology, such as how satellite dishes must generally point south to properly pick up the feeds coming from orbit. The same idea is found in the *Book of Changes*, which also determines the south as the source of all communication and knowledge. If you're having health problems, it means you are misaligned with your original star on the north-south axis. The north-south plane determines your health. If your star's location is too high up away from your body to have a clear connection, then you will have health issues. However if you're having difficulties in your career, that means you are misaligned with east and west. You star is too far off to the side of your body's location. Based on whatever problem you are facing, you need to adjust your alignment with the original soul.

There are two ways of making this adjustment. First of all is qigong. Practicing qigong softens your body. Diligent practice will bring you to the point where you are like an infant, very soft and malleable. When you reach that level of fluidity, you will be able to adjust your opportunities and adjust yourself.

The second way to align yourself is based on using position and colors to make the adjustment. For instance, if you're having health issues that are causing sleep disorders, what direction are you sleeping in? Normally when people are not sick, they can follow the seasons to determine the direction of their head when they sleep. Commonly, in spring and summer you should lie on your side so that you face east. For fall and winter, you should be lying on your side facing west. That's a general rule of thumb.

But whatever side you lie on, your head should be facing south and your feet should be facing north. That's the direction in which you should sleep at night. These are the basic standard principles in terms of what direction you should sleep. If you were born in spring and you're not sick, it's fine if your head is positioned in the east, rather than the south. If you do become sick, then you have to regulate your sleeping habits and make sure your head is in south. These are examples of the adjustments you would need to make for health issues.

There are different adjustments to be made for career. Remember that it's very rare that heaven will give you both perfect health and a successful career. It's very unlikely that a person will achieve both in perfect balance. But because of its rarity, it gives us the opportunity to take a path through the middle and have a moderate amount of both health and material success. This is the Daoist way of finding an opportunity within the limitations of circumstances.

How do we adjust the ratio so we take the best of the two? We can find the best mixture through the practice of qigong. Dr. Wu illustrated this idea with by making an expanding ball with both hands, as in pulling the fingers out from the Taiji ball, then cupping the left palm and making a five finger peak mudra with the right hand, with its point pointing into the center of the palm about an inch above the left palm's center indentation. This is an interesting hand posture when you think about collecting then sending out qi from the fingertips, using convex and concave body postures. To practice qigong, we need to practice with heaven, earth, and trees. Other forms of gongfu will not help you in this. It cannot change. Also *Book of Changes* calculations can help you, which is why they appear again and again shaping the movements of qigong. Without these two elements, it's very difficult to make the changes you need.

If you have an immediate career situation that you need to be successful, such as a big business meeting in the morning, then your head should be positioned in the east as you sleep and your feet should be facing west, then also lie on your side facing south. This will definitely help you in terms of your career. The colors you wear and surround yourself with in your home and daily life should also be based on the color of the correct directions for your needs. The idea is to generate a qi field around you from correct positioning and additional assistance from matching color vibration. This field will then resonate at the pace and angle to best alter the trajectory of your star and bring it back to your body.

To understand this concept is to understand how qigong practice realigns yourself with your celestial star. Chinese culture has taken this very seriously for millennia. We've talked before about how much study, repetition and then sheer drive is involved to discover truly important new inventions. It was because of the seven of the nine stars that were visible to the eye, that the compass was created. This is how deeply ingrained the belief and desire for uniting the two parts of our consciousness, the human and the celestial, truly is for the practice of qigong.

The practice of Nine Palaces Qigong is the only thing that is necessary to find the location of your star. There is no need for astrological calculations or complicated apparatus. You will feel it with your body. Everything you do in this world is in one sense or another either indirectly controlled or directly dictated by your celestial star. That's why there is a Chinese saying, *touren sanshe ling*: "Three feet above your head spirits and gods are looking over you." That sensation of a three foot distance above you is something we develop with qigong practice. As you are practicing, you and your celestial star will find each other again and unite. Just as we realign our car tires so that we can drive straight and safely to our destination, through the Nine-Five Maintenance of Qi we are connected to our best source of guidance to help us navigate our lives. You must practice to gain your own awareness and appreciation of this assistance.

Because changes can't come overnight, we must accept this is a gradual process. Even after you change yourself at your root, new opportunities come gradually. It requires patience and also acceptance. You must be able to recognize that if you change yourself for the best, and things still do not improve, that means the will of the heavens is dictating your timeline. A Daoist can face that sometimes destiny is an inexorable force. There will be some reason why things don't change for the best, even after you have gone to great lengths to surround yourself with the ideal Fengshui. If the will of heaven is involved, that means no matter where you live, no matter what kind of charms and talismans you employ, heaven dictates your fortune.

Of course to discuss the will of heaven, all of its separate meanings and manifestations, and all the different measures and countermeasures you can take, you could fill a dozen volumes with the details or more. To sum it up for our purpose is simple. If what is happening in your life is the will of the heavens, just wait. You could spend a lot of money changing and rearranging, but it won't matter.

Don't think your life will always be difficult just because your experiences are difficult now. Just let time pass and things will be better. This is because the essence of all things is yin and yang. The peak of your success in itself is the turning point towards a catastrophe that will befall you. And when you hit rock bottom, just at the infinitesimal moment where you can't fall any lower that is when fortune will come to you. It's an oscillation, a wave passing along the timeline of our lives. The pinnacle of your victories is the beginning of your descent and when your life is in ruins and nothing seems to be working that will spark a new cycle of better things to come.

This is why some people never aspire to be at the lead, but strive to be further back in the pack, so they can stay in the game a little longer. But you really have to understand the philosophy behind it. You have to sit and think and ask why and how. It's human nature for a person to make a million dollars and then immediately aspire to make two or three or five million the next year. The drive always trying to get to the top is common thinking for many. It's not a bad thing to think this way, but if this relentless ambition for bigger, better and more is your single motivation, then one day something wrong will happen, and it will be difficult to handle. The very thing that drove you to your goal might not be always the right thing for what your life needs, because life is always changing around and inside of us.

The philosophy of Nine-Five Maintenance of Qi is distilled from the personal reflections of Laozi in conjunction with immutable patterns found within *Book of Changes* calculation. Just know that the tallest tree is the tree that is most prone to fall. Be a tree, but not the tallest in the forest. This is some of the Daoist theory that guides the practice of qigong. The *Book of Changes* is clear on the fact that heaven will not give you everything. To have a beautiful face, lots of money and perfect health is rare to be found and if one has it all, then the chance for trouble goes up as well. Something is bound to go wrong in one of those three areas. Maybe bankruptcy, or unexpected health problems or an early death. You can't have all three, longevity, money and good health. It's our innate human nature to strive for all three. Only through your physical efforts and practicing qigong can bring you close to this ideal, by bringing more balance and more harmony to your perspective.

We perform Nine-Five Maintenance of Qi in front of the sun. We are trying to be seen. We want to universe to notice us. The *Book of Changes* will show you a set number of years you are meant to live, but when you do good thing, it lengthens your predetermined time. If you do something bad it cuts down the time, as well. A whole book in the Daoist cannon was written devoted to just this one topic. When you go into a dense forest, the sun is very hot, but the trees are sheltering you from being burned by its rays. Can you see the meaning in this? When you adopted a stray cat or dog, you saved a life. Then you are able to enhance your own lifespan.

Dr. Wu knows a woman with a lot of adopted stray dogs. Every month her paycheck goes towards feeding all these animals. She owns a convenience store in a good location but the business has been not doing that well. Liquor stores in the area are doing well, but hers hasn't done much in over twenty years. She's dedicated her whole life to her animals. Why it didn't help her work, she wondered to Dr. Wu. Had she been so bad in a previous life that the dogs couldn't help? Dr. Wu told her, you have done well by helping these animals, but to activate their blessing, her good deed must combine with the practice of qigong. You may believe in Guanyin Bodhisattva, but if you don't pray to him, will he hear you? If you're in class but you never ask the teacher a question, will the teacher know you're there? You have to connect your communication to nature and to heaven.

Burning a stick of incense in a temple or making the sign of the cross are like making a phone call to god. The gods will be able to know you're calling. She cares for all these dogs, but the heavens didn't know about it. You need to do qigong to let the universe know about your good deeds. Then you gain the benefit of them. You have to give something up to gain something new. You can increase your life beyond your allotted time by doing this practice, as much as by saving the lives of humans and animals. Daily practice of Nine-Five Maintenance of Qi can in general allow you to increase your total lifespan by a third. It combines with the patterns and rhythms of the *Book of Changes* to start changing things for you. It involves a lot of esoteric Daoist philosophy underneath, but the simple way to put it is, if you want something, you have to give it up first. Make room for something new to come in.

We are asking for help from the universe. We need humility and a sense of proportion. The Nine-Five Maintenance of Qi is a practice for protection, so it is true you are asking for something. This is why we work so hard to unite our human needs with heaven and earth. We may not be able to see the full scope of their larger purposes, but if we work in harmony with their rhythms, we find our requests will fit within the grand movements of the universe. Practicing qigong confers many insights and new forms of power. This is a responsibility to be humble in the face of. New challenges may arise as the old problems wash away.

A statue of many-armed Guanyin Bodhisattva is treasured and revered and kept in a golden temple. Did you ever think how this sculpture had suffered through a thousand strikes and sustained a thousand cuts before it was carved into its current form? This Buddha withstood the pain of these blows before it was able to attain a form that is an inspiration to all. The difficulty of the process is what led to such a radiant effect.

This is the central theme of Daoist thought. We worship her not for her perfection, but for the trials that make her worthy of worship. Be accountable in putting the good of the universe and of others in the forefront of your mind, so that you will be doing right by all you come in contact with, as you develop yourself personally. When you practice qigong, it's a personal journey but because it is a journey of harmonizing heaven, humanity, and earth, you are also practicing for the world as well as for yourself. A kind, open heart will be your best guide and protection when learning qigong. Learn to grow your qi and your feeling at the same time. The one will automatically grow with the other, but awareness will allow the changes to take root and flourish.

Qigong is a journey. It is a journey within yourself, to recognize your wishes and fears and find the balance between struggle and acceptance. You travel through the maze of difficulties and pains within your body, towards a new understanding of your potential. You see yourself clearly as your highest self, a star in the celestial firmament, as well as a speck in the indifferent shifting of the cosmic tides. It lasts your entire life. Finding your star and finding your place here on earth are its twin goals. Does the union of heaven, humanity, and earth result in the realization of cosmic awareness? Daoists believe there is a whole new journey to be experienced past life on earth, where we each take a role befitting our attainment. The Union of heaven, humanity, and earth is not an end in and of itself, it's the first step taken on the road in the cosmic journey of existence. Nine-Five Maintenance of Qi teaches us that as there is a place for us here and now in our life, there is also a place for us in grand order of the universe. It just takes that one step forward to begin a journey of qigong. Practice well and believe.

Appendix

Nine-Five Maintenance of Qi

Movement List

Welcome the Qi
1. Stand with feet together
2. Spread feet shoulder width
3. Four heartbeats – one inhale/exhale
4. Relax the thirteen points, shoulders, elbows, hands, hips, knees, feet and head while facing the sun.
5. Hands in triangle at *dantian*
6. Hands come down to the sides with the thumbs being covered with the fingers.
7. Hands come up in first bow – right hand fist into open slanted left palm.
8. Switch to second bow – prayer hands palms together.
9. Switch to third bow – left hand traces down outside edge of right forearm then reaches being cupped up under the *dantian* with the right hand still up in prayer position.
10. Hands turn over palms down naturally from these places and come to the sides.
11. Hands go in fists at sides.
12. Right hand comes up, arm bent towards the center line then extend, then do left.
13. Hands open up with sense of it coming from the center then palms turn over face up.
14. Form the fists over the thumbs, bowing the head down into it.
15. Bring hand down, fist in arm bent, then to side then open the hand. Then do the other side (right then left).
16. Repeat all steps nine times. Three times or one time after you have mastered the practice.

Intake of Qi
17. Visualize yourself as a huge tree.
18. Suck qi up through soles of feet up the back of the body to top of the head then continue growing it up as far as it can go.
19. When the qi and tree is as high as it can go, then bring the qi down the front of the body to the lower *dantian*, then split it at the *dantian*, moving down the legs

and out through the soles of the feet. Do nine times total, trying to grow the tree higher each time.

20.   On the ninth repetition, instead of guiding the qi down and splitting it down the legs, instead dissolve completely like water into the earth. Repeat two times more, for three times trees + total dissolving.

21.   Grow the sprout from deep in the ground until it's the size of your body then inhale through nose and Baihui until chest is full then dissolve like water, out through fingers and toes and relaxing anus and urethra three times.

22.   Clench teeth and rotate tongue nine times clockwise and nine times counterclockwise.

23.   Bite teeth down twenty-four times then swallow the saliva down to the lower *dantian*.

Adjustment of Qi

24.   Clasp hands and starting from right, circle up ear, across back of head, down other ear, and hit lower *dantian* fifty times, then from left fifty times.

25.   Interlace fingers and bring up to chest, palm up, exhaling through mouth, then flip over and lower to lower *dantian*, inhaling through nose, fifty to one hundred times. Can forcefully blow air up and out when exhaling to relieve frustrations.

26.   Swallow any saliva in the mouth down to the lower *dantian*.

Tonification of Qi

27.   Feet are shoulder width, toes pointed inwards. Tongue is on the upper palate naturally.

28.   The hands clasp with the fingers hooked with the left back of the hand facing out with thumb on top and the right back of the hand facing the chest with the thumb on the bottom.

29.   inhale through nose while pulling out with the clasped fingers until you can't inhale any more, then count, holding your breath (stop pulling out) up to 200 count. Focus on your upper back while doing all of this. Then, relax muscles and exhale gently through the mouth.

30.   Repeat inhale and pull, focusing on the sides of the ribcage (full length of ribcage).

31.   Repeat inhale and pull, focusing on the lower *dantian*.

32.   Repeat all three inhales/pulls three to nine times.

Utilization of Qi

33.   Tap the ears with the tips of the fingers.

34.   Put palms over ears and rub circularly counterclockwise (outwards from the jaw line) fifty times.

35.   Then, cup hands to emphasize the center point of the palms then place over but not touching the ears and hold till the ears feel warm and clean..

36.   Repeat these steps around the eyes- hands will rub outwards.

37.   Repeat around the nose and nostrils. Also can insert the index fingers into the nostril to do this.

38.   Repeat around the mouth (this will treat the uterus as well).

39.   Repeat for genitals- woman tap/rub around the perimeter of the vagina, men do on the head of the penis. Can do one hand first then the other.

40.   Repeat around the anus, tapping with both hands but circling with the left hand (first two fingers). Also can use the middle finger slightly inserted into the anus.

41.   Optionally you can treat other sick parts of the body, tapping then rubbing counterclockwise over the affected area.

42.   After you've done the nine openings of the body, put your hands in triangle on the lower *dan*. Think of what you want; if you want to be more beautiful, think about your face, if you want to focus all the sun's energy on your hands or on a sick part of your body, you think of that spot- you are focusing the sun's rays, harvesting the energy from the sun to one part of your body.

Nine Palaces Facing Heaven – Dragon Shape Form

43.   Hands at sides making thumb fist.

44.   Arms come up to chest level with fists facing down and elbows bent, right arm a little higher and in front for women, left for men.

45.   Rotate forearms in a circle around each other (front arm coming down and back while back arm goes up and over) until back to starting position three times.

46.   Hands open up from fist (thumbs down, fingers spread).

47.   Rotate forearms again with hands open three times.

48.   Push up with right hand so that it's palm up over the top center of the head holding up heaven, while the left hand goes down cupped under the genital area, with the knees lowered and pointing in. You are trying to combine the qi of heaven and earth- you can't grab heaven or hold earth, but you can go with nature and bring them together. So hold up heaven, don't try to pull it down.

49.   Flip over upper hand and straighten up bringing up lower cupped palm and down the upper cupped palm to form the Taiji ball at stomach level (right below middle *dan*).

50.   Hold ball until you feel heat coming from the hands into the stomach.

51.   Flip ball with the lower hand coming up in the front to get to the top (important) then repeat sensation of heat.

52.   open ball so that palms are facing, feel sensation then pull out and push back in hands three times then hold ball till you feel sensations again (do this three pulls three times for 9+5 *Book of Changes* numbers)

53.   Once you feel the sensation strongly in the palms that are still facing, put hands on upper chest then wipe down front of body to knees (with fingertips pointing down as you pass the chest), then around to back of knees, then up to kidney where hands start to cup up till runs along sides then the underarms, so that they come to the front with backs of palms facing and almost touching before flipping hands around in prayer position.

54. Prayer position flips to pushing hands (start push going left) *yuan heng li zhen* nine times then switch hands and push opposite direction nine times. The vertical hand is the pushing hand, so pushing to the left, the right hand is vertical.

55. Hands go to triangle in lower *dantian* then step left foot to the right foot.

About the Authors

Dr. Baolin Wu is a traditional Chinese medicine (TCM) doctor, research neurophysiologist, martial artist and Daoist master from the White Cloud Monastery, Beijing, which for almost a thousand years has been one of the most respected centers in China for the study and practice of Daoist philosophy and medicine. At age four he was brought to the monastery to live spending the next twenty years under the direct tutelage of the abbot, Master Du Xinling, learning techniques of which few people today are even aware. He is the 17th generation lineage holder of the Dragon Gate Sect of Complete Reality Daoism, of which Nine Palaces Solar Qigong is the principal practice.

Dr. Wu is an internationally recognized authority on the practice of traditional Chinese medicine and also has a thorough understanding of Western Medicine, as evidenced by his training and experience. Dr. Wu received his medical degrees from the most esteemed schools in China, graduating from the National College of Traditional Chinese Medicine in Beijing, holds a master's degree from the China Academy of Traditional Chinese Medicine and became an attending physician at Guang'anmen Hospital, China's foremost combination Western/Chinese medical institution. Dr. Wu has presented before many prestigious international TCM organizations, including The World Federation of Acupuncture – Moxibustion Societies (WFAS), also serving on their 9th Executive Committee as representatives to the World Health Organization, the China Association of Traditional Medicine (CATCM) and the American TCM Association (ATCMA).

To understand Dr. Baolin Wu's excellence in his field, one must go beyond academic credentials. He hails from one of the most prominent medical families in China. His renowned ancestor Wu Jutong, an imperial doctor of the Qing Dynasty, was the author of "Wen Bing Tiao Bian" (1798) Treatise on the Differential Treatment of Warm Disease, (viral illness, transmission, treatment and epidemic containment), one of the classic "Four Pillars" of modern Chinese medicine. Xi Zhi Wu, Dr. Wu's paternal grandfather, was the personal physician to Pu Yi, the last emperor of China. Dr. Wu's mastery has been shaped by the wisdom of seven generations, passed down to him by his family. In addition, the Daoist principles instilled in his young days have given Dr. Wu a sensitivity towards his patients as well as a holistic understanding of the nature of healing.

Jessica Eckstein is a longtime student of Dr. Wu. She has studied qigong, feng shui, martial arts and Yijing under his supervision for thirty years. Together, they have written *Lighting the Eye of the Dragon: Inner Secrets of Taoist Feng Shui*, voted one of "10 Best Feng Shui Books in English"- www.fengshui.co.uk and *Qi Gong for Total Wellness: Increase Your Energy, Vitality, and Longevity with the Ancient 9 Palaces System from the White Cloud Monastery*, the classic introduction to the essentials of Daoist qigong practice and theory.

Dr. Eric Di Wu (MBBS, DC) is a Medical Doctor (China), a Chiropractic Doctor (USA) and the son of Dr. Baolin Wu. He is also a lineal descendent of the renowned Traditional Chinese Medicine physician, Wu Jutong, Imperial Doctor of the Qing Dynasty and was the author of the "Wen Bing Tiao Bian" (1798). Under the direct guidance and tutelage of his father, Dr. Eric Di Wu has been practicing and cultivating the Daoist Arts since the young age of nine years old. His experiences from practicing Nine Palaces Solar qigong have been transformative.

Made in the USA
Middletown, DE
30 July 2021

45055089R00118